Basic
Guide
to
Flower
Arranging

Illustrations by
Marietta Kust

McGRAW-HILL BOOK COMPANY

New York   St. Louis   San Francisco   Düsseldorf
Johannesburg   Kuala Lumpur   London   Mexico   Montreal
New Delhi   Panama   Rio de Janeiro   Singapore
Sydney   Toronto

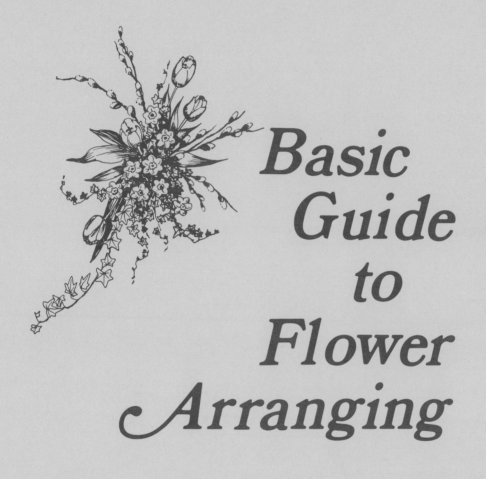

Basic Guide to Flower Arranging

Florence Bell Hillier

Basic Guide to Flower Arranging

Copyright © 1974 by McGraw-Hill, Inc. All rights
reserved. Printed in the United States of America. No
part of this publication can be reproduced, stored in a
retrieval system, or transmitted, in any form or by any
means, electronic, mechanical, photocopying, recording,
or otherwise, without the prior permission of the
publisher.

Library of Congress Cataloging in Publication Data

Hillier, Florence Bell
  Basic guide to flower arranging.

  1. Flower arrangement.   2. Gardens, Miniature.
3. Flowers—Drying. I. Title.
SB449.H48   745.92   73-8634
ISBN 0-07-028907-7

Book design: *Richard A. Roth*

Foreword

It is fun to arrange flowers! It provides the delightful satisfaction arising from accomplishment, followed by a quiet and enduring enjoyment of an ever-changing natural beauty enhanced by the personal artistry of the arranger. I really believe those words and have seen the great pleasure people derive from well-arranged flowers, yet I have also seen the bewilderment of the young housewife confronted with a bunch of flowers, an empty vase, and a blank space on her dinner table. I have spent most of my life helping people overcome that initial bewilderment and leading them to the joys of flower arranging.

This book is just another step. It is a practical book with a very different approach from that of the many other books that have been written on the subject. I believe that my ideas are sound, and the pleasures of flower arranging will become available to anyone who has a minimum of interest.

A familiar form of television commercial goes like this: "If they can put a man on the moon, why can't they make . . . ?" Of course, the advertiser then goes on to show that his company already has. The form of this book evolved from a real-life example of such a query.

For thirty years I have been lecturing on flower arranging, training new employees, and demonstrating to garden clubs and professional florist groups. I have watched students advance steadily from their first terrified moments in front of an empty vase to gaining confidence and beginning to create acceptable arrangements. I have even seen several of the best go on to win blue ribbons. My students have often posed the question: "Where can I get a book that will give me all this information?" When I suggested several titles from the wide range of books on flower arranging that were already available, I found that I was not satisfying their need. It seemed as though there was simply no substitute for demonstration with real flowers. Then I found myself wondering why this was so.

Certainly I could cook a reasonably good meal with the guidance of a cookbook. Or I could successfully make a dress or knit a sweater simply by following the instructions contained in appropriate written material. It began to be clear that flower-arranging books have not succeeded in the same way. They describe general principles, and the better ones give many of the practical techniques of handling flowers, but they all stop short of giving detailed instructions for constructing specific types of arrangements. Instead, they use examples that depend on short descriptions and either line-drawing or photographic illustrations. Thus they fail to provide the student with one of the most critical steps in the learning process—being able to retrace each step to learn where an error was made that prevented the finished arrangement from coming up to expectations. This line of thought led to the idea of writing a book on flower arranging that would be the counterpart of a cookbook or sewing book, with "recipes" or "patterns" that would give the student step-by-step instructions for the construction of many different types of flower arrangements.

Fired by these thoughts, I enthusiastically set about developing recipes for flower arrangements. My enthusiasm soon changed to disappointment. The recipes were wordy, and even worse, when my students tried to make an arrangement from them, even with the illustrations in front of them, the results were far from satisfactory. The idea was not yet fully developed.

The arranging of flowers requires that each flower be properly placed in three-dimensional space. The English language is clumsy when one is trying to describe precisely where to put an object in three dimensions. Moreover, I began to realize that a two-dimensional photograph or drawing of a three-dimensional arrangement is also too often ambiguous as to size, position, or angle of the flowers. I now began to appreciate why other writers had not followed the course to which I was committed.

Then an inspiration came. One night an old Air Force movie came on television. At one point the pilot's voice rasped from the intercom, "Enemy planes at nine o'clock high!" There was the answer—a way to indicate direction that, with the length of the flower, would completely define its position in space. Just two numbers added to each step in the instructions would permit me to use brief and standardized instructions and would remove all ambiguity from the illustrations. I was delighted to find that even my husband could quickly put together very passable arrangements from such instructions. He became so enthusiastic that he became the official tester of each recipe as it was developed.

I am now convinced that this approach provides a precise means of communication with both the beginner and the experienced florist. If, by this means, I am able to bring the pleasures of flower arranging to a broader group of people, I will feel that all the effort was worthwhile.

No book is ever written without the direct or indirect participation of many others. Mine is no exception. I am particularly indebted to my wonderful husband, without whose inspiration, encouragement, and understanding tolerance this book would never have been completed. Special thanks must also go to Marietta Kust, who, in developing the illustrations for the book, spent many long hours away from her family ensuring the accuracy of the drawings for each recipe.

FLORENCE BELL HILLIER
Princeton, New Jersey

Contents

1   The Principles of Floral Design   1

2   Containers, Figurines, and Stands   45

3   Mechanical Aids   57

4   The Preparation and Care of Cut Flowers   83

5   The Mechanics of Preparing Flowers for Arranging   103

6   Step-by-Step Procedure for a General Flower Arrangement   111

7   Recipes   117

    Appendix A: Dish Gardens and Water Gardens   251

    Appendix B: The Art of Preserving Flowers   258

    Index   274

The Principles
of Floral
Design

□Flower arrangement is a recognized art form based on several fundamental principles. Mastery of the art demands a thorough understanding of the principles and continued practice in their application. True, some people have a flair for flower arranging and produce excellent effects without formal training. But most of us must master the principles, and even our more gifted friends benefit from familiarity with them.

In any art form the elements of good design include scale, shape, balance, color, rhythm, and harmony. Each of these elements will be discussed individually as it applies to flower arranging. However, the fundamentals cannot be considered in isolation, since each one interacts with all the others and subtly influences the overall esthetic effect.

A basic rule in arranging flowers is to apply the principles of good design to the total picture. First of all, the principles of design must be satisfied within the arrangement itself. But any flower arrangement is also an integral part of a larger environment. It complements and accents the decor of the room where it is displayed and can adapt its setting to the mood of a season or an occasion. Thus the principles of good design must be satisfied in this more complete environment as well.

Careful analysis of any successful arrangement will reveal that each of the elements of design has been taken into account. Although no two flower arrangements are ever identical, every successful one interprets the fundamental principles in a unique and satisfying way.

In your first attempts at arranging flowers, follow the principles as closely as possible; but, as you become familiar with them, remember that rules are made to be broken. Eventually you will enjoy a disciplined ability to take liberties that will place the stamp of your personality on your work. Some great paintings defy all the rules of perspective, composition, and color, yet still possess an intangible something that makes them outstanding. Such works are not the product of ignorance of basic principles, but rather of a sure knowledge as to when the principles may safely be ignored. In the same way, when a master designer casts aside one of the principles of floral design, it must be with full understanding. The result may then prove to be something fresh, charming, and spontaneous.

Even with a knowledge of the principles involved, your first creations may not be superb, but do not lose heart. With practice you will gain freedom in applying your knowledge and your work will improve. You could not be working in a better medium. Flowers are so beautiful in themselves that it is almost impossible to make an unattractive arrangement.

As you develop confidence in your understanding of the principles of design and skill in handling flowers, you will begin to consider the host of intangible factors that contribute to truly successful flower arranging, such as the tone of the occasion, the personality of your home, your own personality, and the personalities of those who will view your creation.

Perhaps the most important bit of advice for any arranger, experienced or beginner, is to plan ahead. Before starting an arrangement, take a few minutes to form a clear mental image of your completed arrangement in its selected location and in relation to the occasion and the individuals who will view it. In this way you will avoid false starts and make the correct decisions as your arrangement materializes.

Location

Where do you plan to use the arrangement you are about to make? This is a crucial decision, for your arrangement must be designed, constructed, and placed so that the whole creation and each flower in it are shown to the best advantage. The viewing point is a very important consideration. Will your arrangement be seen from below, from above, or at eye level? For instance, a centerpiece for the dining-room table will be below eye level and will be viewed from

Fig. 1. The viewing point is a very important consideration. Will your arrangement be seen from below, from above, or at eye level?

all sides, while an arrangement for a buffet table is normally seen from the front and sides only, usually with the viewer standing. An arrangement for a coffee table will be below eye level and in intimate association with the viewer. An arrangement for a hall table, on the other hand, will be seen from the front and the sides with the back visible only if it is placed in front of a mirror. An arrangement placed on a mantel, in contrast, meets the viewer at eye level as he enters the room. But when he sits or stands below it and looks up, he must see something pleasing—not the coarse underside of foliage or the harsh lines of the container. (Fig. 1)

Scale

"Scale," or "proportion," refers to the size relationship of all the component parts of your arrangement to one another and to the relationship of the whole to its surroundings. There is no precise rule dictating size, but it is a problem that requires serious consideration. Most arrangements should be large enough to look important and yet not be overpowering. However, if you are making an intimate bouquet, it should be rather small to impart a feeling of closeness. In any case, the arrangement should not be hemmed in or crowded by its surroundings.

A good way to decide on the size of an arrangement for a particular location is to visualize one that is too small and then mentally let it grow until it is definitely too large. Do this a couple of times to narrow the range and then select a size that is midway between the too-large and the too-small images. Later you will learn to account for the different size impressions made by the color, shape, and size of the flowers. If you find it difficult to produce this mental image, you might cut out various sizes and shapes of cardboard and try these in the chosen location. But remember that this is a mechanical approach, lacking the effect imparted by the light, natural, feathery feeling of flowers.

If your room is large and the furniture is massive, your arrangement should be large enough to withstand all this competition. An arrangement for a grand piano, a large console, or a big table must be large. On the other hand, you would not overbalance a delicate table or overpower a small room with a bold and assertive arrangement. However, if your large room happens to include a small table, you could use a small arrangement in proportion to its immediate surroundings.

An arrangement for a coffee table does not necessarily have to be large even if the table is massive, since other items, such as ash trays, candy dishes, or magazines, are often present. However, if the coffee table is uncluttered and is the focal point of the room, the arrangement can be more assertive. In the same way the size of the mantel or console and the number of accessories determine the size of an arrangement for these locations. Often there is a picture over the mantel. Do not cover any portion of it with flowers. Your arrangement should be wide and flowing, enhancing rather than competing with the painting both in design and color. (Fig. 2)

A useful guide in designing a centerpiece for the dining-room table is to have the flowers and the candelabra occupy the central third of the table. The centerpiece should not exceed eight inches in height, unless it is very light and airy, or it will interfere with seeing across the table. An exception to this is a centerpiece designed for a formal dinner party. This may be as high as you wish, since etiquette demands that guests converse with their adjacent dinner companions rather than with those across the table. For an informal table, consider placing candles and flowers at one end of the table—provided, of course, that no guests are to be seated there.

ACCEPTABLE

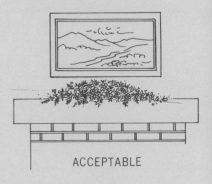

ACCEPTABLE

NOT ACCEPTABLE

Fig. 2. An arrangement should be right for the setting.

Fig. 3. The tallest flower should be one-and-one-half times the height of the container.

Scale within the Arrangement

Once you have chosen the location and determined the size of your arrangement, you must select an appropriate container. While scale is only one of many factors influencing this decision, you must consider the size relationship of your container to its environment and to the flowers. Here you would be wise to be guided by the widely accepted principle that a pleasing proportion is achieved when the flowers are at least one-and-one-half times the height of their container (Fig. 3). Remember that actual dimensions are not the only consideration. A container of heavy material carries more visual weight than one of similar size made of more delicate material or one of more delicate design. Extra visual weight must be offset by greater height in the flowers and greens.

If you are using a shallow container, a pleasing height for the flowers is the sum of the width and the length of the container (Fig. 4). You can use a tape measure to determine these dimensions, but it is much easier to use the container itself as the measure. Just place the stem of the

Fig. 4. The tallest flower for this container should be twelve inches above the holder (the sum of the four-inch width and the eight-inch length). (A) When flowers are to be inserted from the sides and the front, use foam that extends at least one-and-one-half inches above the container. (B) A pin-point holder is adequate for a few flowers when none cascades over the rim of the container.

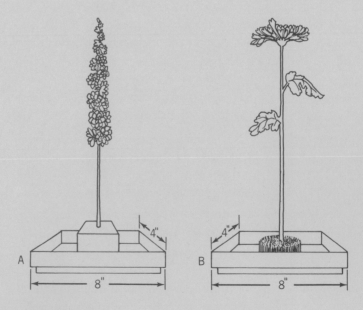

Fig. 5. The concepts of scale and
proportion, illustrated by arrangements
of different sizes in the same vase.
(A) Too small for vase. (B) Still a little
small, but not bad. (C) About right.
(D) Too big.

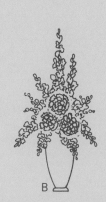
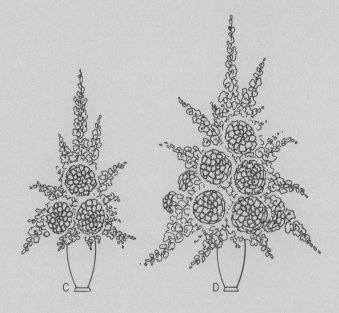

A　　　　　B　　　　　C　　　　　D

key flower lengthwise on the container with the flower tip
even with one edge. Grasp the stem at the other end of
the container, and turn the flower so that it is crosswise
on the container, adding the width you are measuring to
the length already marked off. Cut the stem at this point.
If you want to play safe, you can cut it a little beyond this
point, on the principle that you can always make it shorter,
but never longer.

Now that you have decided on the location, size, and
container for your arrangement, the next step is to select
flowers that are in correct proportion to the container and
to one another (Fig. 5). Large, bold flowers are unsuitable
for delicate containers, as are small, dainty ones for weighty
containers (Fig. 6). Bold and delicate flowers seldom combine well in the same arrangement (Fig. 7). For instance,
gladioli and daisies are a poor combination, as are anthuriums and sweetheart roses, or large chrysanthemums and
cornflowers (Fig. 8).

However, as we have suggested, you can, with ingenuity,

Fig. 6. Large, bold flowers are
unsuitable for delicate containers.

ignore these rules when there is a reason to do so. Perhaps you have received flowers as a gift and are forced to use a normally unhappy combination; or perhaps you have a special color combination in mind. An illusion of size and weight may be gained for your small, dainty flowers by using them in clusters. If you wanted to combine the blue of cornflowers with the color and texture of carnations, you could cluster the cornflowers so that they were in proportion to the larger flowers. They can easily be clustered by bunching them together and tying them with a little piece of the paper-covered wire familiar to all gardeners.

The final consideration in the discussion of scale is the size relationship of the greens to the flowers and to the container. If your flowers are delicate, use delicate greens, and if they are heavy, use bold, heavy greens. Gladioli, for instance, relate better to lemon or huckleberry leaves than to delicate ferns.

Fig. 7. Bold and delicate flowers are a poor combination in an arrangement.

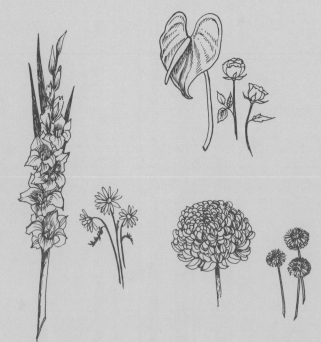

Fig. 8. Examples of poor combinations of bold and delicate flowers.

Shape

In deciding upon a shape for your arrangement, you have a number of basic forms to choose from. You may decide on a linear arrangement that stresses motion and direction in the placement of flowers—a torch (Fig. 9A), an inverted "T" (Fig. 9B), and "L" shape (Fig. 9C), or a reversed "L" (Fig. 9D).

If you want more flowing lines, you might select a Hogarth curve. The eighteenth-century English artist William Hogarth believed that the nape of a woman's neck was the most beautiful shape in nature and called it the line of beauty. The Hogarth curve can most accurately be described as an elongated "S." It can be used horizontally, vertically, or diagonally. (Fig. 10)

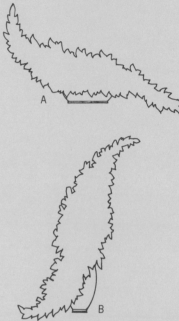

Fig. 10. Hogarth curves.
(A) Horizontal. (B) Vertical.

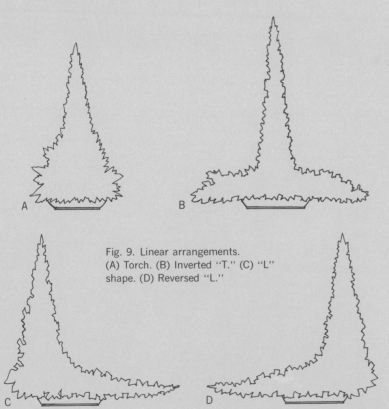

Fig. 9. Linear arrangements.
(A) Torch. (B) Inverted "T." (C) "L" shape. (D) Reversed "L."

If you want a more solid-looking form, select a circle (Fig. 11A), a fan (Fig. 11B), an ellipse (Fig. 11C), an oval (Fig. 11D), a crescent (Fig. 11E), or a triangle. Of all the forms, the triangle is probably the most widely used. There are the right-angled triangles, which point either to the left (Fig. 12A) or the right (Fig. 12B). The equilateral triangle (Fig. 12C) has all sides equal. The isosceles triangle has two sides equal (Fig. 12D), and the scalene triangle (Fig. 12E) has all sides of different lengths. In a symmetrical triangle (equilateral or isosceles) the weight is equally divided by the central axis. The highest point is always the center and is formed by the smallest flower, bud, or thin branch. When an arrangement is to be centered in its surroundings, this is the most pleasing of triangles.

An asymmetrical triangle (right-handed, left-handed, or scalene) can be more interesting. Here the visual weight

Fig. 11. Solid-looking forms.
(A) Round. (B) Fan. (C) Ellipse.
(D) Oval. (E) Crescent.

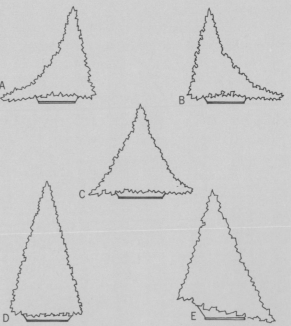

Fig. 12. Triangular forms. (A) Left-handed triangle. (B) Right-handed triangle. (C) Equilateral triangle. (D) Isosceles triangle. (E) Scalene triangle.

is not evenly distributed on each side of the axis. Yet the triangle must appear to be balanced. This effect is accomplished by placing the heavier material close to one side of the axis and the lighter material on the other side, further out or further away from the axis. This effect works on the same principle as the seesaw, where the fat boy must be nearer the center to balance the thin boy who is farther out. In the same way large flowers are placed lower and nearer the center on one side, and smaller lighter flowers extend further out on the other side. Note that here, too, smaller flowers can be grouped to give an illusion of larger size. Sometimes you can gain the extra weight you may need by strategically placing an object such as a figurine or the lid of a container on one side of the arrangement. (Fig. 13)

The term "shape" cannot be taken too literally. It is not intended to describe a firm, hard-lined form which might be cut out of wood. When applied to a flower arrangement it merely indicates the general outlines, since the flowers are never completely contained within the form. Sometimes their buds extend beyond the lines, sometimes they won't quite reach them, and there will be voids and spaces in the outline. This irregularity provides a sense of ease and naturalness, and avoids contrived and static effects. Do not spoil the flowing line by an abrupt transition between your flowers and their container. Unity between the two can be insured by the use of a cascading flower or leaf. (Fig. 14)

Fig. 13. Sometimes you can gain extra weight by placing the lid of a container on one side of the arrangement.

NOT ACCEPTABLE

ACCEPTABLE

Fig. 14. Unity between flowers and container can be insured by the use of cascading leaves or flowers.

Fig. 15. Torch-shaped arrangement.

Selecting a Shape

In selecting a shape, you must take many things into consideration. The shape of an arrangement, for example, plays a part in complementing or enhancing the mood of an occasion, since shape is a phenomenon to which people respond emotionally. Horizontal lines tend to be restful, vertical lines stimulating. The upward movement of a torch-shaped arrangement, for instance, is dignified and exalted, yet restless and moving, while a horizontal arrangement expresses serenity, stability, and repose (Figs. 15, 16). A horizontal arrangement in the center of the dining table imparts a feeling of tranquillity, whereas a sharp triangular arrangement in church suggests exaltation. On the other hand, a bountiful fan-shaped arrangement in church can symbolize God's love and generosity (Fig. 17). In some situations we have come to associate fans with coquetry, and so a fan-shaped arrangement can also imply gaiety, festivity, and good cheer. The circle is found many times in nature, and always imparts a feeling of exhilaration,

Fig. 16. Horizontal arrangement.

movement, and rhythm. A Hogarth curve bespeaks elegance and intrinsic beauty. (Fig. 18)

The spirit and style of your room also must be considered. Most rooms can be categorized as traditional or contemporary. In terms of shape, the difference between the two lies in the clean-cut lines, crispness, and sleekness of the contemporary as opposed to the softer, more intricate lines of traditional furnishings. Whatever the decor, the shape of your arrangement should be in harmony with its setting. The only reliable guideline here is that stark line forms such as the torch (Fig. 19), inverted "T," or "L" shapes are rarely compatible with traditional settings but are very effective with contemporary decors. It is acceptable, though not as effective, to use the fan, the triangle, the circle, and all other shapes in contemporary settings. It is stunning to use an "L"-shaped arrangement and a reversed "L" at opposite ends of a mantel in a contemporary room, perhaps flanking a clock or a painting. In a traditional room, reversed asymmetrical triangles or circular arrangements would seem more at home.

Fig. 18. Hogarth curves using pink carnations and heather.
(A) Horizontal. (B) Diagonal.

Fig. 17. Fan-shaped arrangement.

Fig. 19. For contemporary decor a torch-shaped arrangement of anthurium and sansevieria leaves is appropriate.

If the arrangement is intended to soften some architectural defect, your choice will be comparatively simple. If you wish to emphasize upward lines, choose a tall, upright shape. If you wish to draw attention to the horizontal, choose an arrangement with a horizontal movement. If you want to brighten a dark corner with the illusion of a window to the outdoors, use a flowing, fan-shaped arrangement in bright colors which simulate sunshine. Analyze the defect in your room and plan accordingly.

Occasionally the container determines the shape of an arrangement. For instance, a colonial, fan-shaped vase demands a fan-shaped arrangement, while a teapot calls for a rounded one. Your object is to convey the feeling that flowers and container belong together. If a container has characteristic lines, the flowers must conform to them. (Fig. 20)

Often the flowers themselves dictate the shape of the arrangement. Some flowers, such as gladioli, delphiniums, and snapdragons, lend themselves to triangular and fan-shaped arrangements, whereas sweet peas, daisies, and miniature roses are naturals for round and crescent arrangements. Occasionally even the natural curves of the flower stems may determine the shape of the arrangement. Straight-stemmed snapdragons, for example, lend themselves to triangular or fan-shaped arrangements; but, should your snapdragons have crooked stems, you would be wiser to select a crescent-shaped form.

In any case, you will probably have to weigh the desirability of one shape against that of another. Suppose, for instance, that the environment calls for a tall, upright arrangement, while your particular flowers suggest a crescent shape. You must weigh the pros and cons and choose accordingly, perhaps being influenced by architectural or decorating details that you wish to enhance or conceal.

Since no two settings are the same, it is impossible to set any rule for the shape of a particular arrangement. Study the environment and decide which of several suitable shapes is best for you. For example, you might plan to place an arrangement at one end of a large console that has a tall lamp at the other end. In this case, you could use a torch arrangement or a tall symmetrical triangle, which would balance symmetrically with the lamp; or it could be a full circle or a fan-shaped arrangement, which would provide a more interesting asymmetrical balance. You could also use a crescent shape, perhaps echoing crescents used elsewhere in the room. Try each on different occasions and decide which is more effective. You will develop taste and judgment as you proceed. Fortunately you will not be changing

Fig. 20. Occasionally the container determines the shape of an arrangement. Here, a fan-shaped colonial vase demands a fan-shaped arrangement.

your settings frequently, so you will have plenty of opportunity for improvement by trial and error.

The Shapes of the Flowers

The most satisfying arrangements are composed of a combination of spike and round flowers. Spike flowers, such as gladioli and snapdragons, have multiple florets of graduated size along a single stem (Fig. 21). Round or face flowers, such as carnations and daffodils, have a single flower at the end of the stem (Fig. 22). Feature flowers often function as the focal point (Fig. 23). They are the aristocrats of the flower kingdom, so outstandingly beautiful that they need no other flower to enhance them.

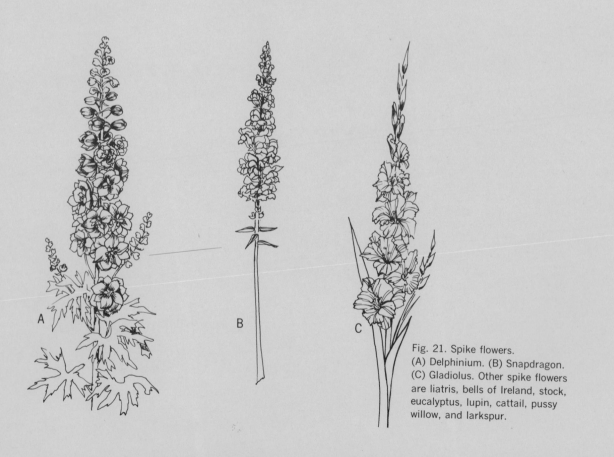

Fig. 21. Spike flowers.
(A) Delphinium. (B) Snapdragon.
(C) Gladiolus. Other spike flowers
are liatris, bells of Ireland, stock,
eucalyptus, lupin, cattail, pussy
willow, and larkspur.

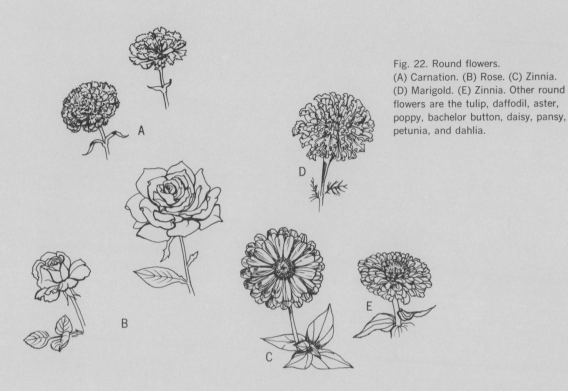

Fig. 22. Round flowers.
(A) Carnation. (B) Rose. (C) Zinnia.
(D) Marigold. (E) Zinnia. Other round
flowers are the tulip, daffodil, aster,
poppy, bachelor button, daisy, pansy,
petunia, and dahlia.

Fig. 23. Feature, or specimen,
flowers. (A) Lily. (B) Tuberous
begonia. (C) Magnolia. (D) Gerbera.
(E) Clematis. Other feature flowers
are the orchid, proteus, open tulip,
gardenia, camellia, and hibiscus.

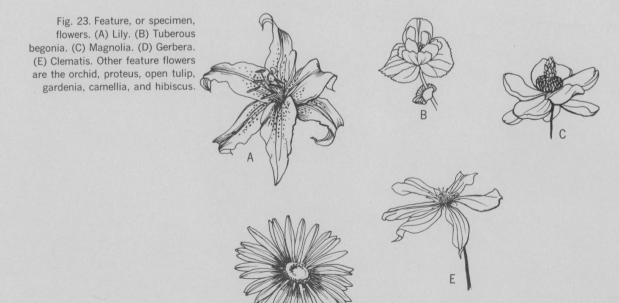

Once you have decided on the shape of your arrangement, you should use spike flowers to establish its skeleton framework. Place them first to define the dimensions, then fill in the spaces with more spike flowers, working down toward the center and base with round flowers and fillers. If you must use all round flowers, place some of them so that they will be seen from the side rather than full face, in order to avoid a polka-dot effect (Fig. 24). A flower is beautiful from every angle and provides the opportunity to avoid monotony. A contrast of form may also be achieved by careful selection of your greens.

Fig. 24. If you must use all round flowers, place some of them so that they will be seen from the side rather than full face in order to avoid a polka-dot effect.

Sometimes the distinction between spike and round flowers is not so obvious as it is in the case of snapdragons, gladioli, delphiniums, and larkspurs in the first group and roses, carnations, dahlias, and zinnias in the second. Some roses, for instance, are essentially pointed in character, while others are rounder. With ingenuity you can use your flowers so as to make them appear either round or spike. Three daffodils placed so that the flowers form a straight vertical line assume the form of a spike flower, whereas clustered they will look like a round flower (Fig. 25). Sometimes you can make spike flowers appear more like face flowers by breaking off the tips. However, having once identified a flower as spike or round, you should use it in the same way throughout your design.

Balance

The dictionary defines balance in art as the composition or placement of elements of design such as figures, forms, or colors in a manner that produces an esthetically pleasing or harmoniously integrated whole. In flower arranging, a sense of balance is achieved through the proper placement of flowers, both as to color and form, and through the proper selection of a container. A well-balanced arrangement appears to be physically stable in its environment. It does not look as though it will tip over or fall apart.

The most important aspect of balance is the matter of visual weight. Large flowers or leaves appear to be heavier than small ones, and solid flowers or leaves have more visual weight than lacy ones. In the same way, dark colors have more visual weight than light ones. Your objective should be to create an arrangement with more visual weight near its base and an impression of balance from side to side and from front to back. Even though the arrangement may be asymmetrical, the balance point falls near the center of the

Fig. 25. Some flowers can be used to achieve either a spike or a round effect. (A) Three flowers placed in a straight line can serve as a spike flower. (B) Three flowers clustered together can serve as a large round flower.

Fig. 26. Try to achieve good balance when combining spike and round flowers.

container. If the results are to appear stable, you must also take the visual weight of the container into account.

The concept of visual weight can be illustrated by considering the combinations of a carnation and a slender gladiolus. If the carnation is large and placed above the gladiolus, it will make your arrangement appear top heavy. Directly below, it will form an unsightly bulge. In either position it destroys balance. (Fig. 26)

If, on the other hand, you first position your gladiolus, and then place a somewhat larger flower, a miniature carnation, for example, below it, and follow that with a still larger flower, you will have the beginning of a balanced arrangement. We can in fact learn much from observing nature. The gladiolus and snapdragon are themselves perfect examples of gradual transition in the size of the flowers, tapering as they do from slender tips with unopened buds through partially opened flowers to large full-blown flowers at the base.

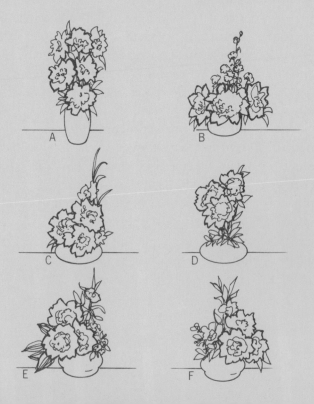

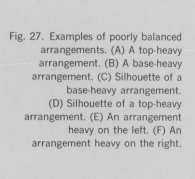
Fig. 27. Examples of poorly balanced arrangements. (A) A top-heavy arrangement. (B) A base-heavy arrangement. (C) Silhouette of a base-heavy arrangement. (D) Silhouette of a top-heavy arrangement. (E) An arrangement heavy on the left. (F) An arrangement heavy on the right.

How to Achieve Balance

To create a balanced arrangement you should use smaller flowers, buds, or bits of fine greens at the top and edges of the arrangement and have a gradual transition in the size of the flowers from the top to the bottom and from side to side, forming a smooth, integrated whole without steps or bulges. There should be a gradual transition, not only in the size of the flowers but also in the size of the spaces between them, with the spaces diminishing toward the base of the arrangement. In other words, the edges and top of your arrangement should be light and airy, with the visual weight gradually increasing as you descend to the base. This effect is best achieved by using spike flowers to outline the arrangement and gradually changing to round flowers as you approach the center from the top and from the sides. (Figs. 27–30)

If by chance it is necessary to use round flowers to outline your arrangement, you should use them as sparsely as possible in order to achieve a light, airy line. As the form takes shape, be careful not to use the round flowers full face, but as you approach the base of the arrangement show more and more of the full faces and place the flowers closer together. In this way the spaces between them will be gradually and naturally decreased.

Where spike and round flowers are being used in combination, and your round flowers seem too small to achieve a perfect balance, remember that you may cluster them to create the illusion of larger, heavier flowers. Note also that physical size alone cannot dictate your choices. A daisy, for instance, may actually be larger than a carnation, but appear lighter because of its lacy character. Learn to judge visual weight. Aim for a gradual transition in the weight of

Fig. 28. Note that the transition in the sizes of roses used gives balance to the arrangement.

Fig. 29. The transition from small to large flowers gives stability to an arrangement.

Fig. 30. A cluster of open roses at
the bottom of the arrangement
adds weight.

flowers from the sides of the arrangement to the center, thus avoiding any apparent tendency to tip one way or the other.

In an asymmetrical arrangement, of course, the major visual weight is off center. You can balance the major weight by extending lighter material further out in the opposite direction and perhaps by using more of the light material. If you are still not satisfied with the balance you have achieved, you may modify it by judiciously placing a figurine, an attractive lid, or a glass bubble near the spot where you feel an added illusion of weight is required— either by the major weight or at the end of the extending arm.

Good balance also depends on slanting the flower stems at the correct angle. All the stems must appear to spring from a common source, and the spine of the arrangement must stand erect. As flowers are added, they should gradually tilt outward, until as they approach the base they are nearly horizontal. (Fig. 31)

Color is an important factor in achieving balance, since different colors have different visual weights. Pastels appear relatively light, while darker flowers appear heavier. It is best to place the pastels at the top and sides of an arrangement, with a gradual transition to darker colors near the base. The gradation should be from tints to hues, to tones, to shades. (These terms are discussed in the following section.)

You may, of course, encounter a practical problem here, if the spike flowers you plan to use to outline your arrangement are dark in color and your face flowers are lighter. The best solution is to compensate for the light visual weight of your face flowers by using more of them, thereby offsetting the greater visual weight of the spike flowers above.

Color

Of all the elements of flower arrangement, the proper use of color is probably the most important, the most challenging, and yet the most difficult to describe. Color arouses your imagination and releases your creative instincts. More than anything else in a flower arrangement it reaches out to the beholder. It is the feature to which the observer responds with the greatest sensitivity. A flower arrangement can lack many qualities, but if the color is pleasing it can be a thing of beauty and very appealing.

Color adds an extra dimension to almost every facet of our lives. We have developed emotional responses to different colors since early childhood, and they have become symbols of our feelings. In our culture white has taken on the connotation of purity. Angels and cherubs are always clothed in white. This idea has carried over into the realms of flowers, and thus the bride's bouquet is usually composed of white flowers. White also implies purity and holiness, and so white flowers in church are always appropriate.

Yellow is a color that we tend to associate with happiness. Just as we are filled with joy on a sunny day when everything is bathed in the golden glow of sunlight, an arrangement accented with a touch of yellow has an element of gaiety.

Whenever we think of babies or delicate china, on the other hand, the color pink comes to mind. Thus pink bespeaks fragility, delicacy, and daintiness, and we use pink flowers when we want to set this mood. The red of fire, in contrast, is terrifying, and the brilliance of sunset is exciting. In the same way, red flowers evoke strong emotions and signify strength.

If you want to evoke a feeling of repose and peace, use green, the color of the quiet forest glade and gentle meadow. To fill the observer with tranquillity and serenity,

Fig. 31. In this arrangement, which uses zinnias, marigolds, or asters, flowers are placed so that all stems radiate from a single point.

rely on the blue of quiet seas and friendly skies. For a hint of mystery, use the purple that we find in deep waters. Since we also associate purple with royalty, a bouquet in tones of purple has a regal air. When a gentleman wants to make a lady feel like a queen, he should present her with a purple orchid. Lavender, however, reminds us of grandmothers in lavender shawls, and so lilacs and lovely old ladies seem to belong together.

In addition, we regard some colors as cool and others as warm. Warm colors are the yellows, oranges, pinks, and reds, suggestive of the warmth of the sun. All contain a large proportion of yellow or red. Cool colors are blues, greens, and purples, reminiscent of the coldness of the sea and the coolness of the forest. They contain a large proportion of blue.

Colors also have a feeling of dimension or depth. The artist sometimes calls this movement. To our eyes some colors appear to be closer than they are and others appear farther away. Warm colors appear to advance and cool colors recede. Thus, you can enhance the three-dimensional effect of an arrangement by using warm colors in the foreground and cool colors toward the back. Sinking cool colors deep into your arrangement also will enhance its depth.

As we have already mentioned, color can play an important role in harmonizing your arrangement with the general spirit of a room. Just as important, it can enhance the mood of the occasion for which you are preparing the arrangement. Since a gathering can be dignified, solemn, gay, frivolous, or elegant, you should choose flowers of a color or colors that will complement or enhance the mood. Follow your own emotional reaction to colors. In this way you will transfer your own personality to your arrangements. It is a process like this that makes creating a flower arrangement such a personal experience and the result a true expression of your personality.

The Uses of Color

As you try to develop arrangements for particular locations from the selection of available flowers, you are certain to run into very specific and practical problems in the use of color. Although it would be impossible to describe all the possibilities that can arise, some examples of the more common situations can give you a good start in solving some of the problems.

Suppose, for example, your room is essentially blue and you want to introduce an air of gaiety, warmth, and friendliness. In this case, you should select yellow or pink flowers. If instead you want to add dignity, choose a color related to blue, such as violet. If you are seeking elegance or you are uncertain of your ability to play with colors, use all white flowers. White flowers are never incorrect, but do not expect them to arouse the wonderful excitement of color.

If your room is a warm color such as yellow or gold, you would still use warm colors to add a note of gaiety. Your arrangement would effervesce with color and add to the already happy atmosphere. If, for some reason, you want to tone down the warmth of the environment or make your arrangement more conspicuous, you would introduce cool colors. White would still be the choice to impart elegance.

If, on the other hand, the room is neutral, bright and intensely colored flowers would be the most dramatic. Visualize, for example, a linear arrangement of anthuriums or red carnations against a white or gray wall.

Of course, you cannot choose color solely to evoke emotion or set a mood. No arrangement exists as a separate entity. Since it becomes an important part of your decor, its color must be keyed to the total environment. In some cases, you may want your arrangement to blend with the background. This treatment makes an arrangement appear larger as it radiates color to its surroundings in a halolike manner. Or you may want it to stand out in strong contrast, in which case you would choose flowers of a complementary color. Perhaps you want to harmonize it by having it pick up or repeat a color used elsewhere in the room. Sometimes for variety you might want to choose the color of your arrangement from an accent color used in the room.

Flower arrangements assert themselves more when they are used against plain walls and away from figured wallpaper or fabrics. If you must use your arrangement in front of a patterned wallpaper, it is better to repeat a color, flower, or leaf found in the wallpaper in order to minimize any conflict with the paper's design. If you have a particular spot where you like to use flowers and the wallpaper presents too much of a problem, consider placing a mirror behind the arrangement, which will not only solve your background problem, but will double the size and depth of your arrangement as its finished back is reflected. You might also place a small folding screen behind the arrangement to break the pattern of the wall covering. (Fig. 32)

To some extent, your color choice may be determined by the available containers. The colors of the flowers must relate to the container in some way, either complementing it, blending with it, or echoing a color in its design.

In a centerpiece, the color of the flowers is determined mostly by its closest neighbors, the china and linen. It is very effective to repeat in the centerpiece a color that appears in the china, especially if you choose to echo a subtle color. Repetition of a color in the place mats is another excellent way to achieve harmony in the overall effect.

Combining Colors

The beginner often wonders how many different colors to use in an arrangement. In general, unless you are putting together one of those old-fashioned bountiful bouquets, it

is best to limit yourself to two or three colors. Just as a
fine painting always has a characteristic color, an arrangement usually is predominantly of one color. To this is added
a smaller amount of a second color along with a dash of
a third color, to provide a nice balance. The dash is usually
a strong vibrant color, and very likely it will be the focal
point. For the sake of harmony and balance, it is best to
arrange the colors in related groupings rather than spotting
them polka-dot fashion throughout the arrangement.

Obviously it is much easier to obtain color harmony with

Fig. 32. To break the pattern of the
wall covering, place a small screen
behind the arrangement.

just a few colors. Each time you add a new color you run the risk of creating discord. However, when you have gained a great deal of experience, the addition of subtle color notes can enhance your arrangement.

But exactly how do you go about selecting actual color combinations from the flowers available to you? A simple yet effective approach is to combine flowers that share a common color ingredient. A more precise method, and one which will offer more opportunities for exciting color combinations, depends on your becoming familiar with the "color wheel."

Following the first method, you tentatively select the group of flowers you would like to use. Analyze them to determine the different colors that nature has combined to arrive at the specific color for each type of flower and then search for one color common to all of them. If you are able to find one common color shared by a group of flowers, you can use them together effectively. For example, if you selected a group of flowers in yellow, orange, and bronze you could use them together, since yellow is present in all of them. In the same way, you can use the red of a carnation but not the red of a rose with yellow flowers, since the scarlet of a carnation contains yellow, while the red of a rose does not.

There is a prevalent theory that pink and yellow or pink and red should not be used together. In both cases these combinations are entirely possible since both of the flowers have a color in common. A warm pink—one which contains yellow—can be combined with either a warm red or yellow. A cool pink—one that contains blue—can be combined only with a cool red, such as a rose, or a cool yellow, such as a snapdragon.

Nature is always one step ahead of us in her ingenuity. Green is a combination of yellow and blue. In most flowers we find either yellow or blue and so the green of the foliage always enhances them. It is a further tribute to nature that no foliage combines with a flower as effectively as its own, not only in color but also in texture. Where could you find a leaf that enhances a geranium more than its own yellow-green ruffled leaves? Or what could compare with the beauty of roses enhanced by their own particular foliage? Could you possibly find anything to emulate the blue-green foliage of the carnation?

A further extension of this common ingredient theory is to select a color and add varying degrees of black, white, or gray. This is called a monochromatic color scheme. A combination of pale pink snapdragons, deep pink carnations, and still deeper pink roses would fall into this category. The concern of the arranger would be to use the colors in the most pleasing proportions—light colors in abundance, medium colors in smaller quantity, and dark colors sparingly. She would also use the lighter colors near the tops and the sides of the arrangement.

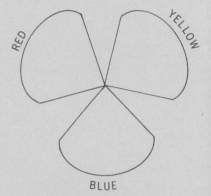

Fig. 33. The primary colors: red, yellow, and blue.

Using the Color Wheel

Useful as this simple formula is, you can expand your choices and begin to acquire the confidence of a master arranger if you will take the time to familiarize yourself with the color wheel. You will be surprised at the exciting color combinations you can create. Experimentation and practice on your part can make you a color specialist.

You will understand the color wheel and the terms used to describe its function if you first learn how it was developed. It may be easier to remember if you think of it in terms of a family circle. First, there are three ancestors: the primary colors—red, yellow, and blue (Fig. 33). These ancestors united with their neighbors and the secondary colors emerged. Red united with yellow and formed orange. Yellow and blue combined to give us green. Blue and red together gave us violet (Fig. 34). The primary and secondary colors then combined to produce the intermediary

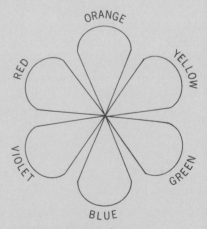

Fig. 34. The secondary colors, orange, green, and violet, are formed from combinations of the primary colors.

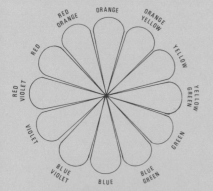

Fig. 35. The intermediary colors are produced by mixing the primary colors with the secondary colors.

colors. That is, each gap was filled by mixing the colors on either side of it. And now we have the whole family circle. (Fig. 35)

The colors adjoining each other on the wheel have a lot in common. They are first cousins, and they are very happy when they are seen together. You can go as far around the color wheel as you wish combining all these cousins. For example, an arrangement of red, red-orange, orange, and orange-yellow would be a pleasing combination. Arrangements using adjacent colors are said to have analogous color schemes.

Complementary colors are those directly opposite each other on the color wheel—for example, blue and orange or blue-green and red-orange. These are distant cousins and they remain distant, always trying to pull away from each other. Their characteristics are so different that when they are used together the result is a strong contrast. A natural example of a complementary color scheme is in the poinsettia, where the red of the blossom pulls away from the green of the foliage, thus eloquently asserting itself. An arrangement of violet flowers against a yellow background also would stand out and be very conspicuous.

In a traditional setting, where the colors are more muted and the effects softer, arrangements against a complementary background are not particularly pleasing. Yet, in a contemporary setting, where the color notes are more strident, the use of an arrangement against a background of a complementary color is very striking.

You could also use a near-complementary color scheme. Choose a basic color—blue, for example. Find its complementary color—orange—and then shift to either side of it, to orange-yellow or red-orange. When used together these form a color combination that is vibrant but not quite as strong as the pure complementary combination.

Another alternative is the triadic color scheme, which combines three colors equally spaced around the color wheel, such as orange-yellow, green-blue, and violet-red. By the same token, the use of four colors equally spaced on the color wheel also is permissible. All in all, it is apparent that if you select combinations from the color wheel in a somewhat orderly fashion you will end up with interesting and pleasing color combinations.

So far we have been discussing only pure colors, or hues, but the colors on the color wheel have other dimensions. These are the colors obtained by adding various amounts of white to produce tints, by adding grays to produce tones, and by adding black to produce shades.

Although it would require a very complex three-dimensional model to represent the full range of possible colors, the simplified two-dimensional representation of the color wheel is quite adequate for flower arranging. In it the tints with the maximum amount of white are placed on the perimeter of the wheel. As you move toward the center, the amount of white is reduced until you reach the band of the hues. These are pure colors without the addition of black or white. Continuing to move inward, you pass through the band of tones, produced by adding grays to the basic colors. As you reach the center of the wheel, you move into the shades, produced by adding increasing amounts of black to the basic colors. (Fig. 36)

You must be careful in using these variations in color. Their proportion of white, black, or gray has an emotional effect on us. An arrangement of only tints is a happy arrangement, bursting with light and the joy of life. An arrangement of hues alone is strong and vibrant but can be too powerful in its impact. An arrangement entirely of tones is subdued and fills one with peace and serenity, while an arrangement of shades alone is depressing.

The best arrangement is one with a variety of each type of color. For example, you can remove the depressing effect of shades of a color by interspersing some hues and tints. You might also add interest to an arrangement of tints by

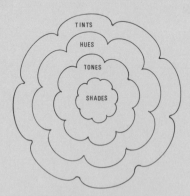

Fig. 36. In addition to the pure colors, or hues, the colors on the color wheel have other dimensions. Tints are produced by adding white to colors, tones by adding grays, and shades by adding black.

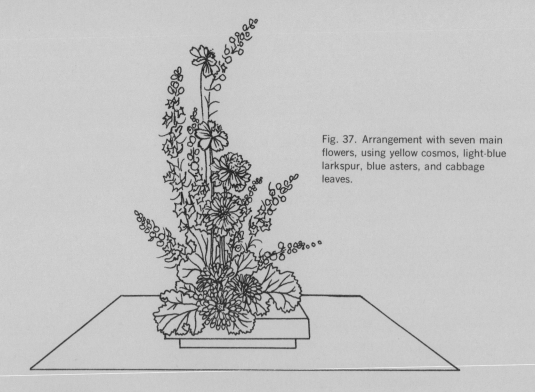

Fig. 37. Arrangement with seven main flowers, using yellow cosmos, light-blue larkspur, blue asters, and cabbage leaves.

introducing hues or tones, or relieve the monotony of a tonal arrangement with a dash of the hue of a color.

Rhythm

Rhythm in art is the harmonious recurrence of a design element—and it is just as much a part of a distinctive flower arrangement as it is of a choice painting or a tastefully decorated room. In a fine painting recurring color notes and forms invite your gaze to move from one to the next until you have experienced a rhythmic passage through the whole. Likewise, spots of similar colors and shapes draw your eye pleasantly around a skillfully decorated room. The same is true of a rhythmic flower arrangement: your eyes move from one flower to the next, up and down, from side to side, and in and out. A flower arrangement without the excitement of this kind of motion is dead and static.

The most important way to achieve this desirable yet elusive quality is through the proper placement of your

Fig. 38. Note the sense of rhythm achieved by the placement of these six flowers.

flowers. The repetition of flower forms and colors, the progression in spacing between flowers, and the subtle repetition of planes and curves all make their contribution to leading the gaze on a pleasant passage through the arrangement. For example, if a flower appears in one position in the arrangement, it must appear elsewhere and be echoed again and again throughout the arrangement so that your eyes move rhythmically from one flower to the next (Figs. 37, 38). Since you are striving for a repetition of color and form, you obviously would never design a bouquet with only one each of several kinds of flowers, for the result would be a disturbing and unattractive hodgepodge.

Although rhythm implies repetition, repetition can also lead to monotony. To avoid monotony you must strive for repetition of more than one type of form. The ideal combination, and the one that provides the most rhythmic motion, is a combination of spike and round flowers. At times, you may not be fortunate enough to have both types, but, as we have seen, you can place your round flowers in line to create an illusion of spike flowers. You can also position round flowers so that some are viewed from the side, others at an angle, and still others full face. Turn your round flowers at the top and edges of your arrangement to give them a more spikelike appearance and gradually turn them at an angle as they descend in the arrangement until, near the base, they show themselves full face. This treatment not only relieves the monotony but also provides motion throughout the arrangement. (Fig. 39)

If you have only spike flowers, you can provide variety by making some of them appear less spikelike than others. Select the thinnest and sharpest spikes for the edges and top of your arrangement, and use the blunter ones farther down. If necessary, break off some of the top buds and tips to give your spikes a rounder form.

Fig. 39. Rhythmic placement of ten flowers. Position round flowers so that they can be viewed from the side, at an angle, and full face.

Fig. 40. Arrangement using seven flowers (Queen Anne's lace), all radiating from one point.

The rhythm of your arrangement really achieves beauty when you depart from repetition in various ways. For example, you should create a progression in the size of the flowers, using the smallest flowers and buds at the top, sides, and front of the arrangement, and gradually progressing to larger flowers as you move downward and toward the center. If all the flowers happen to be the same size, you can use delicate greens to achieve a light and airy feeling on the edges of the arrangement. You can also give an illusion of size difference by clustering your flowers in groups of various sizes.

You should also vary the spacing between flowers from top to bottom, side to side, and front to back in the arrangement. Spaces between flowers should be largest at the top and edges of the arrangement and become progressively smaller toward the base and from the edges to the center of the arrangement. The same sort of progression applies to color. The lighter flowers should be at the top and edges of the arrangement, with a gradual transition to darker colors low in the arrangement and deep in its interior.

Besides repeating individual forms, you should strive for a repetition of planes, curves, and lines. Your arrangement should have one dominant line or curve, with each flower stem contributing to this general line or curve. In addition, all the stems should appear to well up from a common source, never crossing each other or conflicting in any way with the general direction of movement. Whatever shape you are designing, every curve and line in the arrangement must contribute to the envisioned form, with no opposite movements to interrupt the rhythm. (Figs. 40, 41)

Incidentally, you should beware of placing your flowers so that they form squares, since the square is such a static form. Seek instead more interesting patterns such as curves,

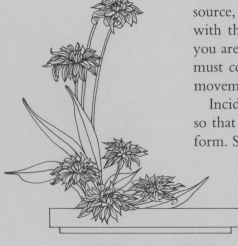

Fig. 41. Each flower contributes to the dominant curve. The stems should appear to well up from a common source.

triangles, and circles. This does not mean that you may not use an even number of flowers, a prevalent conviction that probably originated in Japan, where flowers are normally used in groups of threes and fives. Although beginners invariably ask if they must always use an uneven number of flowers, the answer is simply, "No." Your success depends not on how many flowers you use, but on how you use them.

Creating a Focal Point

If you have achieved rhythm in your arrangement, your eyes will dance with pleasure from one flower to the next. In any type of arrangement except a centerpiece, however, your attention should tend to be drawn to a point just above the edge of the container. This is where all the lines, curves, and progressions in the arrangement appear to converge and be tied together. This is the crescendo in your rhythmic movement, and it is called the focal point. (Fig. 42)

Since the focal point is such an important element in the success of any arrangement, it obviously must be composed of something very special such as a choice flower, an unusual piece of green, or a close grouping of flowers that you have used elsewhere in the arrangement.

If you select a single choice flower, or an unusual piece of foliage, it must relate to the rest of the arrangement in some way, whether in color, form, or texture. Since the focal point serves to tie everything else together, it certainly cannot consist of some entirely foreign element. Instead it should echo either flowers or foliage found elsewhere in the arrangement or the texture or color of the container.

Color is very important. The focal point may be the darkest flower in the arrangement, but it should be only

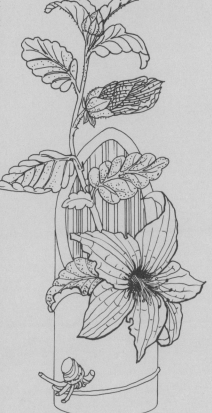

Fig. 42. The focal point in this arrangement is the specimen hibiscus just above the rim of the container.

slightly darker than its neighbors. If it is too dark, the transition in color will be too sudden and cause a break in the visual motion.

If, for your focal point, you choose a selection of some flowers or greens you have used elsewhere, they must be used in a close group, and they must be the choicest of their kind in order to give your focal point the importance it deserves. This center of interest must be attractive and eye-catching—but it must also be of the correct proportion

Fig. 43. Arrangement with twelve flowers. The focal point is the fully developed rose just above the edge of the container.

so as not to overwhelm the arrangement. Since it is low in the arrangement, it should tend to be roundish in shape. (Fig. 43)

Now that you have achieved a rhythmic movement in your arrangement, culminating in a focal point that falls just above the edge of the container, you want the feeling of unity to continue as your eyes move on to the container. This is accomplished primarily by choosing a container of the correct size, shape, and texture. So important is the choice of a container that a later chapter is devoted almost entirely to the subject.

Rhythm is also important in a good centerpiece. Since it will be viewed from all sides, however, it cannot have a single focal point. In many cases, in fact, the centerpiece itself is the focal point of its setting. In this case, the designer applies the principles of rhythm to lead the eye of the observer around the centerpiece and back to the setting, without necessarily creating a focal point. With experience, you will find ways of introducing three or four subtle focal points symmetrically around the arrangement so that the eye of the observer will be momentarily attracted to the one that is visible.

Perhaps a description of an ideal arrangement will be helpful in clarifying the subtleties of rhythm. Spike or spikelike flowers are at the top, edges, and front of the arrangement. As your gaze moves downward, crosswise, and backward, round flowers begin to appear and become larger near the focal point. The colors also become darker. Every change is gradual, though. There are no sudden transitions in color or size which might result in color jolts and physical bulges. The larger and darker flowers, sunk into the arrangement, peek through to give a three-dimensional effect. As with a great fan, all lines travel toward and converge at a point just above the edge of the container. Since it is so enchanting, this focal point holds your eye momentarily; but, since it is related to the rest of the arrangement, it releases your gaze and lets it move again on a pleasant journey among the flowers. You are aware of the container, but it is so much an integral part of the whole arrangement that it does not compete in any way with the beauty of the flowers. You sense only pleasure when you behold the arrangement, for it is a symphony of harmonious notes. (Fig. 44)

Harmony

The dictionary defines harmony in art as a completeness in the relationship of things to each other. In practice, however, harmony cannot be defined explicitly, for it is concerned with elusive, spiritual values. Even so, it is not difficult to sense its presence or be aware of its absence in a flower arrangement. It is more a sense of "belonging" that the viewer feels and appreciates rather than analyzes. In flower arranging, harmony results from the successful application of all the principles we have been discussing, so that the parts of the arrangement "belong" to each other and to the total setting in which the arrangement is placed. Through color, shape, balance, and rhythm, the arrangement captures the total spirit of the environment and the occasion.

To achieve harmony, the discerning flower arranger must begin by selecting a type of arrangement that is in the same spirit or style as its environment. A "traditional" flower arrangement, for example, bursts with an abundance of beautiful and lovely blooms, giving a sense of richness and elegance. It is soft and free flowing and does not appear

Fig. 44. An ideal arrangement featuring the rhythmic placement of flowers. It consists of ten lilacs or buddleias, seven tulips (one forced open), six garden irises, and baby's breath for fill.

Fig. 45. Example of a "traditional" arrangement with wildflowers.

to be contrived in any way. It looks almost as though the flowers were nonchalantly placed in the container. This type of arrangement is most compatible with the traditional home. If the appointments are fine and a formal atmosphere prevails, you would use flowers of the more formal type. If your home is more modest, more casual flowers might be used. (Fig. 45)

An "oriental" arrangement, in contrast, stresses line in its design and uses flowers very sparingly, sometimes with interesting foliage. It creates a mood and imparts a feeling of restraint and contemplation on the part of the arranger. An oriental arrangement is happiest in the simplicity of a contemporary setting. (Fig. 46)

Fig. 46. An "oriental" arrangement, with branches from small fruit trees such as crab apple, cherry, or blue-red-yellow plum.

Fig. 47. A modern arrangement.

Fig. 48. A container appropriate to the environment and the flowers. The ceramic fish is light blue and pink; the fans of coral are maroon with pink highlights.

Modern arrangements, with their attention to line, have been influenced by the oriental, but they also lean toward the traditional with their use of masses of flowers. In a modern arrangement you sense the skill and experience of the arranger, and you sense his comprehension and application of the principles of flower arranging, but you are also aware of his great love of flowers by the joyful way in which he uses them in rich abundance. A modern arrangement can be your choice if your setting is modern or contemporary. As with traditional arrangements, the degree of formality of a modern arrangement would be determined by the formality or informality of the setting. (Fig. 47)

Once you have determined the style of an arrangement, you must decide upon the mood or spirit it is trying to create. It can be lovely, it can be dramatic, it can be dignified, it can be sweet. But it must be definitely something. It must be alive and possess a personality of its own. A church arrangement, for example, should be solemn and uplifting. An arrangement in a recreation room, on the other hand, is gay and happy, while an arrangement in a gracious room is dignified and elegant, and one for the patio is casual and friendly.

To achieve these somewhat abstract and spiritual qualities, you must select flowers that are appropriate to the mood you are trying to create. Just as some people are dignified and proud while others are casual and cozy to be with, certain flowers tend to be formal and aloof while others are less pretentious and more casual. The exact "personality" of a flower is not easy to define, yet it is something one senses rather easily. Large, simple flowers, for example, are more formal in feeling than small, dainty, and complex flowers. It is just as difficult for a sweet little daisy to assume great dignity as it is for a woman under five feet tall to appear stately. In addition flowers that are grown professionally seem to be more formal than those we grow in our gardens or see in the fields. Formality does seem to have a certain connotation of quality.

A few examples should help you develop your own sense of this distinction. The formal flowers include such stately types as large specimen snapdragons, tall hybrid delphiniums, carnations, roses, large chrysanthemums, fuji mums, and calla lilies. More casual flowers are small snapdragons, single delphiniums, carnationettes, daisies, cornflowers, marigolds, zinnias, and petunias.

Harmony also depends on the use of a container that is appropriate to both the environment and the flowers. It will be formal, casual, elegant, simple, Victorian, modern, or exotic in accordance with the effect you are seeking. A formal, traditional arrangement calls for an elegant container fashioned of crystal, silver, or fine china. A Victorian container will be busy and ornate. A container for the outdoors will be of pottery or wicker. A container for a modern setting will have simple lines and texture. Whatever your choice, however, it must suit the flowers, the environment, and the mood. (Figs. 48, 49)

In striving for harmony, you should remember to avoid monotony. Try to introduce some contrast, whether in the interplay of flowers and foliage, or in the contrast between flowers, greens, and containers. Use rough-textured materials with smooth ones. The smooth foliage of camellias, for example, is more handsomely displayed in a rough-textured bowl than in a smooth one. By the same token, the rough texture of marigolds is more interesting in a smooth bowl.

When all is said and done, however, perhaps the best way to explain the concept of harmony at work in flower arranging is by means of a few examples. Imagine, for instance, a formal dining room. The table glows with crystal and fine silver displayed on a beautiful damask cloth. The

Fig. 49. An exotic arrangement using birds of paradise, dracenas, Ming ferns, and eucalyptus. The shape of the dracena leaves echoes the shape of the flowers and therefore contributes to their importance and expansiveness. The other greens are placed so that they contribute to a feeling of flight, in harmony with the birdlike character of the flower.

setting practically demands a crystal or silver bowl filled with roses or carnations. A party on the outdoor terrace, in contrast, would call for an entirely different treatment. Here a rough-hewn table with textured place mats, colorful tumblers, and stainless steel flatware would offer a warm welcome, with the mood enhanced by a centerpiece of daisies casually placed in a pottery or wicker container. The container might be a casserole dish of the correct proportions, color, and texture, or even a metal bucket. (Fig. 50)

A neighbor in the Victorian house might choose an ornate container bursting with a multitude of flowers and colors. But the young bride with a bold modern decor would choose a container with simple clean lines and use simple flowers such as gladioli, strelitzia, bright carnations, or anthuriums (Fig. 51). If her environment is far from formal, she could use large daisies, chrysanthemums, dahlias, or zinnias instead.

In a more traditional house that is charming in its simplicity, good choices would be plain and simple containers of china, pottery, brass, or copper and garden-variety flowers such as daisies, sweet peas, marigolds, or geraniums. Whatever your choices, however, you will know that you have achieved harmony when you sense complete compatibility among all the elements. Everything looks as if it belongs.

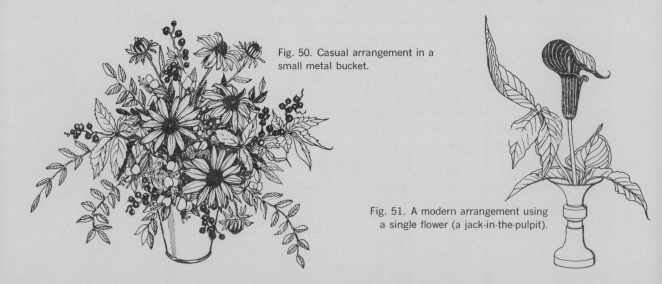

Fig. 50. Casual arrangement in a small metal bucket.

Fig. 51. A modern arrangement using a single flower (a jack-in-the-pulpit).

2 Containers, Figurines, and Stands

☐ A flower arrangement that achieves perfection in every detail is indeed a rarity. The selection of quality flowers may be excellent, the application of the principles of design exemplary, and yet the final arrangement may fall quite short of perfection. Frequently, the difficulty will be with the container.

The container that is ideal in every respect in relation to the flowers and the setting is a rare find. The average flower arranger has only four or five containers on hand; but, whether she has five or fifty to choose from, she is rarely likely to find one that has exactly the right shape, size, color, design, and pattern for both the flowers and the setting. So the selection of a container often must be a matter of compromise, with the arranger adjusting her design to the best container available.

Even so, a few guidelines will enable you to select appropriate containers from your collection and aid you in purchasing new ones to enlarge your collection. Remember first of all that the container is a significant and integral component of the design of any arrangement. It must also function properly as a receptacle for water and must provide mechanical support and stability for the arrangement. In

Fig. 52. An "oriental" hanging flower arrangement. Note that the container harmonizes with the environment and the flowers.

the floral composition it represents the earth from which the flowers appear to emerge. This is why containers of earthy tones and textures seem so natural.

Choosing the Right Container

In selecting the container for a specific arrangement, choose the one that best fits the mood and style of the arrangement you are about to create. Obviously it must also be the right size for the arrangement you have visualized. Remember here our rule of thumb that in the finished arrangement the tallest flowers and greens should be at least one-and-one-half times the height of the container. In a low arrangement, the tallest flowers should equal the sum of the length and width of the container. Shape is also important, for the lines of the container must harmonize with the lines of the arrangement. For example, if you are designing an arrangement dominated by curves and circles, you should use a circular or oval container or one with soft flowing lines. A rectangular container would obviously be inappropriate for such an arrangement.

The container must also be in harmony with its environment. It should be as formal or casual, as elegant or simple, as its surroundings and the flowers it holds. Some flowers and some environments radiate luxury and elegance while others seem less pretentious. The container must always complement the prevailing impression. (Fig. 52)

Fig. 53. A fan-shaped arrangement using orange cosmos. This is not a good arrangement: the flowers overpower the vase; the arrangement is top heavy; and the branching flowers, all cut the same length, have a monotonous effect.

The next thing to consider is the visual weight of the container. Is it in proper proportion to the flowers you are going to use and to the surrounding space? Will it give stability to the arrangement without dominating? Keep in mind that vases of heavy pottery, copper, brass, or wicker have more visual weight than those of the same size but of more delicate materials such as fine porcelain, crystal, or silver. Dark colors also have more visual weight than light ones. (Fig. 53)

The whole question of color, of course, is complex and calls for application of all the principles of color harmony discussed in Chapter One. The simplest course is to use black, white, gray, or green containers, for they are nearly always appropriate. Black is the absence of color and so does not compete with the color of the flowers. White is a combination of all colors and so possesses an inherent unity with all of the colors in your flowers. Gray, a combination of black and white and essentially a neutral color, is never offensive. Most greens are excellent since there is always some green in the stems and leaves of any arrangement.

In any case, the color of the container must always create a sense of unity with the flowers. There must always be some color note tying them together. If the two are of pure complementary colors, they will tend to pull apart. For instance, if you placed bright red carnations in a pure green vase, the flowers would visually separate from it. However, if you were to select a more muted green (with the green toned down by the addition of red), the two colors would be compatible and you would have a distinctive combination. Similarly, pure orange flowers would pull apart from a pure blue vase. Since orange is a combination of red and yellow, you would be better off to use a vase of green, which is a combination of blue and yellow. In this case there would be an easy passage from the yellow in the flowers to the yellow in the vase, and unity and rhythm would be achieved.

Fig. 54. An example of harmony, unity, and rhythm. The pink laurel blossoms are displayed in a soft gray rectangular dish lined with the same pale pink of the laurel flowers. Pussy willows have been used to give height to the arrangement.

If you want your arrangement to appear larger, use a container of the same color as the flowers. Short women apply this principle when they wear just one color in order to appear taller.

In the case of shallow containers, pay particular attention to the color of the interior. If it is an attractive color, it can be extremely effective to allow some of the color to show and be echoed in the colors of the flowers. Imagine pale pink laurel blossoms displayed in a soft gray rectangular dish lined with the pink of the blossoms. Your eyes would travel back and forth from flowers to container, and you would have a perfect example of harmony, unity, and rhythm. (Fig. 54)

The texture of the container must also be taken into account, for it can introduce variety or contrast or it can create a sense of unity. Smooth flowers, smooth greens, and a smooth container will result in unity and an overall large appearance. On the other hand, variety in texture between the container, the flowers, and the foliage can add interest, provided unity has been achieved in some other way.

If you have picked up an exotic container on your travels, emphasize its origin by using material similar to that which you would find in its native country. Flowering branches, for instance, are effectively used in Japanese bowls, while sprays of small orchids combine well with containers from the tropics. Tulips also are attractive in pottery containers shaped like Dutch shoes. (Figs. 55–57)

With practice and experience you will discover many congenial combinations of flowers and containers. In a formal foyer, living room, or dining room, crystal and

Fig. 55. An "oriental" arrangement using flowering branches (bridal wreath).

silver containers are more at home, but they demand the more elegant flowers—roses, carnations, hybrid delphiniums, large snapdragons, and orchids. In more casual settings, fill brass, copper, or wicker containers with the simpler flowers such as daisies, cornflowers, sweetheart roses, zinnias, pansies, marigolds, single delphiniums, miniature carnations, and small snapdragons.

As a general rule, the container should be as simple as possible in order not to detract from the flowers. However, on some occasions you may want to emphasize a particularly handsome container rather than the flowers. One way to do this—and still achieve unity and harmony in the overall design—is to select some characteristic of the container and echo it in specific flowers or greens. For example, if there is pink in the container, include some pink flowers, and your eye will automatically be drawn to the container. This trick is more effective if you echo a subtle color rather than a dominant one. If the vase is decorated with specific flowers, try to include some of these in your bouquet. A generous bunch of violets placed in a teacup decorated with violets is a fine example of unity and harmony achieved in this way.

If the lines of your container are interesting, let them dominate by placing the flowers and greens so that they more or less repeat the lines of the container. An arrangement in a teapot, for example, can be very charming. Arrange your flowers so that the spout and handle are evident and, even better, lay the lid to one side so that it becomes part of the overall design (Fig. 58). (Do not place it too far from the teapot, however, or it will no longer be meaningful. This precise placement applies to any accessory you might use.) When completed, your arrangement should sing, "Look! I am a teapot full of flowers!"

By the same token, if you are arranging flowers in a teacup, mound them so that the essential shape of the cup

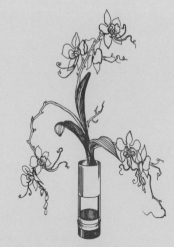

Fig. 56. Small orchids are effective in containers from the tropics.

Fig. 57. An arrangement of tulips in a wooden shoe achieves unity and harmony.

Fig. 58. Teapot arrangement balanced by lid.

Fig. 59. Arrangement in a teacup.

Fig. 60. Arrangement of dried flowers in a pitcher.

Fig. 61. Basket arrangement using tulips and mimosa.

dominates, the handle is evident, and the saucer provides the proper visual weight (Fig. 59). If your choice is a pitcher, take care to emphasize the spout and the handle. Place the flowers high on the handle side and let them cascade toward the spout without obscuring it. (Fig. 60)

Baskets also are ideal and popular containers. But to maintain their identity as baskets you should emphasize their most obvious features, the handles. A good way to design an attractive basket arrangement is to place the basket in front of you so that you are looking along the handle. Position the highest vertical flower close to the handle and then place the longest horizontal flower so that it points away from the opposite side of the handle. From this skeletal framework build an asymmetrical arrangement that seems to flow through the handle. In this way you can avoid the common error of having the handle stand alone with flowers sticking out on each side like the horns on a cow. (Fig. 61)

If you are using containers shaped like birds or other animals, select flowers that allow you to emphasize their lines and reveal their forms (Fig. 62). Their characteristic identities must never be submerged. In the case of religious figurines, take care not to subordinate their beauty or significance, but do compose a unified design. What is more striking than the head of the Virgin Mary backed by a halo of calla lilies? The flowers add to Her own intrinsic beauty and peace, without detracting from Her in any way.

If you want to achieve a feeling of visual separation between the flowers and distracting surroundings, use a special vase. For instance, on a dinner table loaded with food and accessories, flowers in a pedestal vase are lifted above the clutter and eloquently assert themselves. Pedestal vases, whether in a formal or casual environment, always show your flowers off to advantage and make them something very special. Note that the pedestal is included in measuring the overall height of your container.

The Container Collection

If you are to be a serious flower arranger, you must start to collect a supply of suitable containers with adequate variety. Concentrate first on the basic shapes (round, rectangular, and upright) and select neutral colors such as white, off-white, yellow, green, grey, black, and beige. Start your collection with classic materials, such as plain pottery, and then expand it to include silver, copper, brass, crystal, milk glass, and wicker containers. Try to select textures that will be happy in your settings. (Figs. 63, 64)

As you expand your collection, keep in mind the locations in your home where you might want to place your arrangements. As you enlarge your color selection to fit your environment, remember also that you will want to be able to take advantage of the various flowers available throughout the year, particularly the flowers you may grow in your own garden. Finally, you can add figurines, animals, and other containers in diverse shapes. Keep searching for unusual containers, always seeking something new and unique or something that fills a void in your collection.

Fig. 62. Dried flowers arranged in a ceramic container in the shape of a pheasant. The arrangement emphasizes the lines of the container.

Fig. 63. Basic containers of various shapes.

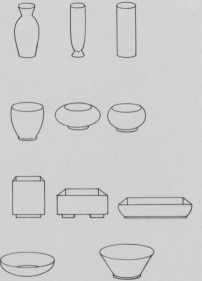

Fig. 64. Handmade pottery containers, with their earth tones and rough textures, are useful for many arrangements.

Remember, too, that many objects not intended as containers can be used with charming results. Do not be disturbed if you find an interesting object that will not hold water. You can always add a glass or a small can such as a tuna fish can to hold your flowers (Fig. 65). Attach the tin to the container with floral clay and cover it with moss or drooping leaves to hide its crudeness. You could also make it less obvious by painting it with tempera in a shade that blends with that of the container. In fact, you can change the color of any container or vase by applying tempera paint. It will readily wash off any time you wish to make a change.

You can also give a container an interesting texture by spraying it with shellac and immediately rolling it in Vermiculite or sand. This will produce an interesting surface which can then be painted. With this method it is easy to convert an ordinary tomato can into a rather elegant vase. (Fig. 66)

Fig. 66. Sand or Vermiculite coatings give an interesting texture to a container. (A) and (B) Sand for texture. (C) and (D) Vermiculite for texture. (E), (F), and (G) To change the color of your container, use tempera paint.

Fig. 65. Buddha statue with cherry branch and blossoms. (A) This arrangement shows how to conceal a water container that has been attached to a figurine. (B) Back view of Buddha figurine.

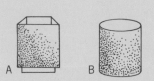

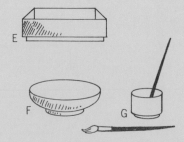

As we have seen, arrangements are often more attractive in a pedestal vase. You can transform an ordinary vase into a pedestal vase by attaching it to an inexpensive candlestick with floral clay. If you wish, you can then spray or paint the whole thing the same color. You can also create a handsome compote by attaching a large shallow container to a candlestick of the correct proportions. (Fig. 67)

Epergnes—centerpieces for table decoration consisting of several grouped dishes or receptacles—are always very attractive when used with flowers, but they are usually very expensive. You can make one by stacking inexpensive sherbet glasses of graded size inside a base consisting of an inexpensive shallow bowl. With floral clay or warm paraffin unite the base of the largest sherbet glass to the inside of the bowl. Then fasten the base of a smaller sherbet glass inside of the bowl of the first glass. If you wish, you can add a third and still smaller sherbet glass (Fig. 68). Now spray the entire construction with paint or gilt. It is even more effective to spray lightly with color and then lightly with gilt. Flowers and greens cascading from each receptacle in soft, graceful lines will create an overall impression of a magnificent shower of flowers spilling over in great abundance.

Fig. 67. An ordinary vase can be transformed into a pedestal vase by attaching it with floral clay to an inexpensive candlestick.

Figurines and Accessories

Figurines and accessories can often provide a flower arrangement with an extra physical or spiritual dimension. Physically, they are sometimes necessary to provide visual balance by extending the length, depth, or height of an arrangement to a dimension that could not be achieved with the flowers alone. They are placed wherever the extra weight is needed. Spiritually, a figurine or accessory can add to the atmosphere, suggest or enrich a theme, or tell a story.

Fig. 68. An epergne made of a bowl and two sherbet glasses.

Fig. 69. In this arrangement the flowers are secondary to the figurine, which is the dominant element in the design.

Since accessories are always used to enhance an arrangement, they must be selected with great discretion as to size, good lines, harmony, and usability. It is always worthwhile to buy figurines of good quality, for you will enjoy them much more and find yourself using them more often. In general you will find it more effective to use figures that are in repose rather than physically active ones, since the activity can be a disturbing element that distracts attention from the flowers. Remember too that figurines and accessories must harmonize with the flowers, the container, and the environment, and they must be consistent in quality and degree of formality.

To function well, a figurine must be in correct proportion to the arrangement. There is no hard and fast rule governing this, but the figurine ought to provide the comfortable feeling of being an integral part of the arrangement rather than a dominant factor. In general, figurines should be no more than one-quarter to one-third the height of the arrangement. Like all rules, however, this one can be broken. It is quite possible to have a good reason for emphasizing the figurine rather than the flowers, in which case it can be so large as to become the imposing and dominant element in the design (Fig. 69). Generally, if you want the flower arrangement to retain dominance, you should limit yourself to one or two accessories in any design. Here, too, the rule can be broken if you want the flowers to play a subordinate role in the total design.

The lines of the accessories must not conflict with the lines of the arrangement, but rather flow easily into the design and function as a pleasing accent or complement. Often something as simple as a book, either closed or open, will add the touch you need. It is particularly effective if the cover has a color accent that matches some color in the flowers.

Accessories are usually placed on the table to one side of the arrangement, but on occasion you can use them in the water in your container. Do not place the figurine in water unless you would normally find it there. You might rightly immerse a frog or a swan, but a female figure would look pretty silly shivering and dragging her skirts through water. If it is necessary to place a figurine in close contact with the water in your container, do not overlook the possibility of placing it on a flat rock in the water. Remember, however, that the rock will add visual weight to your design.

Finally, a word of warning: Never use a figurine just because you think it is attractive by itself. If it is not possible to make it an integral part of an arrangement, do not use the figurine.

Flower stands or bases are other useful accessories. Their main purpose is to add height or weight to an arrangement so that better balance is achieved. The stand must be at least a little larger than the diameter of the vase. Otherwise, it will be out of scale and merely make the arrangement look

Fig. 70. A flower stand provides a finished, professional touch that lifts an arrangement out of the ordinary and makes it truly distinctive.

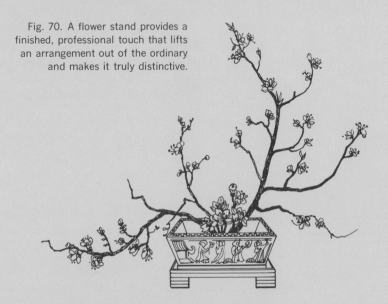

top heavy. Needless to say, the stand must harmonize in style with the vase, flowers, and environment. Use stands whenever you can, for they provide a finished, professional touch that lifts an arrangement out of the ordinary and makes it truly distinctive. (Fig. 70)

In many cases, an arrangement can also be enhanced by placing it on a table mat of an appropriate material such as linen, straw, or fibers. Select mats as to size and color with the same care that you select any accessory. When a design includes both an arrangement and an accessory such as a figurine, a table mat frequently serves to unite the two into a coherent whole. (Fig. 71)

Fig. 71. An arrangement can be enhanced by being placed on a table mat.

3 *Mechanical Aids*

☐In flower arranging, a basic technical requirement is to have some means enabling you to place flowers precisely where you want them and to have them stay there while still obtaining water and nutrients. A wide variety of commercially manufactured mechanical aids are available for these purposes, and there are many others that you can make yourself.

The perfect mechanical aid would provide you with complete flexibility in placing your flowers and would hold them firmly in place once you had positioned them. It would also allow you to change your mind and reposition flowers and would be suitable for use with the whole range of flowers you might have available. Unfortunately, such an ideal device does not yet exist.

Even so, the increasing interest in flower arranging has stimulated manufacturers to develop a great variety of mechanical aids that are suitable for different situations. It is a good idea to keep alert for the latest development, since any mechanical aid that will increase your joy and ability in arranging flowers is well worth the price. New mechanical aids usually first appear at flower shows. Go to the shows, visit the commercial displays, and linger in the areas

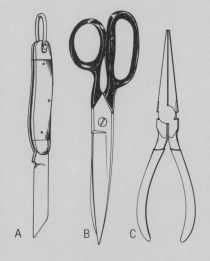

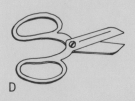

Fig. 72. Tools and aids. (A) Florist's knife. (B) Household scissors. (C) Needle-nosed pliers. (D) Wire-cutting shears. (E) Saw.

devoted to garden club work. You can learn a great deal by studying the outstanding entries of garden club members. By analyzing their arrangements, you will see how they have executed the principles of design with the help of mechanical aids.

Because of the upswing of interest in flower arranging, many florists now offer a wide selection of mechanical aids for sale. Most of them will be happy to give you professional advice on their use. However, you should check first to see if your florist is unusually busy. Even if he is cordial, he is not likely to give you much attention if you approach him near important holidays or on any day when business is overwhelming.

When it comes to using mechanical aids in specific situations, you will frequently find that you have to improvise. For best results, you should have the right tools and materials at hand. A pair of good household scissors, a pair of wire-cutting shears, a pair of long-nosed pliers, a small, inexpensive saw, an ice-pick, and a sharp knife are all desirable. Useful materials to have on hand are floral clay, waterproof tape, corsage thread, floral tape, chenille stems, "Twistems," glass chips, sheet moss, and flower wires, all of which are available from your florist. Other useful materials you can find around home include paraffin wax (partly used candles are fine), transparent Scotch tape (the waterproof variety if you can find it), miscellaneous pins and nails, aluminum foil, newspapers, and small stones. (Fig. 72)

And, of course, you must have an assortment of flower holders, including pin-point holders of various shapes, sizes, and pin separations; blocks of plastic foam sold under the trade names of "Oasis" and "Quickee"; chicken wire with one-inch openings, preferably plastic coated; hardware cloth with one-quarter- and one-half-inch openings, also preferably plastic coated; blocks of white or green rigid polystyrene foam; shredded polystyrene foam; and Vermiculite. All of these are available from your florist.

Before we discuss the uses of the various kinds of flower holders, you should know some of the characteristics of these special ancillary materials.

Floral Clay

No floral kit is complete without floral clay, a green clay very similar to the modeling clay we all used in kindergarten. Because of its adhering qualities, it can be used to form seals or to fasten one article to another or to a surface. Keep in mind that it adheres well only to surfaces that are completely dry and clean.

Floral clay is used primarily for securing flower holders to the bases of vases or bowls but it has a number of other uses. You can seal a container that is not waterproof by applying a thin layer of floral clay to the inside. You can make a cracked vase watertight by pushing floral clay into the crack and applying a thin layer over the crack on the inside of the vase. You can also use it to secure figurines or vases in precarious positions. Simply apply a patch of floral clay to the clean, dry base of the figurine and press it into the desired position. Floral clay is also useful for securing candles in candlesticks. Place a small ball of clay in the cup of the candlestick, insert the candle, and, as you press it home, give the candle a sharp twist. The clay will hold the candle in position indefinitely. (Figs. 73, 74)

Floral clay will sometimes stain or tarnish silver or metal bowls. You can prevent this by lining your bowls with foil or plastic wrap. You can also buy a clay especially made for use in silver containers and guaranteed not to stain. It is reddish brown instead of green and is sold under the trade name of "Posy Clay."

Floral clay cannot be used by itself as a holder for fresh

Fig. 73. Apply a patch of floral clay to the clean, dry base of a figurine to secure it in a precarious position.

Fig. 74. The figurine has been secured to its base by floral clay.

Fig. 75. Floral clay can be used as a holder for dried flowers. In this arrangement a piece of the clay has been pressed against the driftwood.

flowers because it is impervious to water, but it can be used as a holder for dried flowers and foliage or for plastic flowers. It is especially satisfactory for these uses since you can press a piece of any size or shape against the bottom of the container and simply insert the flower stems. Be sure to use a piece of clay large enough to prevent the flowers from sagging after insertion. (Fig. 75)

You can also use floral clay to alter the lines of a piece of driftwood by filling in depressions or accentuating curves. With a combination of clay and driftwood, it is even possible to fashion birds, animals, and other interesting forms. Once the creation has been painted, it is difficult to detect your alterations or additions.

Floral clay can be stored and reused several times. After use, remove any foreign material that may have become attached to the surface or embedded in the mass, then shape the clay into a roll, and squeeze or knead it to remove any moisture. Finally, dry the surface with a paper towel, wrap the roll in foil, and store the clay until you need it again.

Other Accessories

Another useful item to have in your work area is waterproof tape, a very strong tape that comes in half-inch rolls. Like floral clay, it adheres properly only to clean dry surfaces. Although presently it comes only in green and white, in the future it undoubtedly will be available in a variety of colors. For wrapping false stems and a number of other uses, you should also have some floral tape, which is simply a highly waxed, stretchable crepe paper. It is available in one-half-inch-wide rolls and in a variety of colors (Fig. 76). Corsage thread, another invaluable aid, is a very strong, waxy green thread which can be purchased in spools. It is made in two weights, light and heavy.

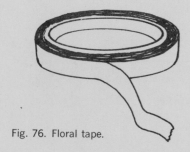

Fig. 76. Floral tape.

"Twistems," simple devices consisting of a sandwich of two narrow strips of kraft paper glued together over a soft iron wire, are used primarily as substitutes for tying with thread or string. Instead of being tied, the ends are simply twisted together, usually by just one full turn. They have gained popularity because of the ease with which they can be handled, essentially with one hand, and the precision with which the tension can be adjusted. They are extremely strong but gentle fasteners, yet can be removed easily. "Twistems" are available cut to various lengths or in continuous rolls.

Flower wires are another staple of the arranger's workroom. They are simply straight lengths of soft iron wire, either plain or painted green, and can be curved, bent, or twisted at will without springing back. Flower wires come in twelve- and eighteen-inch lengths and in a wide range of gauges.

Finally, for decorative purposes you may want to have a supply of chenille stems of the type that florists use for decoration in corsages and wedding bouquets. They are made in the same way as pipe cleaners except that the fibers are longer and are made of rayon or nylon. They come in twelve-inch lengths and a great variety of colors.

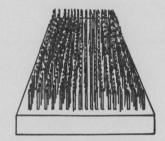

Fig. 77. Pin-point holders.

Pin-Point Holders

The most important mechanical accessories you will need are holders of various types. One of the most versatile and popular for the home flower arranger is the pin-point holder, which in some areas is called a "frog." A pin-point holder is a device with an evenly spaced array of upright pointed pins secured in a heavy metal base. Flowers are held in place by impaling the ends of the stems on the upright pins. Pin-point holders are manufactured in several sizes, shapes, and pin spacings. Some of them are made in inter-

Fig. 78. Pin-point holders can be secured in place by floral clay.

locking segments so that you can create holders of different sizes and shapes as you need them. Exercise judgment in selecting pin-point holders. Do not hesitate to pay a few pennies more for one with closely spaced pins, since this makes it much easier to control your flowers. Holders with brass pins also are more satisfactory than the usual iron or steel varieties since the pins are sharper and do not rust. (Fig. 77)

As with any holder, the pin-point holder must first be positioned and secured in the container you have selected for your arrangement. In general, the holder will be the place from which the flower stems appear to radiate. Thus, if you begin by visualizing the completed arrangement, you will be able to determine exactly where the holder should be placed. In a round bowl, the holder normally should be placed on the bottom in the center. In a shallow traylike container the proper position again will probably be on the bottom, but not necessarily in the center.

In either case, the pin-point holder can be attached by means of floral clay. Roll a small piece of clay between your hands until it resembles a worm about a quarter of an inch in diameter and five or six inches long. Lay the clay in a circle on the bottom of the holder and place the holder in the desired position in the container. Then press the holder firmly with a twisting motion to fasten it securely.

If your container is very shallow and you want to keep the holder as low as possible, you can use a different method. Place the pin-point holder directly on the bottom of the container, lay the "worm" of clay snugly around its base, and then press the clay so that it adheres to both holder and container. You can even make the clay look like an integral part of the holder by using the eraser on a pencil to make a scalloped design around its edge. (Fig. 78)

Obviously a pin-point holder will remain secure only in a container with a reasonably flat base. If you want to use one in a round-bottomed container, pour melted paraffin into the bowl to form a platform for the holder at the desired level. Place the pin-point holder in the wax before the wax has become completely solidified. As the wax hardens, the holder will be fixed in place.

Although we in the Western world use clay to secure pin-point holders, the Japanese hold them in place by setting the holders on small squares of wet newspaper. The wet paper prevents the *kenya* (as the Japanese call the pin-point holder) from sliding, and they believe the ink in the newspaper makes the flowers last longer. If you have no floral clay, you might try this method. Remember, however, that the arrangement will be less stable, so that you will have to be more careful while constructing or moving it.

Using Pin-Point Holders in Tall Vases

It is practically impossible to use a pin-point holder at the bottom of a tall vase, since you cannot direct long stems all the way to the desired spots in a holder that you probably cannot even see. If your vase is opaque, you can overcome this difficulty by stuffing it partly full with newspaper that has been soaked in water, then squeezed almost dry. Top this foundation with several layers of newspaper cut to the same diameter as the vase. Pour melted paraffin into the vase until the paper has become impregnated with wax and a layer about a quarter of an inch thick is resting on top. When the wax begins to congeal, sink your holder into it. With your pin-point holder secured near the top of the vase in this way (Fig. 79), you will have no difficulty placing your flowers exactly where you want them. If you are planning to use heavy material that might make the arrangement top heavy, put a layer of pebbles in the bottom of the vase before you fill it with newspaper. (Stones, of course, can be substituted for newspaper as the basic filler.)

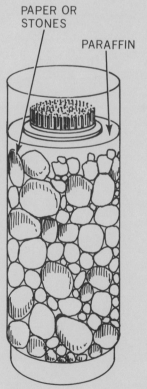

PAPER OR STONES

PARAFFIN

Fig. 79. Pin-point holder in tall opaque vase.

If your tall vase is transparent, you must use a different method, since you would not want pebbles or wet paper to be visible. One approach is to support your pin-point holder on a platform made of hardware cloth and suspended from the top of the vase (Fig. 80). Begin by cutting a cross from hardware cloth, making the arms about an inch wide. The overall size of the cross from tip to tip of opposite arms should equal the diameter of the vase, plus twice the depth at which you want to place the pin-point in the vase, plus two inches. If you make the arms too long at first, you can trim them to the proper length after you have folded the cross and fitted it to your vase.

Now place a pin-point holder of appropriate size and shape at the center of the cross. Lay a wire between two rows of pins, draw the ends under the cross, and twist them until the wire is taut. Two such wires approximately at right angles should be enough to secure the holder. Next bend the four arms of the cross upward so that the whole assembly just slides into the vase. Adjust the height of the holder so that the tops of the pins are at least a half-inch below the water level in the vase and bend the arms of the cross down over the edge of the vase. At this point you

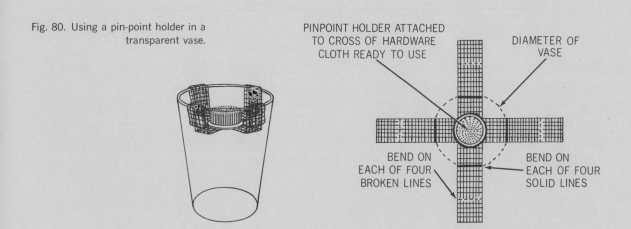

Fig. 80. Using a pin-point holder in a transparent vase.

PINPOINT HOLDER ATTACHED
TO CROSS OF HARDWARE
CLOTH READY TO USE

DIAMETER OF
VASE

BEND ON
EACH OF FOUR
BROKEN LINES

BEND ON
EACH OF FOUR
SOLID LINES

can cut the arms if they seem too long. For extra security, wrap a length of Scotch tape around the vase and over the ends of the arms.

Note that, with this method, the platform itself can function as part of the holder. If you insert some of your longer stems through the holes of the hardware cloth, they will show in the lower part of a transparent vase and appear as part of your design. Besides presenting a convincing appearance, the stems in the vase add visual weight and physical stability. Long stems that are too large for the hardware cloth can be inserted in the openings at the corners of the cross. These openings can also serve for holding foliage you might use to conceal your mechanics.

With this method not much water is available to the flowers in the pin-point holder, so it must be replenished frequently. Obviously the lower you position the holder in the vase, the more water your flowers will be able to absorb and the less attention they will require. But you must not place it so low that it shows through the vase.

Problems with Pin-Point Holders

As you construct your arrangement, there is a good chance that you will have difficulty impaling some of the flower stems on the pins of the holder. Delicate, pulpy, or hollow stems in particular can cause problems.

Delicate stems do not have enough body or firmness to hold them in position after they are impaled. One way to overcome this difficulty is to use a heavy, firm, hollow stem as a reinforcing sleeve for the delicate stem. If you have no hollow stem you can make one by inserting a nail or ice pick up the center of a short length of a heavier stem.

Fig. 81. A fine stem has been placed into a gladiolus stem to give it better support on a pin-point holder. The gladiolus stem can be disguised with greens.

Fig. 82. A fine stem has been wired to a piece of gladiolus stem to give it better support on the pin-point holder. The stem can be disguised with greens.

Thread the finer stem through the opening and impale the whole thing on a pin-point holder (Fig. 81). Another satisfactory method is to tie the delicate stem to a short length of heavier stem with corsage thread. Hold one end of the corsage thread against the stems at the point where you want them fastened and wind it around the stems several times. Be careful not to pull the thread so tight that it cuts the stems. On the last turn, pull the thread up between the ends of the stem and cut it off. (Fig. 82)

With both these methods, you must make sure that the end of the finer stem reaches the water. Also, the heavier stem should be as short as possible so that it will not be obvious to the viewer. It will give sufficient support even if it is no longer than the pin itself. The mechanics of these operations should be camouflaged with a small piece of foliage tucked in the right place.

Flowers with soft pulpy stems sometimes slowly become disengaged from the pin-points. You can prevent this by taping the soft stem to a short length of firm stem to provide the support necessary to keep it in place.

Hollow stems present another problem. To make one stay firmly in place, you should take a solid stem of the right size, slide it inside the hollow stem as far as it will go, and cut it off even with the end of the hollow stem, thus transforming the hollow stem into a solid one. If you do not have a long enough solid stem, you can impale a short length on the pin-point and then slip the hollow stem over it, making certain that the end is in water (Fig. 83). Note, however, that the hollow stems of some bulb flowers tend to split and must be tied with corsage thread or raffia.

The most serious limitation of pin-point holders arises when the design of your arrangement calls for flower heads to cascade below the level of the holder or for stems to be horizontal or nearly so. For such an arrangement, it is generally better to use either plastic foam or a chicken-wire holder, or at least to add a ball of chicken wire above the pin-point holder (see page 74). The chicken wire should rise above the opening of the vase and can be attached to the vase with two or three strips of waterproof tape. If these devices cannot be used, the only approach is to massage the flower stems into appropriate curves. If the stems are hollow, you can insert wires to make it easier to shape them.

The pin-point holder almost always presents a discordant note if it is visible in your finished arrangement. The most effective way to camouflage the holder is to hide it behind some leaves from the foliage of your flowers. If you have planned your arrangement carefully, this foliage will become part of the visual balance. If foliage is not appropriate, you can obtain interesting effects by covering the holder with sheet moss, pebbles, rocks, or glass chips of various colors. Or you can wrap the base of the holder with floral tape of an appropriate color. You might also paint your holder to match the container, although this makes the holder less versatile by tending to restrict its use to one particular container.

When you discard an arrangement, remember to include the pin-point holder in the wash-up. Hold it under briskly running hot water to dislodge the debris that collects between the points. After frequent use, the points of your holder are likely to be bent. They can be straightened with a special Japanese tool called a *kenzan naoshi* which has a hollow end that fits over the pins, enabling you to bend the tips back into position. Its other end is pointed for removing debris caught between the pins. If you cannot find a *kenzan naoshi,* you can straighten the pins with long-nosed pliers or with heavy eyebrow tweezers.

Fig. 83. Hollow stem placed over small firm stem.

Fig. 84. Blue Ribbon holder.

Other Ready-made Holders

While the conventional pin-point holder is by far the most popular of the commercially manufactured holders, many other types are available. A very useful one is a combination pin-point and mesh holder, with the mesh forming a dome over the pin-point base. This has the advantage of supporting your flower stems at two reasonably separated points and enabling you to insert stems almost horizontally.

You can also purchase a pin-point holder attached to the base of a metal cup large enough to provide water for your flowers. This is designed for use in bowls you do not want to risk staining with water. Since the flowers do not get a great deal of water, however, you will probably want to remove the arrangement when it is not on display and place it inside another bowl filled with water to a level well above the rim of the cup.

A specially designed mesh holder also is available for use with heavy-stemmed flowers. It is usually a die-cast metal structure consisting of an open grid base attached to an inverted cup-shaped grid. If the mesh holes are so big that your flowers flop around, you can make them secure by adding reinforcing stems as described above.

Another excellent device, called the Blue Ribbon holder, consists of a series of concentric rings of florist's greening pins standing upright in a heavy base. Greening pins resemble hair pins except that they are wider and only about one-and-one-half inches long and are made of heavier soft iron wire. They are so malleable that they can easily be bent in any direction. Normally the stems are simply inserted between the prongs of the pins, but you can attain more precise control by bending the wires, even to the point where the prongs actually grasp the stems. The Blue Ribbon holder does not work well with delicate stems, al-though they can be reinforced as described above. After the holder has been used, you can bend the prongs back to their original positions and use the holder again for entirely different arrangements. (Fig. 84)

Finally, you should be warned to avoid those common glass holders with all the holes pointing straight up. Even the most talented arranger can do nothing with them.

Plastic-Foam Holders

A real boon to flower arrangers is the development of a green spongy plastic material that absorbs water. It is sold in florists' shops under several trade names, such as "Oasis" or "Quickie," and comes in bricks that can be cut to any desired shape or size. All but the most delicate stems can penetrate the foam and, once inserted, will be held exactly where they were placed and still be supplied with water.

The first step in using plastic foam is to cut an appropriate block for the arrangement you have in mind. You can easily make the major straight cuts with a heavy knife or crude saw and then sculpture the block to any shape with your florist's knife. Although the foam can be cut when wet, it is best to cut it while it is still dry.

A good rule of thumb for determining the size of the top of the block needed for any arrangement is to make each edge equal to twice the diameter of the bunch you obtain when you hold all the stems of the flowers and foliage tightly together. This assumes that the top of the block is square. If it is any other shape, it should have about the same surface area as the square. To determine the depth of the block, assume that no more than one inch of the block will protrude above the water line of your arrange-ment and not less than one inch will be below it. Never

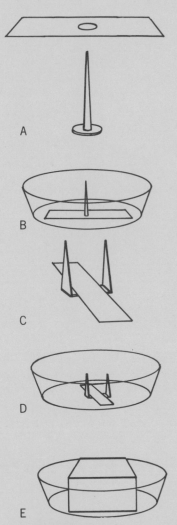

Fig. 85. Securing a small piece of foam in a shallow bowl: (A) Tape with hole cut for nail. (B) Nail taped to bottom of shallow container. (C) Tape placed over staple nail. (D) Staple nail taped to bottom of shallow container. (E) Foam impaled on nail or staple nail in a shallow container.

use a block less than one-and-a-half inches deep. Increase the depth for large and heavy stems.

Before placing the foam in your container, soak it in water for at least five minutes. It is advisable to add a floral preservative to the water in which you soak the foam.

Plastic foam blocks do not have to be secured in shallow containers, bowls, or low vases with large openings. However, if you are using a small piece of foam in a shallow bowl you may experience some difficulty in keeping it stationary. In this case, you can impale the foam on the points of a large double-pronged nail (a staple nail) fastened upside down to the bottom of the container with waterproof tape or floral clay. If you do not have a staple nail, you can use a large-headed roofing nail or even a small pin-point holder to fasten the block of foam in place. (Fig. 85)

In a tall vase, you can support the foam on a cross of hardware cloth cut as was described for the pin-point holder. Make the cross large enough so that about a half-inch of the piece of foam protrudes above the top of the vase. The piece of foam does not have to be secured in any way unless it is small or the arrangement ' going to be top heavy, in which case it can be tied with corsage thread or secured with waterproof tape.

Once the plastic foam is in position, fill the container with water containing floral preservative. The water level should be no more than an inch from the top of the piece of foam. Make sure that the block of foam is not so large that there is no way to replenish the water that is lost through evaporation and absorption by the flowers. If the foam does fill the entire opening of the container, you should cut grooves in the sides of the block so that you can pour water down into the bottom of the vase. When using plastic foam, it is important to replenish the water frequently. Otherwise salts in the preservative solution could become so concentrated in the foam as to be toxic to the flowers.

When you insert the cut ends of flower stems into plastic foam, be careful not to push them all the way through the foam so that they protrude into the water. For some reason the flowers seem to last longer if the ends of the stems are contained in the foam. However, you should make certain that as many of the cut ends as possible reach below water level in the foam block. Even stems inserted horizontally into the above-water portion of the foam can be directed downward to the water level if you massage the stems to give them the necessary curve.

It is better not to disturb the stems after insertion. Pulling the stems out to reposition them creates a vacuum in the cut ends and damages their ability to draw water. If you have to change the position of a flower, cut the stem before reinserting it.

You can use plastic foam in many ingenious ways in flower arranging. For instance, you can make a table center-piece without any container by wrapping a thoroughly wet block of foam in a single layer of aluminum foil, closing the wrap in the center at the top. Insert the stems of your flowers through the foil and into the block of foam, being careful not to penetrate more than halfway through the block. If you are using weak-stemmed flowers, make holes in the foil with an ice pick or a nail before inserting the stems. Do not change your mind about the positioning of the flowers, however, since water can leak from the unfilled holes.

You can make floral wall decorations in much the same way. Wrap the wet foam in a single layer of foil and impale it on a finishing nail driven into the wall. The nail should protrude one to two inches from the wall and be angled upward. With the foam in position, you can insert flowers to create your design. (Fig. 86)

If, for some occasion or just for the fun of it, you want to add some flowers to a green plant, you can attach small foil-wrapped balls of foam to your plant with "Twistems" or dark green chenille stems and insert one flower in each. The flower will receive adequate moisture and your plant will be enhanced.

When you discard an arrangement, you can dry the foam and reuse it several times until the holes made by the stems have become so numerous that the foam is weakened. On subsequent occasions, however, you should use floral preservative only in the water in the container and not in the water used to soak the foam.

Fig. 86. A floral wall or door decoration can be made by using plastic foam wrapped in foil and impaled on a finishing nail.

Chicken-Wire Holders

The principle in using chicken-wire flower holders is to fill the space in a container with a loose network of openings of various sizes through which you can thread the stems of your flowers so that they will be held at two or more points. Since the openings are randomly spaced, it is usually possible to find a set of openings that will hold each flower where you want it. Chicken wire also has the advantage of being so inexpensive that it is feasible to make permanent holders tailored for each vase.

To make a chicken-wire holder, cut a rectangle of small-mesh chicken wire about twice as wide as your container and about seven inches longer than twice its height (Fig. 87A). Lay the wire on a flat surface and fold the two long edges toward the middle to make a flattened roll (Fig. 87B). Do not press it completely flat. Then bend about one-and-a-half inches of one end of the roll upward at a right angle and fold the other end down to meet the first end (Fig. 87C). Stuff this structure into your container, using the flat side as the base (Fig. 87D). The other end should protrude an inch or two from the top of the container. Finally, with a pair of long-nosed pliers, long-bladed scissors, or wire shears, reach into the structure and pull and bend wires to make the spacings of the openings between the wires as uniform as possible.

If the holder is for a shallow container or for the top of a transparent vase, use the same procedure but cut the wire rectangle twice as wide and only four or five inches more than twice the height you want the final holder to be. For shallow containers you can also make a ball-shaped holder of chicken wire. Cut a square or circular piece of chicken wire that is two or three times the diameter of the ball you want. Roll the edges inward and squeeze it into the shape of a ball the way you would make a snowball.

Sometimes a cap of chicken wire is used in conjunction with a pin-point holder to provide extra height and support. Fold a piece of chicken wire in half, taking care to have the wires on the top layer cross the openings on the bottom layer. The object is to make a double layer of wire with smaller openings to provide greater control in positioning your flowers. Cut a square of the double layer about twice as large as the diameter of the cap you intend to make. Press the chicken wire over an inverted bowl of the proper size to mold it into a bowl shape. Trim the edges so the chicken-wire cap has a reasonably true rim, then invert the molded wire form over a pin-point holder that has already been secured to the bottom of your container. Fasten the wire form to the container by pressing its rim into a ring of floral clay that has been pressed in the correct position on the dry base of the container. With this device the stems will be held in place at their ends by the pin-point holder, while the chicken wire supports them at any angle you are trying to achieve.

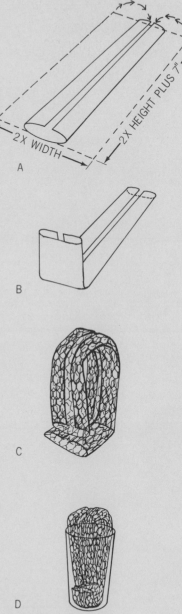

Fig. 87. Steps in making a chicken-wire holder.

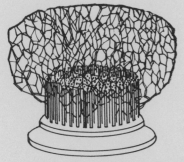

Fig. 88. Pin-point holder with a chicken-wire "cap."

This arrangement is most effective with light delicate flowers. If you plan to use large heavy flowers that need added support, it is better to use a chicken-wire ball in conjunction with the pin-point holder. Make a ball of chicken wire of the proper size and press it down to the base of the pin-point holder, so that it resembles a full bouffant cap on top (Fig. 88). Make sure the wire ball extends one inch or so above the rim of the container. You can attach the chicken-wire cap to the pin-point holder by tightly encircling it with a "Twistem" around the base of the holder. It will be even more secure if you thread wires between the pin-points and around the bottom of the pin-point holder and then attach the whole thing to the base of your container with floral clay.

In normal opaque containers and vases, the basic rolled chicken-wire holder does not usually have to be fastened in place. If it is not secure, you can attach it to the container with two-inch-long strips of waterproof tape. Slip the tape through a loop of chicken wire near the edge of the container. Attach one end to the edge of the container, pull the other end taut, and fasten it to the outside. Three or four such loops around the top of the container will secure the chicken wire (Fig. 89). In shallow containers, you can secure the rolled chicken wire by making a pad of floral clay about one-quarter-inch thick, sticking it to the bottom of the dry container, and then pressing the base of the chicken-wire roll firmly into it.

For transparent containers, you should suspend the chicken-wire holder from the top of the vase where it will not be visible. One way to accomplish this is to place the holder on a wire platform hooked to the top of the container. To make the platform, cut two lengths of heavy florist's wire and cover them with floral tape (Fig. 90). Each piece should be as long as the diameter of the rim of the container, plus twice the depth of the bottom of the chicken wire below the rim, plus twice the length of the hooks that will hang over the edge of the container. Bend each wire into a U shape with the ends turned back to form hooks, and insert them in the container. Be sure the two wires cross at a right angle. Now set the roll or ball of chicken wire on the cross and secure it to the container with water-proof tape. If your dimensions have all worked out, the chicken wire should protrude about one inch above the top of the container.

Fig. 89. Tape used to keep chicken wire secured in place.

Using Chicken-Wire Holders

In using a chicken-wire holder, the objective is to direct stems through the network of openings so that they are held in exactly the desired position. After you start a stem through the first opening, feel your way through the chicken wire until the stem is as far into the holder as you want it. Start with the most important flowers in your arrangement, since, as the holder becomes criss-crossed with stems, it becomes more difficult to find a path for a stem precisely where you want it.

The only major disadvantage of chicken wire is that it does not insure as precise control over the placement of flowers as some other holders do. Since some of the holes may turn out to be too large to hold some of the stems firmly in place, or not in quite the right relationship to one another, you may experience some difficulty in making the flowers stay exactly where you want them. This is especially likely to happen with the first three flowers you place. Yet, since they are the key flowers that establish the outline of the arrangement, they must be very precisely and firmly positioned. If you have trouble, you should first position the flower exactly where you want it. Note the point on the stem where it emerges from the chicken wire and remove it from the holder. Take a three-inch piece of

Fig. 90. The chicken-wire holder can be suspended from the top of the vase.

flexible wire (fine or heavy depending on the thickness of the stem) and wrap it once around the stem at this point. Fasten the wire by twisting the two ends together a couple of times, but do not make it so tight that it cuts into the stem. Now reposition the flower in the holder and pull the ends of the wire in approximately opposite directions. As you hold the flower stem with one hand exactly where you want it to remain, wrap the ends of the wire around the nearest strands of the chicken wire, making them so taut that the stem is held firmly in place.

You can also gain added support by inserting the first three flowers into the chicken-wire holder through the same opening in the top of the mesh. The stems can be further reinforced by wrapping a short wire around all three stems and attaching it to the mesh as described above. Sometimes all that is necessary is a small wire ring to hold the flowers like a bracelet just above the chicken-wire holder.

There is nothing beautiful about chicken wire. Your final step in constructing any arrangement with it should be to make sure that all wires and tapes are appropriately hidden by flowers or foliage.

Hardware-Cloth Holders

Hardware cloth is wire mesh composed of quarter- or half-inch square holes. It is used in much the same way as chicken wire but, since the holes are smaller, is better suited for use with smaller, delicate-stemmed flowers.

Hardware cloth makes a useful holder for tall vases (Fig. 91). Cut a circle two inches larger than the diameter of the bottom of the vase. Make evenly spaced one-inch-long cuts into the edge of the circle and bend the segments down to form legs for the holder. Stand this structure on its legs in the bottom of the vase.

Next cut a circle two inches larger than the diameter of the opening of the vase. Again make cuts into the edge of the circle, but this time place the circle over the top of the vase and bend the cut segments over the outside of the rim. If you want to make sure the top holder is secure, you can wrap a strip of tape around the vase so that it overlaps the edges of the bent segments. You now have two firm anchors for your stems—one at the top of the vase and one at the bottom.

The arranger will find many other uses for hardware cloth. Try it when you arrange pansies in a shallow bowl. Cut a piece of hardware cloth slightly larger than the opening of the bowl, lay it over the top, and press the excess over the sides. Insert delicate greens into the holes, attempting to achieve a flat and soft effect. Then insert short pansy stems into the holes. The result will be a delightful arrangement with all the little pansy faces smiling up at you.

Fig. 91. Hardware-cloth holders on the top and bottom of a container.

The Dragonfly Holder

This useful gadget consists of a piece of exceptionally pliable lead, known as plumber's lead, fashioned into the shape of a dragonfly. Although you can purchase them already made, commercial dragonflies come in just one size. If you want to have a good supply and a variety of sizes at little cost, you can easily make them yourself.

You can purchase the plumber's lead at any plumbing establishment. It comes in flat sheets and can be cut into strips with wirecutting shears or heavy scissors. To make a dragonfly, cut a strip of lead about three-quarters of an inch wide to form the body. Its length will depend on the size of the holder you are making. Then cut three or four strips of equal length and about half an inch wide to form the wings. Lay the wings one on top of the other and place them across the body strip near one end. Finally, loop the short end of the body around the wings and pull it tight to hold the wings in place. You can use more wings if you wish—the more wings you have, the more flowers you can arrange. If you intend to arrange delicate flowers in the dragonfly, reduce all the dimensions proportionately.

To use the dragonfly, bend the body in a flat S shape and hang it inside the vase with the tail of the "S" hooked over the edge. Then, as you place each flower in its correct position in the vase, wrap one of the wings quite tightly around the stem. The end of the wing can be bent over the rim of the vase to give even greater control. Wherever the lead hooks over the edge of the vase it should be covered with a leaf or a flower. If the leaf tends to slip, secure it with a piece of tape. (Fig. 92)

The dragonfly is excellent for positioning large-stemmed foliage, branches of flowering shrubs, or one or two dramatic flowers in a tall vase. It also enables you to achieve interesting underwater patterns with the uncluttered appearance of stems.

The Twig Holder

From the Japanese we have learned how to use a twig as a flower holder. If you cannot find a twig with a natural fork, you can make one by splitting a stem and forcing it into a "Y" shape. Wrap some fairly heavy wire around each arm at the very base of the split and push the wire into the split to keep the arms separated.

To use the twig holder, place it horizontally inside and

BODY LOOPED
OVER WINGS

WINGS SECURELY
LOOPED OVER
FLOWER STEMS

BODY BENT
OVER EDGE
OF VASE

Fig. 92. How to use a dragonfly holder.

near the top of a vase, where its natural springiness will hold it in position. Obviously the twig must be just the right size. The circle defined by its three tips must be slightly larger than the vase at the point where it is going to be suspended. You can achieve the correct fit with a little whittling. (Fig. 93)

The twig is not suitable for bountiful arrangements, but it is particularly successful with large pieces of greens or flowering shrubs. Place the flower stems so that the ends rest on the bottom of the vase and are supported at the top of the vase by the "V" of the twig. Since the twig is so natural-looking, it can be used effectively in either opaque or transparent vases.

Fig. 93. A twig used as a holder fits firmly against all contours of the vase. The flower stem is held firmly in place as it rests in the fork of the twig and on the bottom of the vase.

Waterproof-Tape Holders

Waterproof tape can be used to make a reasonably versatile holder. The transparent type—if you can find it—is particularly adaptable for crystal bowls since it is almost invisible. First be sure that your vase is perfectly dry. Then make a cross-hatching of tape over the mouth of the vase, bringing the ends of each strip of tape down one inch over the edge of the vase (Fig. 94). If you adjust the size of the openings to the size of the flower stems, you are assured of excellent control. For even better control, you can use a cross-hatching of tape at the top of the vase and a pin-point holder in the bottom, thus anchoring your flowers in two places.

Corsage Thread

Corsage thread is particularly useful for dealing with special problems such as arranging flowers in difficult-to-use vases that have small necks and bulging bottoms. The best approach is to make an attractive bouquet in your hand,

Fig. 94. A cross-hatching of tape can function as a flower holder.

extending some of the flowers and nestling others in the arrangement. When you are satisfied with the overall appearance of your hand bouquet, gently wrap the stems with corsage thread just above your hand. Wind the thread around the stems several times, then pull it up between the stems and cut it. Next cut the ends of all the stems so that the arrangement is the desired height. Cut them straight across the bottom so that the bouquet will set squarely in the vase without tipping to one side or the other. The resulting arrangement will not be formal but can be quite charming.

Casual bouquets of larger material can be prepared in much the same way. Arrange the flowers in your hand and then tie them together with a "Twistem," a chenille stem, or even an elastic band. All of these will hold the flowers together as a bracelet would. Cut the stems straight on the bottom so that they will stay in position. After the flowers are in the vase, you can extend some of them and sink others to enhance the three-dimensional effect.

Shredded Styrofoam

Many professional florists use shredded styrofoam as a flower holder. You can buy shredded styrofoam from your florist at a very reasonable price. It works particularly well in tall, upright containers but not at all in shallow ones. It is an excellent filler for opaque containers and not too unpleasant to see in transparent vases. If you want to have a special color visible in your container, you can tint the styrofoam with vegetable color, which will not harm your flowers in any way.

It takes a little know-how to handle styrofoam properly. To grip the flowers well enough, it must be packed very tightly in the container before water is added. Once you have filled the vase with water, test the styrofoam's gripping power with a stem. If it does not hold, add more styrofoam on top and press it into the container. If you are using very heavy flowers, you may want to secure a layer or two of chicken wire on top to add extra strength and to extend the holder an inch or so above the vase for greater control. If you are economy-minded, you can use styrofoam over and over again, keeping it clean by rinsing it under running water after use. (Fig. 95)

Vermiculite

Vermiculite is one trade name for a rooting medium composed of expanded rock. It is used extensively for arranging flowers in upright and tall containers, but its handling requires a little training and experience. Its main advantages are that flowers last well in it and it retains moisture well. Since it is rather unattractive, however, it should be used only in opaque containers.

To prepare an arrangement in Vermiculite, you should fill your container completely with the dry granules and press them down tightly with your hands. Add water to the top and wait a moment until it is absorbed. Then press down again, add more dry Vermiculite, and press this down too. Add more water until all the Vermiculite is saturated. It should now be of the right consistency to hold your flowers firmly in place when you insert the stems. If this is not the case, add more dry Vermiculite until you have provided a very firm base for your flowers.

If you wish to use plastic foam in a tall container, the best and most economical method is to fill your vase with Vermiculite to within two inches of the top. Add water and pack the Vermiculite firmly. On top of this place a piece of foam large enough to rise about an inch above the rim of the container. Finally, fasten the foam to the container with two strips of waterproof tape, forming a cross over the top. (Instead of the block of foam, you can place a ball of chicken wire on top of the Vermiculite and tape

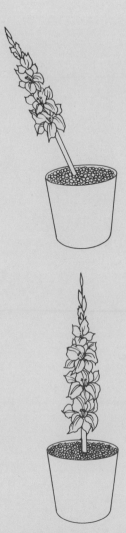

Fig. 95. Shredded styrofoam or Vermiculite used as a flower holder. Test the gripping power of shredded styrofoam or Vermiculite by inserting a flower stem; if it does not hold, add more.

TAPE TO
SECURE FOAM
TO VASE

Fig. 96. Vermiculite and foam in a
tall vase.

it to the vase.) With either of these arrangements you will have the advantages of a good flower-keeping medium combined with material that will give you perfect control over your flowers. (Fig. 96)

When you have completed your arrangement, add water each day so that the Vermiculite remains moist to the touch. Do not attempt to reuse the Vermiculite, however, since it is impossible to clean and becomes odiferous in time. Instead, when you are finished with it, keep it for use as a rooting medium or throw it on your lawn, where it will be a welcome soil conditioner. A final note of caution: Take care not to spill wet Vermiculite on rugs or furniture. It has strong adhesive qualities and is very difficult to dislodge.

Miscellaneous Holders

If you should ever want to arrange flowers and have no holders, do not be discouraged. Almost anywhere you might be, you can find stems or stiff grasses to pack in your container. They should be in an approximately upright position, tight enough to hold flower stems when you insert them but not so tight that they will not accept another stem (Fig. 97). As with all holders, it is a good idea to have the filler stems protrude about an inch above the rim of the container.

Obviously this type of filler is not attractive in a transparent vase. Also, the stems decay rather rapidly, causing bacterial growth which shortens the life of the flowers. Even so, in a pinch it is a workable approach.

Finally, on some occasions you might want to float flowers. Unfortunately, however, they tend to go every which way unless you have some means of restraining them. The ideal way to keep the floating flowers upright is to insert the stems through rings of green cork which are available from florists.

Fig. 97. Vertically placed stems can
serve as supports for flower stems.

4 The Preparation and Care of Cut Flowers

☐ A flower arrangement is a living work of art that starts to change the instant it is completed. As part of its intrinsic nature it has real life, rhythm, and motion, imperceptible at any moment but present nonetheless. It is a very real source of pleasure to see buds open, flowers turn to seek the light, and subtle changes in color develop.

Naturally you will want to enjoy the beauty of any arrangement as long as you can. To prolong its life you must know when and how to cut your flowers and how to treat them to maintain them in prime condition. You must also be familiar with the idiosyncrasies of specific flowers and know how to humor them.

When to Cut Flowers

It is very important to cut flowers at the proper time of day. Early in the morning and late at night are the best times, for this is when the flowers' heads contain the most water and food. The only exceptions to this general rule are roses, which seem to fare better if cut in the afternoon.

Fig. 98. If the rose has developed but still has a hard center, peel off the outer petals until you have a flower that resembles a bud.

Just as important is the stage of development of the flowers you cut. For the sake of rhythm and variety, you will probably want some flowers in tight bud, some approaching maturity, and some completely developed. But you will have to remember that some flowers continue to develop after they are cut while others do not. Thus if you are making an arrangement for a special occasion, you will have to select flowers that will develop to just the right stages of maturity in different parts of the arrangement at the time of the occasion. With a little experience you will be able to do this for any arrangement you have in mind.

Among the flowers that continue to develop after cutting are asters, daisies, gladioli, irises, peonies, roses, and snapdragons. The same is true of most bulb flowers including daffodils, hyacinths, and tulips. It is a good idea to cut these flowers late in the bud stage in order to insure the longest life for your arrangement. The bulb flowers, for example, are short-lived at best, and each extra day of life is to be treasured. Cutting flowers in the bud stage also minimizes the risk of damaging the flowers in handling.

Flowers that develop very little or not at all after cutting include anthuriums, carnations, chrysanthemums, delphiniums, marigolds, orchids, and zinnias. All of them must be cut at the stages of maturity desired for different parts of the arrangement. Although the tight buds of daisies and bachelor buttons will not open fully in water, they do develop into charming miniature blossoms.

Spike flowers that continue to develop after cutting, such as gladioli and snapdragons, are especially interesting to arrange. Irises, common flags, and day lilies also have several buds on one stem which open in sequence, presenting you with a new flower each day. These spike flowers should be cut when the lower florets have just opened and are crisp and fresh, and the upper florets are still in the bud stage. This allows you to enjoy each floret as it opens.

In the case of gladioli, it is usually advisable to cut off the tips of the spikes at the point where the buds are just beginning to show color. This will conserve food and enable the remaining florets to develop to full maturity. You can encourage them to open more quickly if you spray the spikes with warm water and place them in bright light. If you want to make your gladioli even more colorful you can remove the green husks from the florets.

Roses, incidentally, are the one flower whose form you can control. If you want a bud form and your rose is developed but still has a hard center, simply peel off the outer petals until the flower resembles a bud. If your rose is too tight, cup it in your palm and blow lightly into its heart until the petals fall back to form a fully opened rose. (Figs. 98, 99)

Immediate Treatment

The moment you cut a flower, it is disconnected from its source of life-supplying water and chemicals. Somehow these must be immediately replaced and maintained, since a flower dies a little each second that it is out of water. As a matter of fact, one hour without water will reduce the life-span of a flower by a whole day. This happens because the stem of the living flower contains plant juices. After the stem has been cut, the flowers and leaves continue to draw the juices up the stem and draw air bubbles into the cut end. The air bubbles in turn dry out the plant cells and kill them instantly, forming a barrier to the free passage of water. Thus, you should strive to supply cut flowers with water before this process can start—which can be a matter of just a few seconds. For the same reason the stems should be recut if they have been out of water for any length of time.

Fig. 99. To get a more fully blown rose, blow into its heart until the petals fall back.

Fig. 100. One way to reduce bacterial growth is to strip unnecessary foliage from the stems so that none of it will be under the water.

When you are cutting flowers in your garden, it is a good idea to carry along a bucket of warm water so that you can plunge the stems into it immediately. An ordinary bucket is quite satisfactory, but you can also purchase a special carrier composed of several containers of different heights. This enables you to carry both long- and short-stemmed flowers without submerging the short-stemmed blossoms in water.

Flowers delivered from a florist are likely to have been out of water for some time. You should open the box immediately, cut the stems at an angle, and plunge them into a container of warm water. Then leave the container for at least two hours in a cool, darkened room out of drafts.

It may surprise you to be told to place your flowers in warm water. Until recently, it was the custom to use cold water, sometimes even with ice cubes added. However, research in horticultural institutions has proved that warm water rises more readily into the flower heads, and causes less of a shock than cold water. The best temperature is approximately 100°F, but laboratory precision is not necessary. If you do not want to become involved with a thermometer, the best gauge is to use water that feels warm to the touch.

The best tool for cutting flowers is a sharp knife. Do not use pruning shears or scissors, since they tend to squeeze the stems, thus closing the cells and preventing the passage of water. If you do not want to invest in a professional florist's knife, the next best thing is a small, well-sharpened paring knife.

A Note on Cleanliness

Bacterial growth is very harmful to flowers. It clogs the stems, thus preventing the intake of water, and it contaminates the water with chemicals that may or may not be harmful to the flowers. To minimize bacterial growth, you should be sure that all containers are clean, even containers that are used only for temporary storage. All other articles that come in contact with the flowers, such as mechanical aids, holders, and wires, also should be immaculate. All of them should be scrubbed and rinsed with boiling water after each use. However, you must be careful to remove any traces of soap or detergent since these chemicals likewise can be harmful to flowers.

Another way to reduce bacterial growth is to strip unnecessary foliage from the stems before immersing them in water. Any foliage left on the stem below water level provides an ideal growth medium for bacteria as the leaves decay. Note, however, that it is by no means necessary to remove all the foliage. Common practice in the past was to immerse the stems as deeply as possible in water, but in recent years we have learned that flowers absorb little water through their stems. Since only the cut ends are significant, it is possible to place the stems in shallow water and enjoy the beautiful foliage. Strike a balance between providing sufficient water to nourish the flowers and as little stem immersion as possible, since bacteria grows even on the green stems. (Figs. 100, 101)

Hardening Your Flowers

Once you have stripped the unnecessary foliage from your flowers and placed them in clean containers with three or four inches of warm water, you should transfer them to a cool, dark room for several hours, or preferably overnight. Be sure there are no hot or cold drafts to dehydrate the flowers.

This process is known as "hardening" the flowers. The cool temperature slows down osmosis and respiration, while the lack of light prevents photosynthesis. Moderating these

Fig. 101. Water level in a vase. (A) Too high. (B) Less water will keep down bacterial growth.

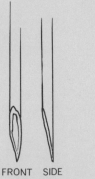

FRONT   SIDE

Fig. 102. Cut flower stems on an angle.

processes permits the flowers to adjust to the sudden loss or change of nutrient and will result in a longer life for your completed arrangement. Generally you can assume that flowers from a florist have already been hardened, and you can start arranging them as soon as you have put them in water.

When you place your flowers in containers for hardening, take care not to crowd them. If they are packed in too tightly, you may damage their blossoms and leaves when you remove them from the container to make your arrangement. Crowding also hinders their further development and increases the risk that mildew will develop if they remain in the container for any length of time.

Whether the flowers are in a storage container or in the final arrangement, it is important to freshen the water each day. If you have used a commercial preservative, you can merely add water; if not, a complete change of water is desirable. Always add warm water to reduce shock and to insure ready absorption.

Cutting the Stems

Always cut flower stems on an angle. In this way you leave more of the stem exposed, increasing the probability of leaving capillaries open and able to take in water. You also lessen the possibility of having the end of the stem resting flat on the bottom of the container, and thus unable to draw in water. Last, but not least, correctly cutting the stem on an angle prevents the knife from cutting into your thumb. (Fig. 102)

If you are using a pin-point holder, it is not necessary

(Opposite) Mounded round centerpiece of fall flowers softened with baby's breath. [Photograph courtesy of Florists' Transworld Delivery Association]

to cut the stems at an angle since in this case there is no problem of having the stem end flat on the bottom of the container. Furthermore, if the ends are cut straight across, they can be supported better on the pin points.

It is worth learning a professional trick for cutting the stem of each flower to the correct length accurately and quickly as you prepare an arrangement. As you select each flower for insertion, hold its head with your left hand at the correct height above the container. Let the stem hang down in front of the container so that it clears the edge of the table. Since you know roughly where the stem will finally be supported in the holder inside the container, you can now place the edge of your knife against the stem at this level and then cut it at an angle (Fig. 103). When the stem is inserted in the holder, it will be the right length. Once you have mastered this trick, you rarely will have to pull a flower out of a partially completed arrangement to adjust its length and in so doing run the risk of disturbing the other flowers and greens.

Fig. 103. How to cut your flower to the desired height.

Chemical Treatments

Over the years researchers have observed that the life and beauty of cut flowers can be greatly extended if certain chemicals are added to the water in which they are placed. The chemicals very likely are the same as some of those that have been supplied by the roots of the living plant. Some of these treatments attempt to adjust the acid–alkaline balance in the water, since some plants like acid soil and others prefer alkaline soil. Other treatments replace the source of nutrition that was lost when the flower was sev-

(Opposite) Three-quarter arrangement in autumn colors of miniature carnations and chrysanthemums, highlighted with cattails.
[Photograph courtesy of Florists' Transworld Delivery Association]

ered from its root system. A number of these treatments appear in the table on page 91. In every case the flowers should remain in the chemical solutions for only eight hours and then be transferred to the permanent arrangement, in a container holding water that has been fortified with a commercial preservative.

If you do not want to become involved with chemicals, you can lengthen the life of your flowers by simply adding one tablespoon of chlorine bleach, one tablespoon of Listerine, or an eighth of a teaspoon of boric acid to each quart of water in your container. This preserves the flowers by sterilizing the water and thus decreasing bacterial growth.

Commercial preservatives provide a more complete treatment. They contain a bactericide that prevents the formation of bacteria in water. They also contain sugar to feed the flowers, and some contain growth-regulating chemicals that retard the development and aging of flowers.

The effectiveness of commercial preservatives depends a great deal on the type of flowers you are treating and the chemical composition of your water. Experiment until you find a brand that offers you the best results. Do not guess at the amount of preservative to use. Follow the instructions and carefully measure the recommended amounts of water and preservative. Finally, use plain tap water to maintain the level of the water in the container. If you continue to add water containing preservative, the mineral salts will become concentrated to the point where they might be toxic to the flowers.

Treatments for Specific Flowers

Certain flowers require special treatments to extend their lives or to develop properly. In every case, however, your lengthened enjoyment of your completed arrangement will amply repay you for the extra effort that is required.

Chemical Treatment of Flowers

	One T* alcohol to two quarts water	One T ammonia to one quart water	One T salt to one quart water	Half Tsp† oil of cloves to one quart water	Two Tsp sugar to one quart water	Two T sugar and one T salt to one quart water	One cup of vinegar to one quart water
Amaryllis		✓					
Anemones							✓
Apple blossoms		✓					
Asters						✓	
Begonias			✓				
Birds of paradise							✓
Chrysanthemum family				✓			
Clematis	✓						
Columbine						✓	
Cosmos						✓	
Dahlias	✓						
Daisies					✓		
Delphinium	✓						
Digitalis	✓						
Forget-me-nots	✓						
Gaillardia			✓				
Gladioli							✓
Grape hyacinths	✓						
Heather	✓						
Hollyhock			✓				
Hyacinths					✓		
Iris					✓		
Larkspur	✓						
Lilies							✓
Petunias						✓	
Poinsettias			✓				
Poppies			✓				
Salvia	✓						
Snapdragons			✓				
Statice					✓		
Sweet alyssum					✓		
Sweet peas	✓						
Water lilies	✓						

*T = tablespoon.　　†Tsp = teaspoon.

Fig. 104. Pounding the stems of woody-stemmed plants, thereby exposing more capillaries to the water, is one method of increasing the water supply to the blossoms.

Woody-stemmed plants, such as flowering shrubs, chrysanthemums, and stock, have a problem transporting enough water to the blossoms to keep them fresh. You can overcome this by cutting a two-inch-long slit into the cut end of each stem, thus exposing more capillaries to the water. Another technique is to place the end of the stem on a solid table and hit it sharply with a hammer about one inch from the cut end (Fig. 104). Either technique may weaken the cut stem so much that it becomes difficult to impale it on a pin-point holder or to make it stand firmly in position in an arrangement. You can remedy this by binding the end of the stem with corsage thread or raffia to make a firm base.

Before arranging woody-stemmed flowers, insert the ends of the pounded or slit stems to a depth of about two inches in wood alcohol and leave them for three to five minutes. This treatment seems to benefit the flowers by preventing loss of nutrients through "bleeding."

"Forcing" flowering shrubs can add another dimension to your enjoyment of flower arranging. Branches of most of the garden shrubs, including rhododendron, andromeda, lilac, quince, forsythia, bridal wreath, pussywillow, and, of course, all the fruit trees, can be gathered when they are dormant and forced to bloom before their normal flowering periods. If properly trimmed and handled, they can bring you fresh flowers through most of the latter half of winter. Gather the branches a few weeks before you want to arrange them. If you continue to gather them at different times, you will have shrubs at various stages of development and your pleasure can be extended.

Once you have cut the branches, pound two inches of the cut ends with a hammer. This will allow water to seep up into the branches. Then submerge the entire branches in warm water and leave them there overnight. (A bathtub is ideal for this.) The next morning, place the stems in warm water containing a preservative, and place the container where it will receive good light, but not direct sunlight. Do not put the container near a radiator. Since the stems absorb water rapidly, you must be conscientious about adding water regularly to maintain the original level. A fine spray of room-temperature water, resembling a soft spring rain, will further hasten development of the buds. Usually you can expect a show of color within two to three weeks.

Lilacs are fragrant, beautiful flowers, but many people consider them unsuccessful as cut flowers since they usually wilt soon after being placed in water. If properly prepared, however, they can provide very satisfactory arrangements. For best results they should be cut at full maturity. Since they are woody, the stem ends must be pounded or slit, then placed in a few inches of denatured alcohol for approximately five minutes. In addition, most of the leaves must be removed so that they do not draw too much water away from the flowers and do not detract from their beauty. However, it is important not to strip off the leaf at the base of the flower since removing it somehow adversely affects conduction of water to the flower head. (Fig. 105)

Fig. 105. Proper preparation of lilacs.

Roses are very fragile flowers. They wilt not only from old age but also as a result of incorrect handling by the commercial grower, by the retail florist, or by the arranger. Yet a few simple precautions will greatly extend their lives. For one thing, the flowers should never be cut in the tight bud stage. Cut them just as the buds are about to unfold and, as we have noted, cut them in the middle of the day, when the buds are filled with food.

If you are cutting roses in the garden, sever the stems just above the first leaf with five leaflets to insure future blooms (Fig. 106). Of course, if you want long-stemmed

Fig. 106. Proper technique for cutting roses.

roses, you must sacrifice future blossoms. This explains why long-stemmed roses are expensive at the florist's.

In roses the water-conducting tissues are between the pith and the bark. If you injure these tissues, water will not be transferred to the flowers. Yet the lower part of the stem must be cleared of leaves and thorns. The best way to do this is to wear a heavy glove and grasp the stem between your thumb and fingers at the top of the length to be cleared. Then pull your hand down the stem to strip off the leaves and thorns. This method seems to cause minimum harm to the water-conducting tissues. Do not crush or scrape the stem since this can damage the tissues.

After removing the leaves and thorns, place the stems in water at 100°F to which a flower preservative has been added. The water should be deep enough to reach just below the lowest leaves left on the stems. After the water has cooled, place the container with the roses in a refrigerator at 35 to 40°F for about eight hours before arranging. If the roses have come from a florist, you can assume that they have been hardened properly. However, if they are delivered out of water it is advisable to cut half an inch from the stems and place them in warm water for an hour or two.

Milky-sap flowers, such as poppies, dahlias, forget-me-nots, and poinsettias, exude a milky substance from their cut stems. To prolong their lives you should first squeeze as much of the milky substance as possible from the stems and then singe the freshly cut stems or treat them in hot water. During treatment, hold a damp cloth around the base of the flower to protect it from the damaging effects of steam or hot air. To singe the stem, hold the cut end in a gas or candle flame until there is no evidence of any discharge and you feel that the stem is sealed. For the water method, dip the stem into boiling or very hot water for a second or two until the end is sealed. (Fig. 107)

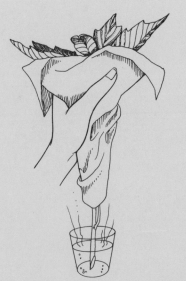

Fig. 107. Treatment of milky-sap flowers.

Once the stem has been sealed, it must not be cut again for arranging, so it is wise to establish the length of the stem before treatment. If you must cut the stem again, it will be necessary to reseal the end.

Poinsettia blooms are always exciting to arrange during the Christmas holidays. This was often disastrous in the past since the blooms collapsed immediately, but in recent years researchers have developed a method for preserving them. First, squeeze as much sap as you can from the cut stems, and then immerse the ends for two minutes in a solution of one pint of water and one tablespoon of alcohol. Here again, however, if you recut the stems while arranging them, you must treat them again in the alcohol solution. (Fig. 108)

Fig. 108. Special treatment for the poinsettia, a milky-sap flower.

Bulb flowers, such as daffodils, irises, and hyacinths, must be cut above the white section on the stems that indicates the earth line. Otherwise they will be unable to draw water. The mucous that oozes from their stems should be squeezed out immediately since it clogs the stems and prevents the intake of water. The stems of bulb flowers tend to curl or divide when they are placed in water, making them difficult to arrange. You can prevent this by binding the ends of the stems with raffia, string, or corsage thread as soon as they are cut. This forms a gentle restraint that keeps the ends from splitting. (Fig. 109)

In the case of tulips and calla lilies in particular, the entire stems tend to curl or bend in water. This can be an advantage since they do provide interesting lines underwater. If you want the stems to remain straight, however, you should roll the flower heads and stems in several layers of wet newspaper during the hardening period. If you do not have time for this, or if you do not feel completely secure about their behavior, you can wire the stems to make sure they will remain straight. (Wiring is explained on pages 105–106.)

Tulips open very quickly and very wide. If your arrange-

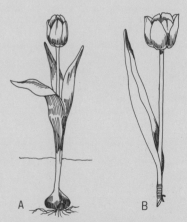

A   B

Fig. 109. Treatment of bulb flowers. (A) Bulb flowers must be cut above the white line that indicates their earth line, or they will be unable to draw water. (B) As soon as bulb flowers are cut, the lower part of their stems should be bound with raffia or string, which forms a gentle restraint that keeps the ends from splitting.

Fig. 110. Brushing egg white or melted wax on the outer petals at the base of the flower keeps tulips from opening quickly.

ment demands tighter buds, you can prevent them from opening by brushing egg white or melted wax on the outer petals at the bases of the buds. Perhaps it is witchcraft, but many people claim that a penny placed in the water used for tulips will make them last longer. Possibly there is a chemical reaction with the copper that is beneficial to the flower. (Fig. 110)

Some Miscellaneous Suggestions

Some flowers benefit from complete immersion. Violets, lilies of the valley, and hydrangea blooms should be immersed in water for four hours before you arrange them.

If you are fortunate enough to have water lilies at your disposal, you can keep them from closing at night by dropping a bit of wax in the center of each bloom (Fig. 111). Passion flowers also close soon after they are cut. They will remain open if you dip the whole face of each flower in warm wax as soon as it is cut.

Although carnations are very durable flowers, some growers claim they will last even longer if you break the stems at one of their many joints instead of cutting them. Note, however, that carnations are sensitive to certain gases given off by members of the narcissus family and even by decaying greens. These gases put carnations "to sleep," making them appear closed and withered. As a result, florists never store carnations near narcissi, and you would be wise to avoid such a combination in your arrangements.

If an important petal should fall from a flower, do not overlook the possibility of fastening it in place with floral clay or one of the many good glues on the market. Scotch tape will also do the job, provided all surfaces are dry.

If a petal falls from a chrysanthemum, the whole flower

will unravel like a piece of knitting when you have dropped a stitch. You can stop this by inverting the flower and dropping candle wax on the base in the area where the petals have become detached. Or you can spray the break with "Make-It-Snow," a brand of aerosol spray used to give a snow-covered appearance to evergreens at Christmas. The spray has good adhesive qualities and is harmless to flowers.

Sometimes a flower will wilt for no apparent reason. Often it is possible to revive it by cutting off the end of the stem and placing it in warm water. If this doesn't help, complete immersion in water at room temperature sometimes proves effective.

Treatments for Greens and Foliage

Preservation of the foliage in an arrangement is just as important as keeping the flowers in good condition. Like flowers, the greens respond favorably to the addition of floral preservatives to the water and benefit from the antiseptic properties of Listerine or Clorox.

Although greens in general tend to be hardier than flowers, some of them require special treatment. As with certain flowers, woody-stemmed greens benefit from having their stems pounded or slit. Most soft-stemmed greens, such as ferns, ivies, galax leaves, and philodendrons, will last longer if they are completely immersed in water for eight hours before arranging. Greens with a fuzzy texture, such as asparagus ferns, do not respond to this treatment; it merely makes them soggy.

Podocarpus, pittosporum, laurel, and rhododendron are very rewarding foliages. With periodic water changes, they will last three or four months and give you much enjoyment. Eucalyptus and magnolia also are good investments.

Fig. 111. Dropping a bit of wax into the center of a water lily bloom helps keep it from closing.

Although they do not remain fresh in water for very long, after a few days they change to a beautiful silvery gray-green and last almost indefinitely in this state. In fact, once they have changed color they do not even have to be kept in water. Even after it has dried, eucalyptus continues to give off its wonderful fragrance for a long time. (Fig. 112)

The life of evergreens can be lengthened by a chemical treatment. Prepare a solution of one gallon of hot water, four teaspoons of chlorine bleach, two cups of light corn

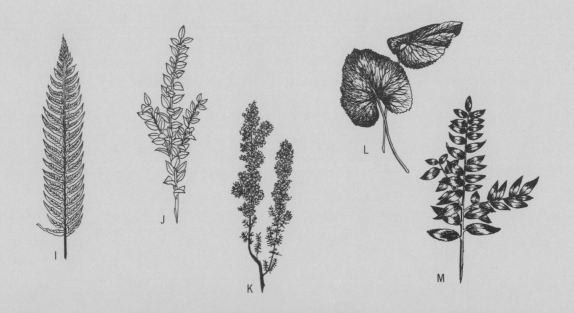

syrup, and four tablespoons micronized-iron plant food. Pound or slit the cut ends of the evergreen boughs and arrange them in two inches of this solution. Add more solution daily as it evaporates in order to maintain the level. To preserve holly, put it in a solution of one cup of brown sugar to one gallon of hot water. Add water daily to maintain the level in your finished arrangement.

A simple way to maintain greens in a waterless arrangement, such as a centerpiece of fruits or gourds, is to insert

Fig. 112.   Types of greens and foliage.
(A) Pittosporum. (B) Spiral eucalyptus.
(C) Flat-leaf eucalyptus. (D) Scotch broom.
(E) Maidenhair fern. (F) Dracena. (G) Emerald fern. (H) Baker fern. (I) Flat fern. (J) Red huckleberry. (K) Heather. (L) Galax.
(M) Huckleberry. (N) False fig leaves.
(O) Skimmia leaves. (P) Ming fern.
(Q) Lemon leaves.

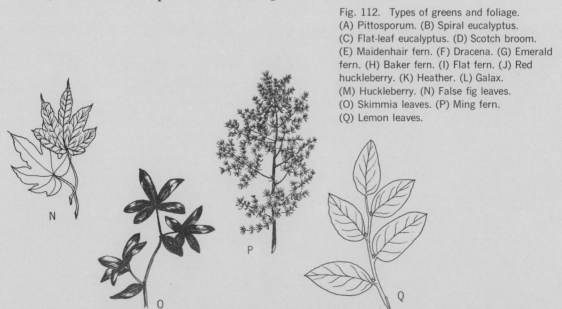

Fig. 113. Inserting the stems of greens into an apple or a potato is a simple way to maintain greens in a waterless arrangement.

each stem in a potato or an apple. This provides the greens with a limited supply of moisture and nourishment and so extends their life somewhat. (Fig. 113)

Extending the Life of Your Arrangement

The period of time an arrangement will last depends on the quality of the environment in which it is maintained and the quantity of water and nourishment it takes in. If you want an arrangement to last for more than one occasion, it is advisable to use flowers that have lasting qualities.

You should never expose an arrangement to direct sunlight or drafts since this will cause water to evaporate from the flower heads faster than it can be replaced and hasten wilting. Since all arrangements benefit from a moist, humid atmosphere, they should be sprayed frequently with a fine mist of water. This treatment is absolutely essential for certain flowers—gardenias, for example—which never feed through their stems. You can purchase fine sprayers for this purpose at most flower shops. (Fig. 114)

When an arrangement is not on view, you can reduce evaporation and maintain constant humidity by covering the whole thing with cellophane or with a plastic bag of the type used by dry cleaners. If possible, it is also beneficial and well worth the trouble to transfer your arrangements at night to a cool but not freezing location. If you have space, the flowers will be very happy in your food refrigerator. The temperature of 40°F which is maintained in refrigerators is ideal for flowers. This is, in fact, the temperature at which florists maintain their commercial refrigerators.

Frequent water changes also are important in prolonging the life of an arrangement. You can easily change the water without disturbing your arrangement by gently tipping the container until the stale water flows off and then replacing it with water containing floral preservative in the correct proportion. An alternative method is to place the arrangement in a sink or bathtub and let water from the spigot run into the container and overflow until there is a complete water change. (Use tap water at the same temperature as the water in the arrangement.) Then add a small quantity of water in which you have dissolved the proper amount of cut-flower food for the full capacity of the container.

If you do not want to remove the arrangement from its location, you can draw off the old water with a syringe or gravy baster and add fresh water containing a preservative. Keep a gravy baster for this use only—otherwise your gravy may take on a new and mysterious flavor.

If your arrangement is in a very small or shallow container, it may not have an adequate supply of water. In this case, when it is not on display, you can place the entire arrangement in a large basin filled with enough water to flow over the edge of the container. Often the most convenient method is to fill the sink with water and place the arrangement in it.

Fig. 114. "Son-of-a-Gun" sprayer.

5 The Mechanics of Preparing Flowers for Arranging

☐ Even if you have mastered all the artistic principles of arranging flowers, you should not embark on the actual construction of an arrangement, particularly of the Japanese or modern type, until you understand some of the mechanical aspects of making flowers behave. Otherwise the step from loose flowers to finished arrangement can be a discouraging and frustrating experience.

Perhaps you want a stem with a special curve, for example, but find that none of your flowers has it. Or you may want a particular flower to stand very erect, only to discover that the flower is too heavy for its stem to support it. Or possibly none of the flowers looks out at just the right angle to give your arrangement the final touch of perfection. Although nature often refuses to provide exactly the materials you need, all these problems can be solved by appropriate mechanical means.

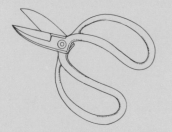

Fig. 115. Japanese loop-handled shears.

Fig. 116. Proper use of a florist's knife.

The Basic Tools

Every flower arranger needs three basic tools to be able to work efficiently in the actual construction of the arrangement: a sharp knife, Japanese loop-handled shears (Fig. 115), and heavy pruning shears. The Japanese shears have short, sharp blades and are used to cut away excess light stems, while the pruning shears are used for heavier branches. The most important tool, however, is the knife. It is ideal for cutting stems since, unlike shears, it does not squeeze them and damage their cell structure, thus preventing the intake of water.

Although you can use an ordinary paring knife or a penknife, the ideal choice is a professional florist's knife. Besides being small enough to hold comfortably in your hand, it has the advantage that it can be worn around your neck; it comes with a loop on the handle through which you can put a string or ribbon. Adjust the length of the string so that the knife falls comfortably into your hand. This gives you freedom of movement and at the same time prevents you from ever misplacing the knife.

Your first attempts to use a florist's knife can be a bloody experience. To use it properly and avoid cutting yourself, grasp the flower head in your left hand and, while holding the knife in the palm of your right hand, guide the knife along the stem to the point where you want to cut it. By changing the angle of the knife so that it cuts into the stem at this point, you can sever the stem without directing the blade at your thumb (Fig. 116). This sounds awkward and is not easy to do at first, but once you have mastered the technique you will find it a most worthwhile accomplishment. Practice the sliding and cutting motions on old discarded stems until you are able to make the cut exactly where you want it.

Obviously it is important to keep your knife sharp at all times. A small electric knife sharpener is excellent for this purpose. You should also keep your shears well oiled so that they will continue to work easily and resist rust. And you will find that it is a good idea to paint the handles of your tools a bright color so that they can be seen easily among the debris that inevitably collects on your work table.

Wiring Flowers

Wiring is without question the commonest method of making flower stems behave. Florist's wires of appropriate gauges are used for this purpose. With a little experience you will learn to select the correct gauge to solve your particular problem. Try to use the lightest wire that will serve your purpose, since it will result in a much more natural appearance.

The basic technique for wiring a flower is to insert one end of the wire as far as possible into the calyx without having it protrude through the petals. Then wind the wire in very long curves along the full length of the stem (Fig. 117), being careful not to catch any foliage under the wire. Use four to six inches of wire for each full turn around the stem. If you want greater flexibility, or if the stem is particularly fine, you should make each turn shorter. If any wire extends beyond the end of the stem, wind it back up or cut it so that it is even with the end of the stem.

With daisies, chrysanthemums, and similar flowers you

Fig. 117. Basic wiring technique.

Fig. 118. Special wiring technique for daisies and chrysanthemums.

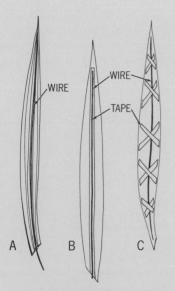

Fig. 119. Wiring large greens. (A) Insert a wire into the spine of a gladiolus or daffodil leaf. (B) Single strip of tape holds wire in place. (C) Wire held in place by crosshatch of tape.

can insert the wire in the calyx, push it through the flower, bend the end into a sharp hairpin, and pull it back into the flower until the hook is tight and invisible. Then wind the wire around the stem (Fig. 118). This gives very strong support to the flower. If your flower has a soft or hollow stem, you can thread the wire up the center of the stem and push it into the flower. The wire will be invisible and the stem well supported.

After the stem has been wired, bend it into the desired curve by gently pulling it several times between your thumb and fingers. With experience, you will quickly learn just how much pressure to apply to achieve precisely the curve you want. Stems can be curved after insertion in the arrangement, but this is usually awkward and imprecise. It is much better to curve the stems before they are inserted.

You can also use wire to straighten flowers with nodding heads or to change the position of a flower at an awkward angle. Simply hold the flower in the desired position in relation to the stem and insert a short length of stiff wire, or even a toothpick, through the flower and into the stem.

Wiring Foliage

The increased control achieved by wiring foliage enables the arranger to create many interesting and unusual effects. Because of the great variety in the structure of leaves, however, you will have to employ a variety of techniques and a bit of ingenuity to achieve the desired results.

Spearlike leaves such as those of daffodils and gladioli are the easiest to deal with. You can strengthen them by simply inserting a fine wire into the spine of the leaf. If the spine is too tough to accept the wire, you can secure it to the back of the leaf with transparent, waterproof tape. You can either run a single strip of tape along the full length of the wire or cross the wire with several short pieces of tape at intervals along the leaf. In either case, the tape must be waterproof and the leaf perfectly dry. (Fig. 119)

Leaves that grow on stems are wired by a method known as sewing. Push a fine wire through the leaf, from back to front, at a point next to the main vein and about halfway along its length. Then push the end of the wire back through the leaf on the other side of the vein. Pull the wire taut around the vein and bend the two protruding ends so that they lie along the back of the leaf and extend along its stem. Then wind one of the wires around both the stem and the other end of the wire (Fig. 120). If there is no stem, you can make an artificial one by keeping one wire straight and winding the second around it, first catching part of the leaf where the stem should be. This artificial stem can be wrapped with green florist's tape to make it stronger and more realistic.

Fig. 120. Sewing individual leaves.

To wire a fern frond, place a stiff wire along the stem and secure it by winding a lighter wire around both the stem and the stiff wire. Be careful to avoid cutting or catching the individual leaflets of the frond with the wire as you wind it.

Once they have been wired, spearlike leaves and fern fronds can be formed into curves in the same way as wired flower stems. Ordinary leaves on stems can be wired or taped in place in your arrangement and can be twisted or bent into any position you want. Since the stemmed leaves will normally be out of water, they will not last as long as the arrangement, but they can be very useful for special occasions. (Fig. 121)

Shaping Flowers without Wires

The easiest way to obtain flowers with curved stems is to search for them in your garden or to ask your florist for them. The florist may consider them a nuisance and

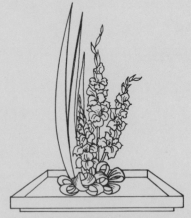

Fig. 121. An arrangement using three flowers. The gladiolus leaves have been wired to form an interesting base.

Fig. 122. A hollow stem can be placed over a small, firm stem to extend the height.

Fig. 123. Florist's picks.

regard them as second grade. He may even charge less for them than for perfect straight-stemmed specimens. Even if you are unable to obtain crooked- or curved-stemmed flowers, however, there are ways of creating them without resorting to wiring. Although these methods are trickier and more troublesome than wiring, you run no risk of having wires visible in your arrangement.

It is often possible to curve a stem by pulling it over your thumb several times, using your fingers to control the degree of bending. Some stems, such as those of calla lilies, tulips, and daffodils, need to be preconditioned for this by twisting them gently, segment by segment. In either operation the correct amount of bending or twisting can only be learned by experience. Practice on some old, worthless stems in order to develop a feel for these rather tricky techniques.

Stems that are too brittle for shaping can be softened by placing them between moist bath towels or wet newspapers. If you are dealing with woody branches such as pussywillows or flowering shrubs, you can immerse them in warm water. After an hour or two, they will become very flexible. Scotch broom, an old favorite of flower arrangers, also responds well to this treatment.

To curve gladiolus leaves or the stems of tulips or snapdragons, place them in a container out of water and let them wilt. After a period of time they will droop over the edge and bend into curves that are permanent. (Cut off the end of the stem before placing it in the arrangement, or it will not be able to draw water.) Some leaves, such as daffodil foliage, can be shaped by wrapping them around a finger and fastening the resulting roll with a bobby pin. When you remove the pin a few minutes later, the leaf will retain a curve.

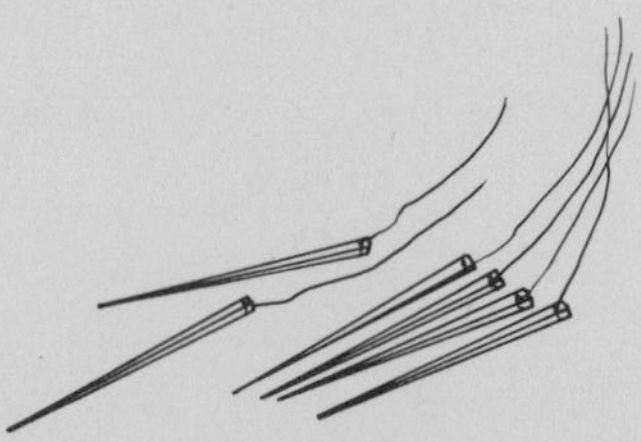

Lengthening Flower Stems

If you should find that the only available flowers are too short to give your arrangement the height or width you desire, it is usually possible to lengthen the stems. You can insert a straight twig in the marrow of any stem with a soft center (pussywillow and forsythia are excellent for this purpose). You can do the same with harder stems if you first make a hole in the end of each stem with an ice pick. Or you can wire the stem to a florist's pick or any straight twig that can serve as a stilt. With all these methods, you must make sure that the end of the actual flower stem reaches the water in your container. (Figs. 122, 123)

In extreme cases, short-stemmed flowers can be put in water picks, test tubes, or surplus pill bottles filled with water and taped or wired to appropriately shaped branches (Fig. 124). Water picks, available at your florist, are essentially miniature plastic vases that provide a small amount of water for the flowers inserted in them. Each water pick consists of a plastic tube about four inches long. The upper end is fitted with a rubber cap with a hole in it to hold the stem of a flower or piece of foliage. The lower end has a sharp point so it can be inserted into plastic foam, Vermiculite, soil, or any other firm material. The stems of tiny flowers that you want to tuck into a large arrangement can also be inserted in small water-filled balloons. Use short elastic bands or wire covered with floral tape to tighten the mouths of the balloons around the stems. This method also works well if you want to keep bunches of grapes fresh in an arrangement of fruits.

Whatever your approach, you should conclude the operation by camouflaging your mechanics. Cover the miniature containers with green floral tape and hide the containers or balloons behind strategically placed leaves.

Fig. 124. Short stems can be lengthened by placing them in a test tube or pill bottle taped to a taller stem.

6 Step-by-Step Procedure for a General Flower Arrangement

☐Now that you are familiar with the principles of floral design, the use of mechanical aids, and the methods for preparing and handling cut flowers, it is time to apply this knowledge and construct some actual flower arrangements. This is by no means a difficult task. Yet there are so many factors to keep in mind that at first you might find it confusing to take them all into consideration without some assistance.

If you were to watch an expert designer creating a great variety of arrangements, whether large or small, traditional or modern, you soon would realize that he was following a rather exact procedure. The major steps in the procedure are listed on the following pages. They will provide you with general guidelines that are basic to the design of all arrangements. They can also serve as a checklist, enabling you to detect oversights and correct any defects in your completed arrangement.

The Basic Procedure

The first two steps involve basic artistic decisions which will determine your precise actions throughout the rest of the procedure:

1. Decide on the location of your arrangement.
2. Clarify your mental image of how the completed arrangement should look.

The next four steps, all mechanical, should be completed sometime before you begin to actually arrange your flowers. They may already have been done if you obtained the flowers from a florist:

3. Strip all foliage from the portions of the stems of the flowers and greens that will be below the waterline in the completed arrangement.
4. With a sharp knife, cut the ends of the stems at an angle.
5. Place the flowers and greens in a container of water at 100°F.
6. Leave the container in a cool, dark room or in your refrigerator for several hours.

Now you are ready to set your stage for the actual arranging:

7. Assemble your tools and mechanical aids, including a copy of the color wheel.
8. Scrub your container with soap and water, rinse it completely, and dry it thoroughly.
9. Equip the container with the proper holder for your flowers and the type of arrangement you are planning.
10. Fill the container almost to the brim with warm water containing the proper concentration of a flower preservative.
11. Place the container on an appropriate work space so

that, as you design the arrangement, you will be looking at it from the same angle that it will be viewed from in its intended setting. The container should be near the front edge of the work table.

Finally, you are ready to work with the flowers:

12. Separate spike flowers from face or round flowers.

13. Critically examine each flower as to stage of development, characteristic line of stem, size of blooms, and color.

14. Wire any flowers that appear weak-stemmed.

15. Review the flowers, one by one, mentally considering where you will place each one in your composition.

16. Select the tallest, straightest, choicest flower in the earliest stage of development and cut it to the correct length for use as the key flower in developing the basic framework of the arrangement.

17. Place the first flower in the holder, choosing a position a little back from the center.

18. Make sure that the first flower is held firmly in place. If it is not, use a mechanical technique to fasten it properly.

19. Add the other key flowers to establish the outline of the arrangement.

20. Insert a few greens to fill in and soften the outline.

21. Place the important flowers to give the arrangement rhythm, depth, and a focal point.

22. Add more greens if necessary to fill in voids or complete the design.

23. Insert filler flowers if the arrangement requires them.

24. Examine the arrangement from all angles and add greens or leaves to fill voids or to cover any mechanical aids that are visible.

25. Check the junction between the container and the arrangement. If necessary, add a few flowers or leaves to soften the line or provide better unity.

A Critical Look at Your Arrangement

When you have finished your arrangement, you should view it with a critical eye to see if it really fulfills your original artistic objective. Check it over point by point to make sure you have not overlooked anything. If it is disappointing in any way, try to analyze how you might improve it:

1. Is the entire arrangement appropriate to its environment?

2. Are the proportions correct? Are the flowers in scale with each other and with the container?

3. Are the colors in harmony with each other, with the container, and with the environment?

4. Are the colors in groups rather than in a polka-dot pattern?

5. Are the shapes of the flowers in harmony with each other, with the greens, with the container, and with the environment?

6. Is there enough variety in the shapes, textures, and colors of the flowers, leaves, and container to provide interest?

7. Are the spike flowers at the top and edges of the arrangement, and the face flowers closer to the center?

8. Is the arrangement well balanced with no apparent tendency to tip?

9. Is the outline good from all vantage points? Are there no sudden size changes resulting in bulges?

10. Do all the stems appear to radiate from a common source?

11. Does the arrangement give a good impression of depth?

12. Are there gradual transitions not only in the size and color of the flowers but also in the spaces and voids between them?

13. Are flowers clustered at the center and base of the arrangement to provide a focal point or center of interest?

14. Have you avoided square patterns of flowers or long, straight line patterns?

Keeping the Arrangement Fresh

Once the arrangement is completed to your satisfaction, you will want to enjoy it as long as possible. Several simple precautions will help you extend its life:

1. Keep the arrangement out of direct sunlight and away from heat and drafts.

2. Add fresh tepid water daily or, better yet, make a complete water change, using water fortified with the correct amount of floral preservative.

3. Spray the arrangement daily with a fine mist of tepid water.

4. Store the arrangement in a cool spot or in your refrigerator at night or when it is not on view. Even better, enclose it in a plastic bag to insure a moist atmosphere and no drafts.

5. Manicure the arrangement daily, removing wilted material and making changes in your design where necessary.

6. Finally, when the arrangement is no longer attractive, use the remaining fresh flowers to make another, simpler arrangement.

7 *Recipes*

☐ In the recipes that follow, each step is described carefully in words, and each important step is illustrated in the accompanying simple drawings. The drawings are in sequence so that the step-by-step development of each arrangement can be followed easily. This method would appear to give ample information for the development of any arrangement; in fact, it serves for many arrangements. However, in many other cases it does not. The success of the recipes depends on the precise placement of the flowers in the arrangements. Unfortunately, the representation of a three-dimensional arrangement by a two-dimensional drawing (or photograph) inevitably contains ambiguities in positions and angles. Language is even more inadequate if it is not to be too technical or mathematical.

In the recipes this problem has been solved by adding two numbers in parentheses at the end of each step involving the placement of a flower or a critical piece of foliage.

Fig. 125 illustrates the use of these numbers. Imagine that the container is placed on the face of a very large clock with the center of the holder at its center and turned so that 12 o'clock points directly backward. The first of the two numbers indicates the hour on the clock face toward which the flower stem is *tilted.* The second number indicates the amount of the tilt of the flower stem above horizontal. Five intervals are used between the horizontal and vertical. (Fig. 126)

In the procedure a typical step might read: "Select spike flower S#2. It should be $\frac{2}{3}$ the length of S#1. Insert forward and slightly to the right of S#1, tilted to the right and slightly forward. (5, 3)"

In the last sentence, the words "Insert forward and slightly to the right of S#1" refer specifically to the *position* on the holder where the tip of the stem of flower S#2 is to be inserted relative to the point where flower S#1 was inserted. The remaining words, "tilted to the right and slightly forward," refer specifically to the *angle* at which the stem is to be inserted. This angle, along with the length of the flower, is the significant determinant of the position the flower will take in the arrangement. By themselves the words describing the angle are much too vague to enable the flower to be positioned with precision. The drawing that accompanies the instruction helps enormously and will frequently be sufficient. The numbers "5, 3" define the angle with reasonable precision and remove all ambiguity.

The numbers are used as follows: Take the designated flower, which has been cut to the right length, and hold it horizontally, with the cut end of the stem at the point where it will be inserted in the holder. Point the flower in the 5 o'clock direction of the imaginary face. Then, keeping the cut end of the stem in position, tilt the stem upward to the angle indicated by position 3 in Fig. 126. This example (5, 3) is shown in Fig. 125.

After relatively little practice, the use of these numbers becomes second nature and the placement of the flowers can be accomplished rapidly and without confusion.

All the recipes that follow have been carefully tested to insure the accuracy of the directions given. However, variations in the sizes and colors of the flowers used might mean that slight adjustments will have to be made in their positions to make the arrangements truly artistic.

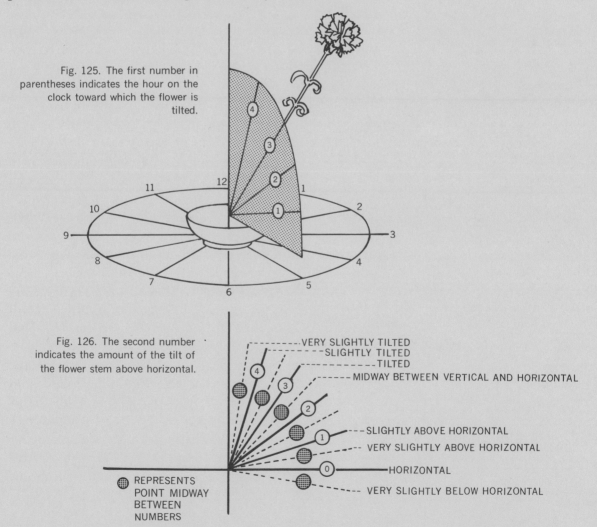

Fig. 125. The first number in parentheses indicates the hour on the clock toward which the flower is tilted.

Fig. 126. The second number indicates the amount of the tilt of the flower stem above horizontal.

VERY SLIGHTLY TILTED
SLIGHTLY TILTED
TILTED
MIDWAY BETWEEN VERTICAL AND HORIZONTAL

SLIGHTLY ABOVE HORIZONTAL
VERY SLIGHTLY ABOVE HORIZONTAL
HORIZONTAL
VERY SLIGHTLY BELOW HORIZONTAL

REPRESENTS POINT MIDWAY BETWEEN NUMBERS

In recipes that involve a large number of flowers, the instructions frequently provide added information regarding the position at which a specific flower should be placed relative to other flowers that have already been inserted in the arrangement. In using these recipes it might be helpful to put number tags on the flowers instead of trying to memorize their identities. Strips of light paper marked with numbers and looped around the stems can be used. Place them near the flowers so that they can be seen and then removed easily when the arrangement is completed. Small squares of ordinary painter's masking tape marked with numbers can also be used. The tape will adhere adequately if it is lightly pressed onto a stem or a leaf, and it can be removed easily.

Arrangement for Single Flower
 # 1

Materials

1. Container—a shallow bowl, a deep bowl, or a tall vase.
2. A holder for flowers—a medium-size pin-point holder or shredded foam or crushed chicken wire for the deep bowl.
3. A fastener for the holder—floral clay to secure the pin-point holder.

(Opposite) Dainty French centerpiece of assorted small flowers in pinks, lavenders, and reds, accented by a velvet bow.
[Photograph courtesy of Florists' Transworld Delivery Association]

4. Flower—hardened and with all foliage below the waterline removed. One feature flower (amaryllis lily, bird of paradise, spider chrysanthemum), or one large round flower (peony, chrysanthemum, large marigold).

5. Foliage—8 to 10 large leaves, appropriate to the flower, that can be built up to form a rosette or a columnar shape (leaves of canna, coleus, funkia, lily of the valley).

Procedure

1. Secure the pin-point holder in the center of the shallow container. If the deep bowl is used, fill it with the shredded foam or the crumpled chicken wire.

2. Fill the container with water fortified with cut-flower preservative.

3. Select the largest leaf and insert it straight up in the center of the container. The length of this leaf should be at least $1\frac{1}{2}$ times the width of the container or $1\frac{1}{2}$ times the height of the deep bowl or tall vase.

4. Select four approximately equal leaves cut to $\frac{3}{4}$ the length of the first leaf. Insert them at a slight angle to the first leaf and equally spaced around it. (4, 4; 7, 4; 10, 4; 1, 4)

5. Select four smaller leaves and cut them to $\frac{2}{3}$ the length of the leaves of the previous group. Insert them close to and evenly spaced around the first five leaves. (5, 3; 8, 3; 11, 3; 2, 3)

6. When the shape of the greens has been established, insert the single flower straight up in front of the first leaf. It should be cut so that when it is inserted, its lowest petal will appear clearly above the tallest leaf. (Fig. 127)

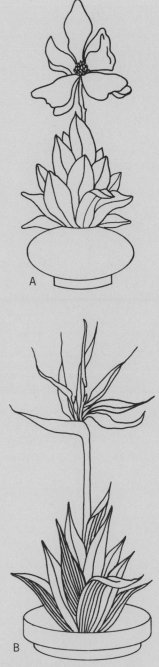

Fig. 127. Arrangement for single flower #1. (A) Magnolia. (B) Bird of paradise.

(Opposite) Elegant candlelight centerpiece of pink gladioli, carnations, and roses—a masterpiece of monochromatic colors.
[Photograph courtesy of Florists' Transworld Delivery Association]

Arrangement for Single Flower
 # 2

Materials

1. Container—a shallow rectangular or circular container.
2. A holder for flowers—a medium-size pin-point holder, or a block of foam 2 inches square and high enough to protrude $\frac{1}{2}$ inch above the rim when it is secured in the container.
3. A fastener for the holder—floral clay to secure the pin-point holder, or a staple, attached in the base of the container with tape, on which to impale the foam.
4. Flower—hardened and with all foliage below the waterline removed. One large, long-stemmed flower (aster, daffodil, geranium, iris, marigold).
5. Foliage—two pieces of tall delicate material (cattails, flame bushes, forsythia, pussywillows, wheat) and a quantity of the natural foliage of the flower selected.

Procedure

1. Secure the holder to the right or left of the center of the container at a position $\frac{1}{3}$ of the width of the container from the side.
2. Fill the container with water fortified with cut-flower preservative.

Fig. 128. Arrangement for single flower #2 (daffodil).

3. Cut the flower so that its length is equal to the length plus the width of the container. Insert it straight up in the center of the holder.

4. Cut tall foliage #1 to a length $1\frac{1}{2}$ times the length of the flower. Insert it close to but to the left of the flower (if the holder is on the left side of the container) and tilted very slightly backward. ($11, 4\frac{1}{2}$)

5. If the natural foliage of the flower is also delicate, cut one stem to a length between that of the flower and foliage #2. Insert it directly behind the flower and tilted very slightly backward. ($12, 4\frac{1}{2}$) If the natural foliage is a broad leaf, omit this step.

6. Cut three stems of the natural foliage of the flower to various lengths, all shorter than the flower. Insert them around the stem of the flower with the tallest behind the stem of the flower and the others on either side, and with the shortest on the outside. All except one should be behind the flower. ($1, 4; 11, 4; 12, 4$)

7. Cover the holder with stones, glass chips, seashells, moss, or greens.

COMMENT: For a more dramatic display of this arrangement, it can be placed on an appropriate mat at a position to the left of the center of the mat. (Fig. 128)

A left-handed arrangement is described here. If the location for the arrangement requires a right-handed arrangement, simply exchange right for left in the procedure.

Arrangement for Single Flower
#3

Materials

1. Container—a shallow circular bowl.
2. A holder for flowers—a medium-to-large pin-point holder, or a block of foam 3 inches square and high enough to be even with the rim when it is placed in the bowl.
3. A fastener for the holder—floral clay to secure the pin-point holder, or a staple, attached in the base of the container with tape, on which to impale the foam.
4. Flower—hardened and with all foliage below the waterline removed. One large feature flower (amaryllis lily, magnolia, orchid, spider chrysanthemum).
5. Foliage—leafy branches that can be bent or pruned or arranged into a triangular shape.

Fig. 129. Arrangement for single flower #3 (magnolia).

Procedure

1. Secure the holder to the left of the center of the bowl at a point $\frac{1}{3}$ the diameter of the bowl from its rim.
2. Fill the bowl with water fortified with cut-flower preservative.
3. Use the branches to design a loosely and uniformly filled triangle. Remember that the flower is to be an integral part of the triangle and that when inserted in the holder, the branches must appear to originate near the base of the stem of the flower. The top point of the triangle should be above the center of the *bowl* and should be more than the diameter of the bowl above its rim. The width of the triangle at its two lower points should be somewhat less than twice the diameter of the bowl.
4. Insert the feature flower upright in the center of the holder. Its highest point should be at a height above the rim equal to $\frac{2}{3}$ the diameter of the bowl. The flower can be placed so that it is facing either upward or forward.
5. Camouflage the holder with stones, moss, etc. (Fig. 129)

Arrangement for Single Flower
#4

Materials

1. Container—a shallow rectangular or circular container.
2. A holder for flowers—a medium pin-point holder, or a block of foam 3 inches square and high enough to protrude $\frac{1}{2}$ inch above the rim when it is placed in the bowl.
3. A fastener for the holder—floral clay to secure the pin-point holder, or a staple, attached in the base of the container with tape, on which to impale the foam.
4. Flower—hardened and with all foliage below the waterline removed. One large flower, round (aster, chrysanthemum, marigold, peony, etc.), or feature (amaryllis lily, bird of paradise, magnolia, orchid, etc.).
5. Foliage—long, straight branches or blades that can be molded to maintain a shape (pussywillows, scotch broom, etc.).
6. Wires—24-inch heavy-weight florist wire and some short lengths of fine wire.

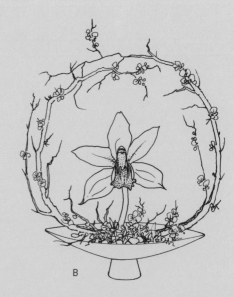

A

B

Procedure

1. Secure the holder in the center of the container.
2. Fill the container with water fortified with cut–flower preservative.
3. Take two pieces of foliage of equal length and weight and bend each into a semicircle, as illustrated. It will probably be necessary to insert a wire into the blades, if they are used. Fasten the two pieces into the holder so that a loop is formed. The diameter of the loop should be at least twice the width of the container. It may be necessary to reinforce the loop by joining the tips of the branches at the top and winding a short piece of fine wire around them.
4. Cut the flower so that when it is inserted in the holder, its center will be at $\frac{1}{3}$ or $\frac{2}{3}$ the height of the loop.
5. Insert some of the natural foliage of the flower around the point where its stem enters the holder.
6. Cover the holder with moss, stones, etc. (Fig. 130)

Fig. 130. Arrangement for single flower #4. (A) Rose framed by foliage. (B) Cymbidium encircled by a branch. (C) Tuberous begonia encircled by a branch. (D) Hibiscus framed by greens.

C

D

Arrangement for Single Flower
#5

Materials

1. Container—a shallow rectangular or circular bowl.
2. A holder for flowers—a medium pin-point holder, or a block of foam 3 inches square and high enough to protrude $1\frac{1}{2}$ inches above the rim when it is placed in the bowl.
3. A fastener for the holder—floral clay to secure the pin-point holder, or a staple, attached in the base of the container with tape, on which to impale the foam.
4. Flower—hardened and with all foliage below the waterline removed. One large feature flower (amaryllis lily, magnolia, orchid).
5. Foliage—a long, light branch, flowering, leafy, or bare, that will lend itself to the desired shape.

Procedure

1. Secure the holder to the left of the center of the container at a point $\frac{1}{3}$ the width of the bowl from its rim.
2. Fill the container with water fortified with cut-flower preservative.
3. Prune and bend the branch to obtain a simple rhythmic line, as illustrated. The bent branch should form a curve extending over both the right and the left edges of the container and appearing balanced over the center of the

holder. The total width of the arrangement should be a little more than twice the width of the container. The total height of the arrangement is not too critical but should be between $1\frac{1}{2}$ and $2\frac{1}{2}$ times the width of the container. Leaves should be removed from the branch to the extent necessary to achieve a delicacy of line. Some leaves should remain at the base to give the branch more weight there. After a satisfactory design has been achieved, fasten the branch to the holder.

4. Cover the holder with leaves, moss, stones, etc.
5. Insert the flower so that it will balance the branch and look important. (Fig. 131)

Fig. 131. Arrangement for single flower #5 (lily with bent branch).

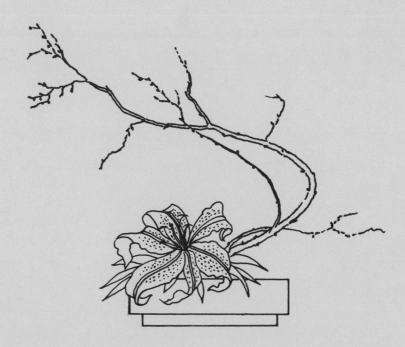

Arrangement for Single Flower
#6

Materials

1. Container—a shallow container of a shape and size appropriately in scale with the branch and flower.
2. A holder for flowers—a medium pin-point holder, or a block of foam 2 to 3 inches square and high enough to protrude $\frac{1}{2}$ inch above the rim when it is placed in the container.
3. A fastener for the holder—floral clay to secure the pin-point holder, or a staple, attached in the base of the container with tape, on which to impale the foam.
4. Flower—hardened and with all foliage below the waterline removed. One large flat flower (amaryllis lily, aster, fuji chrysanthemum, marigold, poinsettia, etc.).
5. Foliage—a large curved branch that can be pruned to shape (blossoming, evergreen, leafy).

Procedure

1. Secure the holder toward the back of the container, directly behind the center.
2. Fill the container with water fortified with cut-flower preservative.
3. Prune the branch so that it has a sweeping curve, as illustrated. Measure it so that when the base is fastened in the holder, the branch will extend beyond the left side of the container by $\frac{1}{2}$ to 1 times the width of the container and will extend at its upper end a like amount beyond the right-hand side of the container. Its height should be at least $2\frac{1}{2}$ times the width of the container.

The arrangement can be given more weight by adding two shorter branches. The first of these should be about $\frac{1}{3}$ the height of the arrangement, inserted upright behind the center of the holder but tilted to the right and slightly backward. (2, 3) The second should be inserted horizontally from the left and should be approximately the same length as the other short branch. (9, 0) It should be chosen and inserted so that its tips curve upward.

4. Insert the flower in front of the base of the dominant line of the branch in a flat position. Cut the stem just long enough to reach well into the water.

5. Insert the natural foliage of the flower around it so that the leaves extend beyond the petals and also hide the holder.

6. Colored glass chips can also be added to give weight to the base of the arrangement and to make interesting underwater patterns. (Fig. 132)

Fig. 132. Arrangement for single flower #6 (spider mum and fire thorn bush).

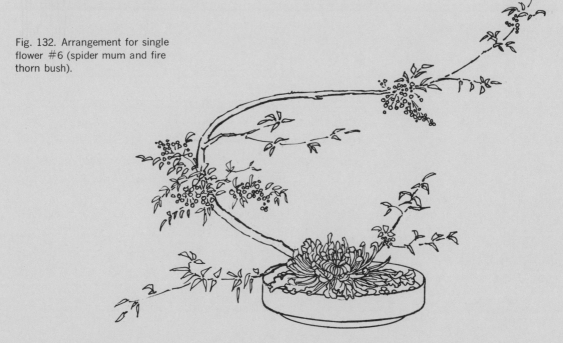

Arrangement for Single Flower
#7

Materials

1. Container—a small shallow circular container.
2. A holder for flower—a small pin-point holder.
3. A fastener for the holder—floral clay to secure the pin-point holder.
4. Flower—hardened and with all foliage below the waterline removed. One large choice spike flower (buddleia, delphinium, larkspur, liatris, lilac, snap-dragon, stock, tritoma, etc.).
5. Foliage—several pieces of appropriate spike greens (cattails, gladiolus leaves, pussywillows, scotch broom, etc.) and some round greens.

Procedure

1. Secure the pin-point holder in the center of the container.
2. Fill the container with water fortified with cut-flower preservative.
3. Cut the spike flower 3 inches below the last floret and insert it straight up in the center of the holder.
4. Cut one piece of spike green so that it will reach to $\frac{1}{3}$ the height of the flower when inserted. Insert it behind the flower, tilted so that it shows to the left of the flower. (10, 4)
5. Cut the second piece of spike green to be a little shorter or a little longer than the flower, but not the same length. Insert it behind the flower and tilt it so that it will become visible from behind the left upper part of the flower. (11, 4$\frac{1}{2}$)
6. Cut the third piece of spike green so that it will be

approximately (but not exactly) halfway between the other two pieces of green. Insert it, tilting it to the left until it appears balanced between the other two pieces of green.

7. Add a few round greens in the holder if they appear to be needed. Favor the side opposite the spike greens. This will add weight and hide the holder. (Fig. 133A)

COMMENT: A larger rectangular or circular container can be used for this arrangement. In this case the holder should be secured to the right or left of center (about $\frac{1}{3}$ the width of the container from the edge) and the spike greens should be placed on the side toward the short end of the container. The container should not be too large. The total height of the arrangement should be greater than the width of the container and preferably $1\frac{1}{2}$ times as great. (Fig. 133B)

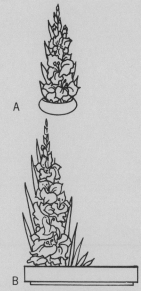

Fig. 133. Arrangement for single flower #7. (A) Gladiolus placed in center of bowl. (B) Spike flower (gladiolus) placed off-center.

Arrangement for Two Flowers
#1

Materials

1. Container—a shallow circular container.
2. A holder for flowers—a medium pin-point holder.
3. A fastener for the holder—floral clay to secure the pin-point holder.
4. Flowers—hardened and with all foliage below the waterline removed. Two flowers, one large and mature, and one smaller and closer to bud stage, either round (asters, carnations, geraniums, gerbera, roses, etc.) or spike (larkspur, lilacs, stock, etc.).
5. Foliage—feathery or spike greens (gladiolus leaves, tulip leaves, scotch broom, etc.), or flat or round greens (geranium leaves, lemon leaves, etc.).
6. Stones.

Procedure

1. Secure the holder in the center of the container.
2. Fill the container with water fortified with cut-flower preservative.
3. Select the smaller or tighter of the two flowers as flower #1. Cut it so that its length is equal to twice the diameter of the container plus 2 inches. Insert it in the holder $\frac{1}{2}$ inch behind center, tilted very slightly to the right. (3, $4\frac{1}{2}$)
4. Cut flower #2 about $\frac{2}{3}$ the length of #1. Insert it in front of flower #1, tilted very slightly to the left (9, $4\frac{1}{2}$)
5. Cut spike foliage #1 slightly shorter than flower #1. Insert it behind flower #1, tilted slightly to the left. (9, $4\frac{1}{2}$)

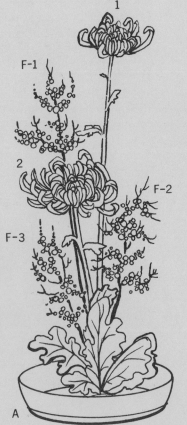

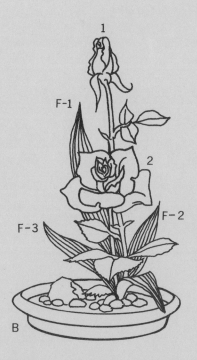

6. Cut spike foliage #2 slightly shorter than flower #2. Insert it to the right of flower #2 and tilt slightly to the right and backward. (2, 4)
7. Cut spike foliage #3 about $\frac{2}{3}$ the length of foliage #2. Insert it to the left of flower #2 tilted slightly to the left and backward. (10, 4)
8. Insert natural or round foliage at the base to add weight and to hide the holder. (Fig. 134A–C)

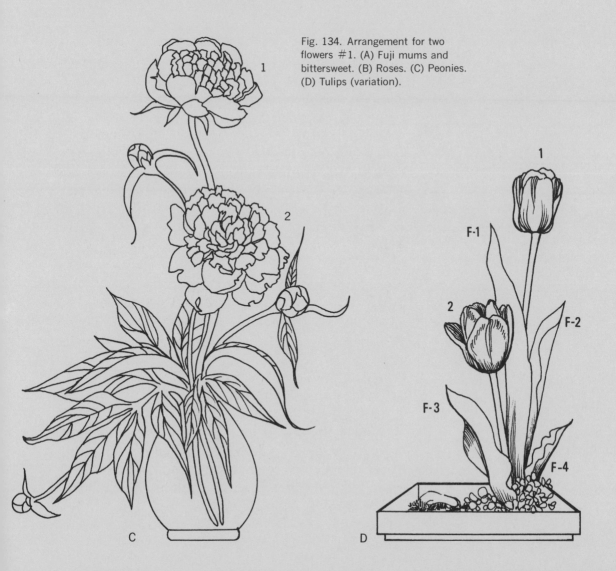

Fig. 134. Arrangement for two flowers #1. (A) Fuji mums and bittersweet. (B) Roses. (C) Peonies. (D) Tulips (variation).

VARIATION

If a somewhat larger container is used (it can be rectangular), this arrangement can be put off-center for added interest. In the following procedure the holder should be placed to the right of the center of the container. If the final location needs a left-handed arrangement, follow the same procedure, simply exchanging left and right.

Procedure

1. Secure the holder to the right of the center of the container. It should be $\frac{1}{3}$ of the diameter of the container from the right edge.

2. Fill the container with water fortified with cut-flower preservative.

3. Select the smaller or tighter of the two flowers as flower #1. Cut it so that its length equals the width plus the length of the container plus two inches. Insert it in the holder $\frac{1}{2}$ inch behind the center of the holder and tilt it very slightly to the right. $(3, 4\frac{1}{2})$

4. Cut flower #2 about $\frac{2}{3}$ the length of flower #1. Insert it in front of flower #1 and tilted very slightly to the left. $(9, 4\frac{1}{2})$

5. Cut spike foliage #1 slightly shorter than flower #1. Its tip should reach a point $\frac{2}{3}$ the distance between the tops of flowers #1 and #2. Insert it straight up behind flower #1. Any natural curve in foliage #1 should be to the left.

6. Cut spike foliage #2 shorter than foliage #1 by an amount equal to $\frac{1}{3}$ the distance between the tops of flowers #1 and #2. Insert it to the right of flower #1, tilted slightly to the right and backward. Any natural curvature should be to the right. $(2, 4)$

7. Cut spike foliage #3 about $\frac{2}{3}$ the length of flower #2. Insert it to the left of flower #1, tilting slightly backward and to the left. $(10, 4)$

8. Cut spike foliage #4 about $\frac{2}{3}$ the length of foliage #3 and insert it to the right of flower #2, tilting to the right and slightly backward. (2, 3)

9. Insert natural or round foliage at the base to add weight and to hide the holder.

10. A small, distinctive stone (no more than half the diameter of the base of the arrangement) can be placed in the left-hand side of the container to add interest and balance. Its exact position will depend on its size and color. Smaller and lighter stones will be further to the left than larger or darker stones. (Fig. 134D)

Arrangement for Two Flowers
#2

Materials

1. Container—a shallow container of appropriate shape.
2. A holder for flowers—a medium-to-large pin-point holder.
3. A fastener for the holder—floral clay to secure the pin-point holder.
4. Flowers—hardened and with all foliage below the waterline removed. Two flowers appropriate to the branch and occasion (asters, carnations, geraniums, peonies, poinsettias, etc.). One flower should be larger and more mature than the other.
5. A branch, or a flowering, leafy, or bare evergreen that has a major and minor line as illustrated and is at least twice as wide as the container and at least as high as the width plus the length of the container.

COMMENT: The procedure for this arrangement is dependent on the shape of the branch available. Three of the most common of the many possible variants are described and illustrated. If the branch desired or available does not match any of the three shown, these general principles will help. Almost any branch can be trimmed so that when it is inserted in the holder, it and the container will define one (Variation 1) or two (Variations 2 and 3) incompletely enclosed spaces. The aim of the arranger is to anchor and balance these spaces visually by proper placement of the two flowers.

If the branch defines only one space, it should be placed in the container so that the space (as further defined by the container) is reasonably balanced on the container. The larger flower is used to complete the balance by compensating for the opening. The smaller flower is used to highlight the space and further refine the balance.

When the branch defines two spaces, it should be pruned so that the spaces defined by it and the container are quite unequal; such an inequality is more interesting and artistic. The branch should be placed in the container in such a way that the amount of the container contributing to each space is proportional to that space. (For example, if the space

Fig. 135. Arrangement for two flowers #2. Variation #1. (A) Clematises and weeping willow branch.

defined on the right is twice that on the left, the branch should be inserted from the left at $\frac{1}{3}$ the width of the container.) The larger flower is used to highlight and balance the smaller space, and the smaller flower is used to do the same for the larger space.

VARIATION 1

Procedure

1. Secure the holder in the center of the container.
2. Fill the container with water fortified with cut-flower preservative.
3. Select and prune a branch shaped such that when the main stem is horizontal, it will curve back on itself. When impaled on the pin-point holder, it should extend over the side (assume right) of the container by an amount equal to at least $\frac{2}{3}$ the width of the container. At the point where it crosses above the container, its height should be between $1\frac{1}{2}$ and $2\frac{1}{2}$ times the width of the container. It should then extend beyond the line of the left side of the container by an amount that balances the extension over the right side. At this point, trim the twigs and do further pruning to achieve the best possible balance.
4. Cut flower #1 (the smaller) to such a length that when inserted in the center of the holder and tilted to the right and slightly backward, it will reach approximately halfway to the branch. (2, 3)
5. Cut flower #2 (the larger) such that when it is inserted, its highest point will reach the halfway point of flower #1. Insert it in front of flower #1, tilted to the left and slightly forward. (8, 3)
6. Examine the arrangement critically for balance and adjust it accordingly. For instance, if flower #1 were larger than as illustrated, it would have to be tilted slightly more to the right.
7. Camouflage the holder with natural foliage, stones, or moss. (Fig. 135A)

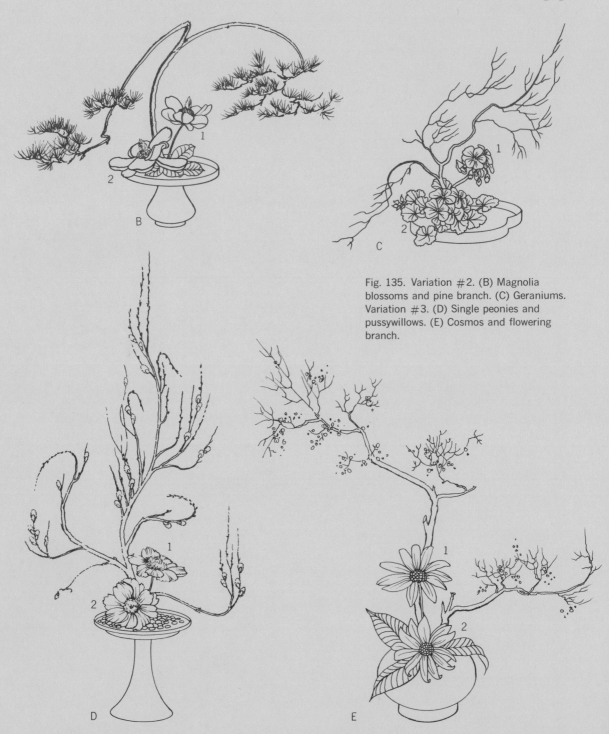

Fig. 135. Variation #2. (B) Magnolia
blossoms and pine branch. (C) Geraniums.
Variation #3. (D) Single peonies and
pussywillows. (E) Cosmos and flowering
branch.

VARIATIONS 2 AND 3

Procedure

1. Select and prune a suitable branch similar to one of those illustrated. When the branch is impaled, its height should be at least twice the width of the container. Its width should be at least twice the width of the container.

2. Test the shape and size of the branch by holding it in position over the container, halfway between back and front. Tilt the branch to the right and left until the angle at which it appears most balanced is determined. Then, holding the branch at the selected angle, slide it to the right and left until the most suitable position is determined. Secure the pin-point holder at this position and impale the branch on the holder.

3. Fill the container with water fortified with cut-flower preservative.

4. Cut flower #1 (the smaller) and insert it in the holder near the base of the branch, and tilted along the line from the holder that divides the *larger* space into two roughly equal parts. Its length should be such that it reaches between $\frac{1}{3}$ and $\frac{1}{2}$ the way into the larger space, according to the size of the flower. A smaller flower should be longer. (3, 3 approximately)

5. Cut flower #2 (the larger) to a length approximately $\frac{1}{2}$ the length of flower #1 and insert it tilted along the line that divides the smaller space into two, and slightly forward. (8, 3 approximately) If the smaller space is quite small and flower #2 is large relative to the space, it can be inserted very close to where the branch enters the holder.

6. Examine the arrangement critically for balance and adjust the positions of the flowers accordingly, or do some appropriate pruning.

7. Camouflage the holder with natural foliage, stones, or moss. (Fig. 135B–E)

Arrangement for Two Spike Flowers

Materials

1. Container—a long rectangular container at least three, but not more than five, times the width of the base of the tallest and fullest flower.
2. Two small pin-point holders.
3. A fastener for the holder—floral clay to secure the pin-point holders.
4. Flowers—hardened and with all foliage below the waterline removed. Two choice spike flowers (buddleia, delphiniums, gladioli, larkspur, liatris, lilacs, snapdragons, tritomas, etc.).
5. Foliage—several pieces of appropriate spike greens (cattails, gladioli, or iris foliage, scotch broom, pussywillows) and some round greens.

Procedure

1. Secure one pin-point holder $\frac{2}{3}$ the distance between the center of the container and the left-hand rim. Secure the second holder $\frac{3}{4}$ the distance between the center of the container and the right-hand rim.
2. Fill the container with water fortified with cut-flower preservative.
3. Cut the taller spike flower 3 inches below the last floret and insert straight up in the center of the first holder.
4. Cut one piece of spike green so that when it is inserted, it will reach to $\frac{1}{3}$ the height of the flower. Insert it behind the flower, tilted so that it shows to the left of the flower. (11, 2)
5. Cut the second piece of spike green to be a little shorter or a little longer than the flower, but not the same length. (Generally, it should be shorter if the flower

has a natural green spike, as a gladiolus does. If it is blunt-tipped like a lilac, it could be longer.) Insert it behind the flower and tilt it so that it will become visible from behind the left upper part of the flower. $(11, 4\frac{1}{2})$

6. Cut the third piece of spike green so that it is approximately, but not exactly, halfway between the other two pieces of green. Insert it, tilting it to the left so that it will appear balanced between the other two pieces of green. $(11, 3)$

7. On the opposite side of the flower add spike greens following the pattern used for those on the left, but insert them somewhat shorter and lower, or add round foliage favoring the side opposite the spike greens.

8. Cut the second flower $\frac{3}{4}$ the length of the first. Insert it straight up in the center of the second holder. The procedure for inserting foliage is the same as that given for the first flower, except that each piece of foliage should be $\frac{3}{4}$ the length of the corresponding piece, and left and right should be interchanged. (Fig. 136)

COMMENT: Since there may be a large area of water, colored stones or glass chips can be added for interest.

Fig. 136. Arrangement for two spike flowers (gladioli).

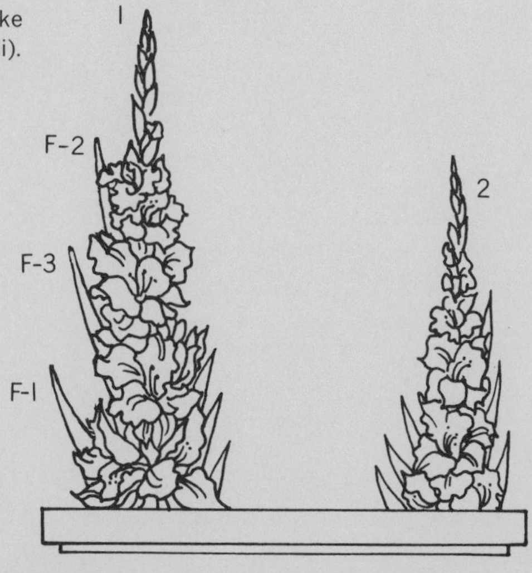

Arrangement for Three Flowers
 # 1

Materials

1. Container—a shallow circular or rectangular container.
2. A holder for flowers—a medium pin-point holder, or a block of foam 2 to 3 inches square and high enough to be even with the rim of the container.
3. A fastener for the holder—floral clay to secure the pin-point holder, or a staple, anchored to the base of the container with tape, on which to impale the foam.
4. Flowers—hardened and with all foliage below the waterline removed. Three flowers of one kind or three pieces of dried material (daffodils, gladioli, irises, tulips, cattails, pampas grass, pussywillows, etc.). There should be some variation in the size or degree of development.
5. Foliage—natural foliage of the flowers used, or other appropriate foliage.
6. Moss, stones, or chipped glass.

Procedure

1. Secure the holder in the center of the container. (A variation is to secure the holder to the right or left of the center of the container. In this case the holder would be about $\frac{1}{3}$ the width of the container from the side.)

2. Fill the container with water fortified with cut-flower preservative.
3. Select flower #1—the smallest or least developed—and cut it to a length at least equal to the width plus the length of the container. Insert it straight up in the center of the holder.
4. Select flower #2—the intermediate in size and development—and cut it so that it is $\frac{2}{3}$ the length of flower #1. Insert it to the left of flower #1, tilted slightly to the back and to the left. (11, 4)
5. Cut flower #3 about $\frac{1}{2}$ the height of flower #1. Insert it to the right of flower #1, tilted slightly forward and to the right. (4, 3)
6. Insert foliage if desired or needed to enhance the foliage already on the flower stems.
7. Camouflage the holder by covering it with moss, stones, or chipped glass. If the holder has been placed off center, it may be desirable to balance the arrangement with an interesting stone or rock placed in the other side of the container. (Fig. 137)

Fig. 137. Arrangement for three flowers #1 (cattails).

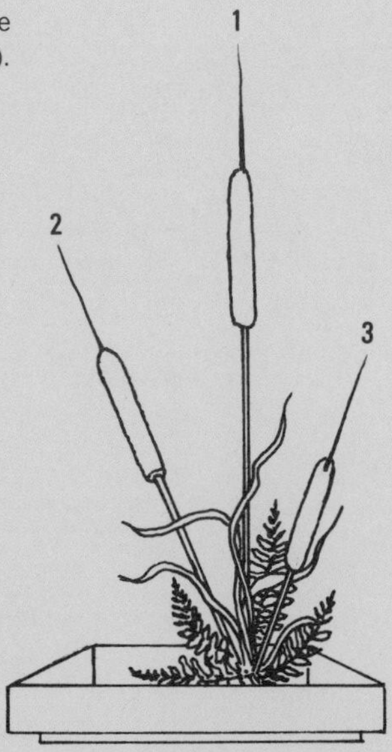

Arrangement for Three Flowers
 # 2

Materials

1. Container—a tall vase with a curved lower portion and a small opening.
2. A holder for flowers—shredded foam, crumpled chicken wire, etc.
3. Flowers—hardened and with all foliage below the waterline removed. Three round flowers of one kind but of different sizes or degrees of development (asters, calendulas, carnations, cosmos, marigolds, roses, zinnias, etc.).
4. Foliage—spike foliage that has been or can be shaped into a curve (scotch broom, eucalyptus, pussywillow, etc.).

Procedure

1. Stuff the holder material into the vase to the tightness appropriate for the stems of the flowers being used— tight enough to hold the stems firmly where they are inserted, but not so tight that insertion is difficult.
2. Fill the container with water fortified with cut-flower preservative.
3. Select a long, smooth piece of foliage. Cut it so that when it is inserted its exposed portion will be $2\frac{1}{2}$ to 3 times the height of the bowl. Wire the foliage so that it can be shaped. Shape the top end of the foliage so that it will curve toward the centerline of the vase. The piece of foliage should finally have the shape of the top part of a Hogarth curve. Insert the foliage, tilted to the left so that its stem forms a continuation of the main curve of the lower part of the vase. (9, 4)
4. Cut a second piece of foliage so that its exposed portion

will be about $1\frac{1}{2}$ times the height of the vase. Wire it and shape it so that when inserted, it will curve sharply over the rim of the vase, to the right and forward, and then sweep down in front of the vase. Insert it with the stem as near to horizontal as possible, making sure that the end reaches into the water. (4:30, 1) Adjust the tip of this piece of foliage so that it forms a harmonious relationship with the curve of the vase.

5. Select the largest and most mature of the flowers as #1. Cut it so that when inserted, it will extend out of the vase by about $\frac{1}{3}$ the height of the vase. Insert it just in front of the stems of the foliage, tilted forward and slightly to the right. (5, 2) Flower #1, with its foliage, should hide and soften the junction of the foliage stems in the vase opening.

6. Select the intermediate flower as #2. Cut it so that when it is inserted, its highest point will reach $\frac{2}{5}$ the distance from the rim of the vase to the highest point of the foliage. Insert it behind flower #1, tilted slightly forward. (6, 4)

7. Cut flower #3 so that when it is inserted, its highest point above the rim of the vase will be twice as high as that of flower #2 above the rim of the vase. Insert it behind and to the left of flower #2, tilted very slightly forward and to the left. (8, $4\frac{1}{2}$)

8. Add one or two pieces of the natural foliage of the flowers in the opening of the vase, but only if it is needed to hide exposed stems. (Fig. 138)

Fig. 138. Arrangement for three flowers #2 (anemones and forsythia).

COMMENT: This is a difficult arrangement to execute properly. Its beauty is derived from the interplay of two curves in a space—a Hogarth curve formed by the first piece of foliage and the vase, and a crescent formed by flowers and the second piece of foliage. Visualizing these curves will help in adjusting the flowers to give the best effect.

Arrangement for Three Flowers
#3

Materials

1. Container—a tall vase with a curved lower portion and a small opening.
2. A holder for flowers—shredded foam, crumpled chicken wire, etc., to fill the vase.
3. Flowers—hardened and with all foliage below the waterline removed. Three round flowers of one kind, but of different sizes or degrees of development (asters, calendulas, carnations, cosmos, marigolds, roses, zinnias, etc.).
4. Foliage—spike foliage (scotch broom, pussywillows, etc.).

Procedure

1. Stuff the holder material into the vase to the tightness appropriate for the stems of the flowers being used— tight enough to hold the stems firmly where they are inserted, but not so tight that insertion is difficult.
2. Fill the container with water fortified with cut-flower preservative.
3. Select the smallest or least developed flower as #1. Cut it so that when inserted the flower will be at a height above the rim of the vase equal to at least $1\frac{1}{2}$ times the height of the vase. Insert the flower straight up just in back of the center of the vase.
4. Select the intermediate flower as #2. Cut it so that when the flower is inserted its head will be slightly higher than the halfway mark between the rim of the vase and the top of flower #1. Insert it just in front of flower #1, tilted very slightly forward and to the left. $(8, 4\frac{1}{2})$

5. Cut flower #3 such that, when it is inserted, its exposed portion will be $\frac{2}{3}$ that of flower #2. Insert it in front of flower #2, tilted forward and to the right. $(5, 3\frac{1}{2})$

6. Select a long, straight piece of foliage and cut it so that when it is inserted its exposed portion will be at least $1\frac{1}{2}$ times that of flower #1. Insert it just in back of flower #1, tilted very slightly backward and to the right. $(1, 4\frac{1}{2})$

7. Select a second straight piece of foliage and cut it so that when it is inserted, its height will be slightly more than that of flower #1. Insert it slightly to the left of flower #1, tilted slightly backward and to the left. $(10, 4)$

8. Select a third piece of foliage and cut it so that when it is inserted its height will be slightly less than that of flower #1. Insert it slightly to the right of flower #1, tilted slightly to the right. $(3, 4)$

9. If needed, add 2 or 3 pieces of the natural foliage of the flowers used in front of and to the sides of the base of the stems. They will also serve to hide the filler. (Fig. 139)

Fig. 139. Arrangement for three flowers #3 (poppies and eucalyptus).

Arrangement for Three Flowers
#4

Materials

1. Container—a tall vase or possibly a shallow container. (See comment below.)
2. A holder for flowers—shredded foam, crushed chicken wire, etc.
3. Flowers—hardened and with all foliage below the waterline removed. Three spike flowers (delphiniums, gladioli, lupins, stock, etc.), or 3 round flowers (asters, carnations, daisies, marigolds, roses, etc.).
4. Foliage—for spike flowers, heavier in scale (natural foliage, dogwood, ferns, gladiolus leaves, podocarpus, scotch broom, etc.), for round flowers, light and airy (natural foliage, asparagus fern, baker fern, pittosporum, etc.), plus some heavy round foliage to give weight at the base (galax leaves, ivy, etc.).

Procedure

1. Stuff the holder material into the vase to the tightness appropriate for the stems of the flowers being used— tight enough to hold the stems firmly where they are inserted, but not so tight that insertion is difficult.
2. Fill the container with water fortified with cut-flower preservative.
3. Select the choicest flower as #1 and cut it so that when it is inserted, the part showing above the vase will be at least $1\frac{1}{2}$ times the height of the vase.

Insert it straight up slightly in back of the center of the vase.

4. Select the next-best flower as flower #2 and cut it so that its visible part will be $\frac{2}{3}$ the length of flower #1. Insert it just to the right of flower #1 and tilted to the right and backward, so that it will be a little more than $\frac{1}{3}$ of the way to horizontal. (2, 3)

5. Cut flower #3 such that its visible part will be a little more than half of that of flower #1. Insert it just to the left of flower #1 and tilted forward and to the left by amounts somewhat greater than the corresponding angles of flower #2. (10:30, $2\frac{1}{2}$) If round flowers are used, flower #1 should be seen in profile, flower #2 should be $\frac{3}{4}$ face to the front, and flower #3 should be full-face to the front.

6. Add foliage as needed to fill obvious voids left by the foliage on the flowers used. (Fig. 140)

COMMENT: If the location for the arrangement requires the opposite asymmetry of that described, all "rights" and "lefts" can be interchanged.

This arrangement can also be put in a shallow container. In this case the arrangement can be made more interesting by placing the holder off center so that it will be $\frac{1}{3}$ the width of the container from the side.

Another variation is to put flower #2 to the left of flower #1, tilted slightly backward and more to the left. (10, 3) Insert flower #3 in front of flower #2, tilted more to the left and substantially forward. (8, 2) Balance the flowers with a concentration of foliage on the right.

Fig. 140. Arrangement for three flowers #4 (gladioli).

Arrangement for Three Flowers
#5
(*Modern*)

Materials

1. Container—a shallow container.
2. A holder for flowers—a medium pin-point holder, or a block of foam 2 inches square and high enough to be even with the rim of the container.
3. A fastener for the holder—floral clay to secure the pin-point holder, or a staple, fastened in the container with tape, on which to impale the foam.
4. Flowers—hardened and with the foliage below the waterline removed. Three feature flowers of the same kind and of the same size and degree of development (anthuriums, cymbidium orchids, fuji chrysanthemums, gerberas, hibiscus, etc.).
5. Foliage—simple spike foliage (eucalyptus, gladiolus leaves, iris leaves, podocarpus, pussywillow, scotch broom, etc.).
6. Moss, stones, etc.

Procedure

1. Secure the holder in the center of the container.
2. Fill the container with water fortified with cut-flower preservative.
3. Cut flower #1 to a length equal to at least the width of the container plus its length plus its height. Insert the flower about 1 inch directly behind the center of the holder and straight up.

4. Cut flower #2 to a length such that when inserted the flower will be about $\frac{2}{3}$ as high above the rim of the container as flower #1. Insert it close to and just in front of flower #1, tilted very slightly forward. (6, $4\frac{1}{2}$)

5. Cut flower #3 so that when it is inserted the space between flower #3 and flower #2 is equal to the space between flower #2 and flower #1. Insert it just in front of flower #2, tilted slightly forward. (6, 4)

6. The treatment of the foliage in this arrangement can be quite variable, according to what is available and the effect desired. The principle is best represented by a fern frond that is straight and has a width no more than twice the width of any flower in the arrangement. Cut it so that when inserted it will rise above flower #1 but not more than $1\frac{1}{2}$ times the height of flower #1 above the rim of the container. Insert it directly behind flower #1, tilted very slightly backward. (12, $4\frac{1}{2}$) Other types of foliage should be cut and inserted in such a way that they closely emulate the position of the fern as described above.

7. Insert two or three pieces of the natural foliage of the flowers used around the point of insertion of the stems to hide the holder. Be careful to preserve the simple lines of this arrangement. If no suitable foliage is available, the holder can be camouflaged with moss or stones. (Fig. 141)

Fig. 141. Arrangement for three flowers #5 (anthuriums and piece of fern).

Arrangement for Three Flowers
#6

Materials

1. Container—a shallow circular container.
2. A holder for flowers—a medium pin-point holder, or a block of foam 2 inches square and high enough to be even with the rim of the container.
3. A fastener for the holder—floral clay to secure the pin-point holder, or a staple, fastened in the base of the container with tape, on which to impale the foam.
4. Flowers—hardened and with all foliage below the waterline removed. Three full spike flowers (gladioli, delphiniums, snapdragons, etc.), or three full round flowers (carnations, marigolds, zinnias, etc.).
5. Foliage—some round foliage (funkia, galax leaves, ivy, natural foliage, etc.).

Fig. 142. Arrangement for three flowers #6 (pansies).

Procedure

1. Secure the holder behind the center of the container at a point $\frac{1}{3}$ of the diameter of the container from its back edge.
2. Fill the container with water fortified with cut-flower preservative.
3. Cut flower #1 to a length equal to $1\frac{1}{2}$ times the diameter of the container. Hold the flower over the holder and tilt it slightly backward and to the right. (1, 4) Holding the flower at this angle, insert the stem so that it points toward the center of the bottom of the holder.
4. Cut flower #2 to $\frac{2}{3}$ the length of flower #1. Hold it above the holder and tilt slightly backward and more to the left. (10, 3) Insert the flower at this angle so that its stem also points toward the center of the bottom of the holder.
5. Cut flower #3 to $\frac{1}{2}$ the length of flower #2. Hold it above the holder and tilt it substantially forward and to the right. (5, 2) Insert the flower at this angle so that its stem also points toward the center of the bottom of the holder.
6. Cut three pieces of foliage, one for each of the flowers, to lengths such that when inserted each will be $\frac{1}{3}$ shorter than the flower with which it is associated. Insert each piece of foliage on the outside of the arrangement and close to its associated flower. The foliage should be inserted on the line from the center of the holder to its associated flower, and in such a direction that the stem points to the center of the bottom of the holder.
7. Add a few pieces of foliage at the base to hide the holder and give the base a little more weight. (Fig. 142)

Arrangement for Four Flowers

Materials

1. Container—a shallow circular or rectangular container.
2. A holder for flowers—a medium pin-point holder, or a block of foam 2 inches square and high enough to be even with the rim of the container.
3. A fastener for the holder—floral clay for the pin-point holder, or a staple, fastened in the base of the container with tape, on which to impale the foam.
4. Flowers—hardened and with the below-water foliage removed. Four flowers, of one kind and of different sizes or different degrees of development, spike (gladioli, lilacs, lupins, snapdragons, etc.) or round (asters, daisies, geraniums, marigolds, zinnias, etc.).
5. Foliage—spike foliage (forsythia, gladiolus leaves, pussywillows, etc.) or round foliage (galax leaves, geranium leaves, ivy, etc.).

Procedure

1. Secure the holder in the container. It can be in the center, behind the center, or to the left or right of center. If it is off center, it should be placed at a point $\frac{1}{3}$ the distance from the center to the edge toward which it is shifted.
2. Fill the container with water fortified with cut-flower preservative.
3. Select the smallest or least developed of the flowers as #1 and cut it so that its length is equal to the width plus the breadth of the container. Insert it about 1 inch behind the center of the holder and straight up.

4. Select the next-largest or next-most-developed flower as #2. Cut flower #2 such that, when it is inserted, the length of its exposed portion will be $\frac{2}{3}$ that of flower #1. Insert it slightly to the right and backward of flower #1, tilted somewhat to the right and slightly backward. ($1, 3\frac{1}{2}$)

5. Select the smaller of the remaining two flowers as #3. Cut flower #3 such that when it is inserted its exposed portion will be $\frac{1}{2}$ that of flower #1. Insert it slightly to the left and forward of flower #1, tilted slightly to the left and somewhat more forward. ($8, 3$)

6. Cut flower #4 such that when it is inserted its exposed portion will be $\frac{1}{3}$ that of flower #1. Insert it between flowers #1 and #2 and slightly forward, tilted sharply forward and slightly to the right. ($5, 2$)

7. Select four pieces of spike foliage of varying weight. Cut the heaviest such that when it is inserted its length will be slightly shorter than that of flower #1. Cut the lightest such that it will be slightly longer than flower #3. Cut the remaining two pieces of foliage to lengths evenly spaced between the longest and shortest. Starting with the longest insert as follows:

F-1. To the left of flower #1, tilted very slightly to the left. ($9, 4\frac{1}{2}$)

F-2. To the right of flower #1, tilted slightly to the right and backward very slightly. ($2, 4$)

F-3. To the right of flower #3 and in front of flower #1, tilted very slightly forward. ($6, 4\frac{1}{2}$)

F-4. Behind and slightly to the right of flower #4, tilted to the right slightly more than flower #2 and very slightly backward. ($2, 3$)

8. If needed, insert two or three pieces of round foliage at the base and on the outside of the arrangement to correct balance and hide the holder. (Fig. 143)

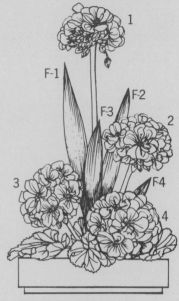

Fig. 143. Arrangement for four flowers (geraniums and iris leaves).

Arrangement for Five Flowers
 # 1

Materials

1. Container—a shallow bowl, a deep bowl, or a tall vase.
2. A holder for flowers—a medium pin-point holder for the shallow container, or shredded foam or crushed chicken wire for the deep bowl or vase.
3. A fastener for the holder—floral clay to secure the pin-point holder.
4. Flowers—hardened and with all foliage below the waterline removed. Five spike flowers (delphiniums, gladioli, larkspurs, snapdragons, etc.), or five round flowers (anemones, daisies, geraniums, roses, tulips, etc.).
5. Foliage—natural spike foliage of the flowers used, or other appropriate spike foliage, and a few pieces of round foliage (natural foliage of the flowers used, or galax leaves, geranium leaves, ivy, etc.).

Procedure

1. Secure the pin-point holder in the center of the shallow holder. If the deep bowl or the vase is used, fill it with the shredded foam or crumpled chicken wire.
2. Fill the container with water fortified with cut-flower preservative.

NOTE: In what follows, all the dimensions will be for the lengths of the flowers showing above the rim of the container. In actually cutting the flowers add to the lengths given the amount needed for insertion into the holder.

3. Select the smallest and least developed flower as #1. Its length should be equal to 2 times the width of the container or more. Insert it straight up 1 inch behind the center of the holder and 1 inch to the left.

4. Select the next-largest or next-most-developed flower as #2. Its length should be $\frac{2}{3}$ that of flower #1. Insert it slightly to the right of flower #1, tilted very slightly to the right and forward. $(4, 4\frac{1}{2})$

5. Select the next-largest or next-most-developed flower as #3. Its length should be a little more than $\frac{1}{2}$ that of flower #1. Insert it slightly to the left of flower #1, tilted slightly backward and to the left. (10:30, 4)

6. Select the next-largest or next-most-developed flower as #4. Its length should be $\frac{1}{2}$ that of flower #1. Insert it just in front of flower #2, tilted sharply forward and somewhat to the right, so that the stem is only slightly above the rim. $(5, 1\frac{1}{2})$

7. Flower #5 should be the largest and most developed. Its length should be just slightly shorter than that of flower #4. Insert it forward of the midpoint between flowers #1 and #3, tilted forward and to the left. (7:30, 3)

8. Cut 5 pieces of spike foliage. The longest should be slightly shorter than flower #1 and the shortest slightly longer than flower #3. The others should be evenly spaced in between. Insert the foliage in order of length starting with the longest, as follows:

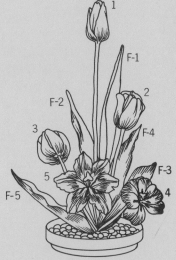

Fig. 144. Arrangement for five flowers #1 (tulips).

F-1. Just to the right of flower #1, tilted very slightly backward and to the right. ($1, 4\frac{1}{2}$)

F-2. Between flowers #1 and #3, tilted slightly backward and to the left. ($11, 4$)

F-3. Behind flower #2, tilted backward and to the right. ($1:30, 3\frac{1}{2}$)

F-4. Slightly to the right of flower #2, tilted to the right and slightly forward. ($4, 3$)

F-5. To the left of the midpoint between flowers #3 and #4, tilted to the left. ($9, 2$)

Insert several pieces of round foliage around and among the bases of the stems to give more weight to the arrangement and to hide the holder. (Fig. 144)

Arrangement for Five Flowers
#2

Materials

1. A shallow container.
2. A holder for flowers—a medium pin-point holder or a block of foam 2 inches wide, 2 inches long, and 2 inches high.
3. A fastener for the holder—floral clay to secure the

pin-point holder, or a staple, anchored to the base of the container with tape, on which to impale the foam.

4. Flowers—five spike flowers (delphiniums, gladioli, snapdragons) or five round flowers (carnations, daffodils, marigolds, roses, tulips).

5. Foliage—spike or round greens appropriate for the flowers used.

Procedure

1. Secure the holder in the center of the container. (If you prefer an asymmetric arrangement, secure the holder $\frac{1}{3}$ of the width of the container in from the right or left side.)

2. Cut flower #1 to a length twice the width of the container plus 2 inches. Insert it straight up at a point $\frac{1}{2}$ inch behind the center of holder.

3. Cut flower #2 to a length that is $\frac{2}{3}$ that of flower #1. Insert it in front of flower #1, tilted very slightly forward. $(6, 4\frac{1}{2})$

4. Cut flower #3 to a height that is $\frac{1}{2}$ that of flower #2. Insert it slightly to the left of flower #2 and tilt it slightly forward and to the left. $(8, 4)$

5. Cut flower #4 a little shorter than flower #2. Insert it to the right of flower #3 and tilt it backward and to the right. $(1, 3)$

6. Cut flower #5 the same length as flower #3. Insert just in front of the junction of the stems in the holder, pointing forward and upward, adding to the graceful curve of flowers #1, #2, and #3. $(6, 2)$

7. Add spike greens, five to seven leaves so as to contribute to the upward line.

8. Camouflage the holder with round greens, moss, or stones. (Fig. 145)

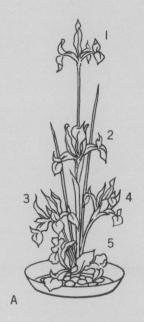

Fig. 145. Arrangement for five flowers #2. (A) Irises. (B) Garden irises.

Arrangement for Seven
Round Flowers

Materials

1. Container—a shallow circular container.
2. A holder for flowers—a medium pin-point holder fitted with a cap of chicken wire large enough to protrude 1 to $1\frac{1}{2}$ inches above the rim of the container, or a piece of foam at least 3 inches square and high enough to protrude 1 to $1\frac{1}{2}$ inches above the rim of the container.
3. A fastener for the holder—floral clay to secure the pin-point holder, or a staple attached in the base of the container, with tape on which to impale the block of foam.
4. Flowers—hardened and with all foliage below the waterline removed. Seven round flowers of one kind (asters, daisies, cosmos, chrysanthemums, marigolds). The most beautiful and most developed flower should be identified and held for the focal point of the arrangement. In this recipe it will be flower #4.
5. Foliage—several pieces of good-quality spike foliage.

Procedure

1. Secure the holder in the center of the container.
2. Fill the container with water fortified with cut-flower preservative.
3. Select a smaller flower with a long, slightly curved stem as flower #1. Cut it so that it is at least twice as long as the diameter of the container plus the extra length required for insertion in the holder. Insert it approximately 1 inch to the left of the center of the holder so that the flower is directly over the point of insertion and any curve in the stem is to the left.

NOTE: In the arrangement described here, the tallest part will be on the left. If the location requires the opposite, simply interchange all rights and lefts.

NOTE: In what follows, the extra length required for insertion will not be mentioned; only the length of the flower showing above the rim of the container will be given. It is to be understood that the length required for insertion will be added in each case.

4. Select flower #2. Its flower should be the same size as flower #1 or slightly larger, and its stem should have approximately the same curve. Its length should be $\frac{3}{4}$ the length of flower #1. Insert it in front of flower #1, tilted so that its flower is directly in front of, or slightly to the left of, the stem of flower #1. Its stem should follow the curve of the stem of flower #1.

5. Select flower #3. Its flower should be slightly larger than flower #2, and its stem should have approximately the same curve. Its length should be $\frac{1}{2}$ the length of flower #2. Insert it in front of flower #2, tilted so that its flower is directly in front or slightly to the left of the stems of flowers #1 and #2. Flowers #1, #2, and #3 should form a curve that enhances the curve of the stem of flower #1.

6. Flower #4, selected as the largest, most beautiful, and most developed flower, is used as the focal point. It is cut very short so that it stands just clear of the holder when inserted. Insert it in the center of the front edge of the holder, tilted forward, halfway between vertical and horizontal. $(6, 2\frac{1}{2})$

7. Select flower #5. It should be the same size as flower #3 or slightly larger. Its length should be such that, when inserted, it is $\frac{1}{4}$ the length of flower #3. Insert it to the left and slightly forward of flower #3, tilted to the left and slightly forward of flower #3, so that

its flower is slightly to the left of the stems of flowers #1, #2, and #3, extending the curve formed by those flowers. (8, 3)

8. Flower #6 should be slightly less than $\frac{1}{2}$ the length of flower #3. Insert it to the right of flower #3, tilted to the right and very slightly backward. $(2, 3\frac{1}{2})$

9. Flower #7 should be $\frac{2}{3}$ the length of flower #6. Insert it to the right of midway between flowers #4 and #6, tilted to the right and slightly forward so that the flower is almost a flower-width to the right of midway between flowers #4 and #6. (4, 3)

10. Select a slender piece of foliage that has approximately the same curve as the stem of flower #1. Its length should be between the lengths of flowers #1 and #2. Insert it slightly to the left of flower #2, tilted so that it is behind or slightly to the left of flower #2 with its curve following that of the flower stems. $(11, 4\frac{1}{2})$

11. Select a similar piece of foliage and cut it so that its tip will be above midway between flowers #3 and #5 when it is inserted. Insert it behind flower #5. (8:30, 4)

12. The third piece of foliage should be about $\frac{2}{3}$ the length of the second piece. Insert it to the left of the second piece, tilted so that it appears behind the left half of flower #5. $(8:30, 2\frac{1}{2})$

13. Two pieces of foliage approximately the same length as flower #6 should be inserted along the centerline of the holder from the right, tilted slightly above horizontal. $(3\frac{1}{2})$ (3, 1)

14. Use flat, broad foliage to cover and hide the holder. (Fig. 146)

Fig. 146. Arrangement for seven round flowers (hibiscus).

Arrangement for Twelve Round Flowers
(Symmetrical Fan-Shaped)

Materials

1. Container—a shallow circular container or a tall vase with an opening at least 3 inches in diameter.

2. A holder for flowers—a medium-to-large pin-point holder for the shallow container, fitted with a cap of chicken wire large enough to protrude 1 to $1\frac{1}{2}$ inches above the rim, or a piece of foam at least 3 inches square and high enough to protrude 1 to $1\frac{1}{2}$ inches above the rim of the container. For the tall vase, use shredded foam as a filler topped with a piece of foam cut to fit the opening of the vase. The block of foam should be 2 to 4 inches high according to the weight of the flowers being used and, similarly, should protrude 1 to $1\frac{1}{2}$ inches above the rim of the vase.

3. A fastener for the holder—floral clay to secure the pin-point holder, or a staple, attached in the base of the shallow container with tape, on which to impale the block of foam.

4. Flowers—hardened and with all foliage below the waterline removed. Twelve round flowers of one kind and of uniform size and development. If there is some variation in the size of the flowers available, use the smaller and least developed flowers for the upper and outer flowers of the arrangement (asters, daisies, cosmos, chrysanthemums, marigolds, roses, zinnias, etc.).

The most beautiful, largest, and most developed flower
should be identified and held for the focal point of the
arrangement. In this recipe it will be flower #9.

5. Foliage—several good-quality pieces of the natural
foliage of the flowers used, or other appropriate foliage.

Procedure

1. Secure the holder in the center of the shallow container.
If the tall vase is being used, stuff it with shredded foam
to a tightness appropriate for the flowers being used—
tight enough to hold the flowers where they are inserted, but not so tight that insertion is difficult. Fit
the block of foam on top of the shredded foam. When
the tall vase is used, the stems of the flowers should
be cut long enough to pass completely through the
block of foam and deeply into the shredded foam. Since
this method anchors the block very securely, no other
attachment is necessary.

2. Fill the container with water fortified with cut-flower
preservative.

3. Select a flower with a very straight stem as #1.
If there is a variation in the size of the flowers, this
should be one of the smallest and least developed. If
the shallow vase is being used, cut flower #1 so that it
is equal to the length required for insertion in the holder
plus twice the diameter of the container, or more. If the
tall vase is being used, flower #1 should be the length
required for insertion plus twice the height of the vase,
or more. Insert it straight up about 1 to $1\frac{1}{2}$ inches in back
of the center of the holder.

NOTE: In what follows, the extra length required for insertion will not be mentioned; only the length of the flower
showing above the rim of the container will be given. It

is understood, however, that the length required for insertion is to be added in each case.

4. Select flower #2. Its length should be $\frac{7}{8}$ the height of flower #1. Rotate the stem until the flower is seen in profile from the front of the arrangement. Insert it just to the right of flower #1, tilted slightly to the right. (3, 4)

5. Select flower #3. Its length should be $\frac{7}{8}$ that of flower #1. Turn it until it appears in profile and insert it just to the left of flower #1, tilted slightly to the left. (9, 4)

6. Select flower #4. Its length should be $\frac{7}{8}$ that of flower #3. Turn it so it will appear in profile. Insert it from the left along the centerline of the holder, so that it is in the same plane as the flowers already inserted, tilted slightly above horizontal. (9, 1)

7. Select flower #5 and cut it the same length as flower #4. Turn it so it will appear in profile. Insert it from the right along the centerline of the holder, so that it is in the same plane as the flowers already inserted, tilted slightly above horizontal. (3, 1) (Fig. 147A)

8. Select flower #6. Its length should be $\frac{3}{4}$ that of flowers #4 or #5. Insert it horizontally toward the center of the holder at an angle midway between the left and the forward directions. (7:30, 0) Before inserting it, turn the flower until it faces as fully forward as possible.

9. Select flower #7. Cut it to the same length as flower #6. Insert it horizontally toward the center of the holder at an angle midway between the right and the forward directions. (4:30, 0) Before inserting it, turn the flower until it faces as fully forward as possible.

10. Select flower #8. Its length should be $\frac{3}{4}$ that of flower #1. Insert it just in front of flower #1, tilted slightly forward. (6, 4) Before inserting it, turn the flower so that it shows the most face somewhat to the right of forward. (Fig. 147B)

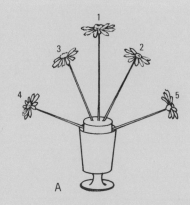

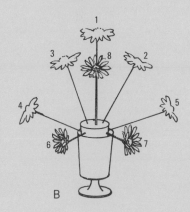

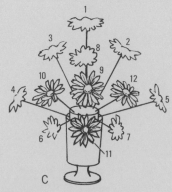

Fig. 147. Arrangement for twelve round flowers (symmetrical fan-shaped arrangement with daisies). (A) Steps 1–7. (B) Steps 8–10. (C) Steps 11–14.

11. Select flower #9, the most beautiful and fully developed flower. Its length should be $\frac{2}{3}$ that of flower #8. Insert it just in front of flower #8, tilted forward. (6, 3) Before insertion, the flower should be turned to face as fully forward as possible.

12. Select flower #10. Cut it the same length as flower #9. Insert it between flowers #4 and #9, tilted sharply to the left and forward, so that it is slightly in front of the plane of flowers #4 and #9 and located slightly closer to flower #4. (7:30, $1\frac{1}{2}$) Before insertion, turn the flower so that it faces slightly forward from its profile position.

13. Select flower #11. Its length should be $\frac{1}{2}$ that of flower #8. Insert it horizontally in the center of the front of the holder, so that the flower points directly forward and the stem is just above the rim of the container. (6, 0)

14. Cut flower #12 the same length as flower #10. Insert it between flowers #5 and #9, tilted sharply to the right and forward, so that it is slightly in front of the plane of flowers #5 and #9 and slightly closer to flower #5. Before insertion, turn the flower so that it faces slightly forward from its profile position. (4:30, $1\frac{1}{2}$) (Fig. 147C)

15. Cut foliage to various lengths, but always shorter than flower #1. Insert the taller pieces behind flowers #1, #2, and #3. Insert the shorter pieces sparingly where there appear to be voids in the arrangement. Insert some small pieces in the front of the holder and between, but below, flowers #4 and #6, #6 and #11, #11 and #7, and #7 and #5. These small pieces should cascade over the rim of the container and should enhance the curve of the lowest flowers of the arrangement. (Fig. 147D)

Fig. 147. (D) Step 15.

Arrangement for Twelve
Conical Spike Flowers

Materials

1. Container—a shallow circular container or a tall vase with an opening at least 3 inches in diameter.

2. A holder for flowers—a medium-to-large pin-point holder for the shallow container, fitted with a cap of chicken wire large enough to protrude 1 to $1\frac{1}{2}$ inches above the rim, or a piece of foam at least 3 inches square and high enough to protrude 1 to $1\frac{1}{2}$ inches above the rim of the container. For the tall vase use shredded foam as a filler topped with a piece of foam cut to fit the opening of the vase. The block of foam should be 2 to 4 inches high according to the weight of the flowers being used and, similarly, should protrude 1 to $1\frac{1}{2}$ inches above the rim of the vase.

3. A fastener for the holder—floral clay to secure the pin-point holder, or a staple, attached in the base of the shallow container with tape, on which to impale the block of foam.

4. Flowers—hardened and with all foliage below the waterline removed. Twelve conical spike flowers of one kind and of uniform size and development. If there is some variation in the size of the flowers available, use the smaller and less developed flowers for the upper and outer flowers of the arrangement (delphiniums, gladioli, larkspurs, liatris, snapdragons, stock, etc.). The most beautiful, largest, and most developed flower should be identified and held for the focal point of the arrangement. In this recipe it will be flower #12.

5. Foliage—Several good-quality pieces of the natural foliage, or other appropriate foliage.

Procedure

1. Secure the holder in the center of the shallow container. If the tall vase is being used, stuff it with shredded foam to a tightness appropriate for the flower being used—tight enough to hold the flowers where they are inserted, but not so tight that insertion is difficult. Fit the block of foam on top of the shredded foam. When the tall vase is used, the stems of the flowers should be cut long enough to pass completely through the block of foam and deeply into the shredded foam. Since this method anchors the block very securely, no other attachment is necessary.

2. Fill the container with water fortified with cut-flower preservative.

3. Select a flower with a very straight stem as flower #1. If there is a variation in size, this flower should be one of the smallest and least developed. If the shallow container is being used, cut flower #1 equal to the length required for insertion in the holder plus at least twice the diameter of the container. If the tall vase is being used, flower #1 should be the length required for insertion plus at least twice the height of the vase. Insert it straight up about 1 to $1\frac{1}{2}$ inches in back of the center of the holder.

NOTE: In what follows, the extra length required for insertion will not be mentioned; only the length of the flower showing above the rim of the container will be given. It is understood, however, that the length required for insertion is to be added in each case.

4. Select flower #2. It should be $\frac{2}{3}$ the length of flower #1. Insert it to the right of flower #1, near the edge of the holder, tilted sharply to the right. (3, 2)

5. Select flower #3. It should be the same length as flower #2. Insert it to the left of flower #1, near the edge of the holder, tilted sharply to the left. (9, 2)

6. Select flower #4. It should be $\frac{7}{8}$ the length of flower #1. Insert it midway between flower #1 and flower #3, tilted so that its flower appears to be midway between flowers #1 and #3, but slightly toward the back. (10:30, $3\frac{1}{2}$)

7. Select flower #5. It should be a little longer than flower #4. Insert it midway between flower #1 and flower #2, tilted so that its flower appears to be midway between #1 and #2, but slightly toward the back. (1:30, $3\frac{1}{2}$) (Fig. 148A)

8. Select flower #6. It should be $\frac{2}{3}$ the length of flower #2. Insert it from the left just above the rim of the container, tilted slightly above horizontal, with the stem pointed toward the center of the holder at an angle $\frac{1}{3}$ of the way from the left to the forward directions. (8, 1)

9. Select flower #7. It should be the same length as flower #6. Insert it from the right just above the rim of the container, tilted slightly above horizontal, with the stem pointed toward the center of the holder at an angle $\frac{1}{3}$ of the way from the right to the forward directions. (4, 1)

10. Select flower #8. It should be slightly shorter than flower #1. Insert it between flowers #1 and #4, tilted so that its flower appears to be between flowers #1 and #4, quite close to flower #1, and tilted slightly forward. (8, $4\frac{1}{2}$)

11. Select flower #9. It should be $\frac{2}{3}$ the length of flower #1. Insert it between flowers #1 and #5, tilted so that its flower appears to be quite close to flower #1, and tilted slightly forward. (5, 4) (Fig. 148B)

12. Select flower #10. It should be a little longer than half the length of flower #1. Insert it midway between flowers #3 and #8, tilted so that its flower appears to be midway between flowers #3 and #8, and tilted slightly forward. (7:30, 3)

13. Select flower #11. It should be the same length as flower #2. Insert it midway between flowers #2 and #9, tilted so that its flower appears to be midway between flowers #2 and #9, and tilted slightly forward. (4, 3)

14. Select flower #12. It should be ½ the length of flower #1. Insert it forward of flower #1, tilted slightly forward. (6, 4) This flower will hide the bare stem of flower #1, and the lower floret or florets of this flower will become the focal point of the arrangement. (Fig. 148C)

Fig. 148. Arrangement for twelve conical spike flowers (delphiniums). (A) Steps 1–7. (B) Steps 8–11. (C) Steps 12–14. (D) Finished arrangement.

Three-Quarter Arrangement of Twelve
Front-Facing Spike Flowers
(Symmetrical Fan-Shaped)

Materials

1. Container—a shallow circular container or a tall vase with an opening at least 3 inches in diameter.

2. A holder for flowers—a medium-to-large pin-point holder for the shallow container, fitted with a cap of chicken wire large enough to protrude 1 to $1\frac{1}{2}$ inches above the rim, or a piece of foam at least 3 inches square and high enough to protrude 1 to $1\frac{1}{2}$ inches above the rim of the container. For the tall vase use shredded foam as a filler topped with a piece of foam cut to fit the opening of the vase. The block of foam should be 2 to 4 inches high according to the weight of the flowers being used and, similarly, should protrude 1 to $1\frac{1}{2}$ inches above the rim of the vase.

3. A fastener for the holder—floral clay to secure the pin-point holder, or a staple, attached in the base of the shallow container with tape, on which to impale the block of foam.

4. Flowers—hardened and with all foliage below the waterline removed. Twelve spike flowers of one kind and of uniform size and development (delphiniums, gladioli, larkspurs, liatris, snapdragons, stock, etc.). If there is some variation in the size of the flowers available, use the smaller and less developed flowers for the upper and outer flowers of the arrangement. The most beautiful, largest, and most developed flower should be identified and held for the focal point of the arrangement. In this recipe it will be flower #12.

5. Foliage—several good-quality pieces of the natural foliage or other appropriate foliage.

Procedure

1. Secure the holder in the center of the shallow container. If the tall vase is being used, stuff it with shredded foam to a tightness appropriate for the flowers being used— tight enough to hold the flowers where they are inserted, but not so tight that insertion is difficult. Fit the block of foam on top of the shredded foam. When the tall vase is used, the stems of the flowers should be cut long enough to pass completely through the block of foam and deeply into the shredded foam. Since this method anchors the block very securely, no other attachment is necessary.

2. Fill the container with water fortified with cut-flower preservative.

3. Select a flower with a very straight stem as flower #1. If there is a variation in size, this flower should be one of the smallest and least developed. If the shallow container is being used, cut flower #1 so that it is equal to the length required for insertion in the holder plus at least twice the diameter of the container. If the tall vase is being used, flower #1 should be the length required for insertion plus at least twice the height of the vase. Insert it straight up about 1 to $1\frac{1}{2}$ inches in back of the center of the holder.

NOTE: Spike flowers should always be inserted face-forward or, if they are conical, the best florets should always show toward the front of the arrangement.

NOTE: In what follows, the extra length required for insertion will not be mentioned; only the length of the flower showing above the rim of the container will be given. It is understood, however, that the length required for insertion is to be added in each case.

4. Select flower #2. It should be $\frac{2}{3}$ the length of flower #1. Insert it to the right of flower #1, near the edge of the holder, tilted sharply to the right. (3, 2)

5. Select flower #3. It should be the same length as flower #2. Insert it to the left of flower #1, near the edge of the holder, tilted sharply to the left. (9, 2)

6. Select flower #4. It should be $\frac{7}{8}$ the length of flower #1. Insert it midway between flower #1 and flower #3, tilted so that its flower appears to be midway between flowers #1 and #3, and slightly toward the back. (10:30, $3\frac{1}{2}$)

7. Select flower #5. It should be a little longer than flower #4. Insert it midway between flower #1 and flower #2, tilted so that its flower appears to be midway between flowers #1 and #2, and slightly toward the back. (1:30, $3\frac{1}{2}$) (Fig. 149A)

8. Select flower #6. It should be $\frac{2}{3}$ the length of flower #2. Insert it from the left along the centerline of the holder, just above the rim of the container, tilted slightly above horizontal. (9, 1)

9. Select flower #7. It should be the same length as flower #6. Insert it from the right along the centerline of the holder, just above the rim of the container, tilted slightly above horizontal. (3, 1)

10. Select flower #8. It should be slightly shorter than flower #1. Insert it between and slightly forward of flowers #1 and #4, tilted so that its flower appears to be between flowers #1 and #4, quite close to flower #1, and slightly forward. (9, $4\frac{1}{2}$)

11. Select flower #9. It should be $\frac{2}{3}$ the length of flower #1. Insert it between and slightly forward of flowers

#1 and #5, tilted so that its flower appears to be between flowers #1 and #5, but quite close to #1, and forward. (3, 4½) (Fig. 149B)

12. Select flower #10. It should be a little more than half the length of flower #1. Insert it midway between, but forward of, flowers #3 and #8, tilted so that its flower appears to be midway between flowers #3 and #8, but slightly forward. (9, 3)

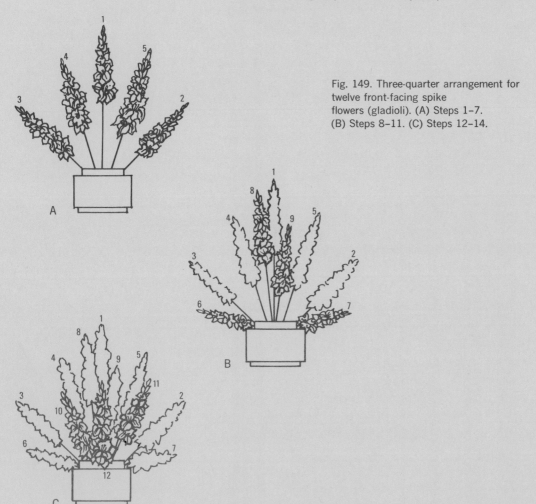

Fig. 149. Three-quarter arrangement for twelve front-facing spike flowers (gladioli). (A) Steps 1–7. (B) Steps 8–11. (C) Steps 12–14.

13. Select flower #11. It should be the same length as flower #2. Insert it midway between, but forward of, flowers #2 and #9, tilted so that its flower appears to be midway between flowers #2 and #9, but slightly forward. (3, 3)

14. Select flower #12. It should be slightly shorter than flower #9. Insert it straight up, forward of flower #1. Flower #12 will hide the bare stem of flower #1, and the lower floret or florets of this flower will become the focal point of the arrangement. (Fig. 149C)

15. Cut foliage to various lengths, but always shorter than flower #1. Insert the taller pieces behind flowers #1, #4, and #5. Insert shorter pieces sparingly where there appear to be voids in the arrangement. Insert some small pieces in front of the holder and between flowers #10 and #6, #11 and #7, #10 and #12, and #12 and #11. These should cascade over the rim of the container and should enhance the curve of the lowest flowers of the arrangement.

COMMENT:

1. If the flowers are very full, or if a larger and more symmetrical arrangement is desired, cut flowers #2, #3, #4, and #5 just a little shorter than flower #1.

2. The length of flower #6 should be $\frac{2}{3}$ that of flower #1. Insert it horizontally from the left on the centerline of the holder and just above the rim of the container. (9, 0)

3. Cut flower #7 in the same way as flower #6. Insert it horizontally from the right on the centerline of the holder and just above the rim of the container. (3, 0) The lengths of the other flowers should be adjusted proportionately.

Asymmetrical Centerpiece of
Twelve Round Flowers

Materials

1. Container—a circular, square, or rectangular shallow container or a tall vase with an opening at least 3 inches in diameter.
2. A holder for flowers—a medium-to-large pin-point holder for the shallow container fitted with a cap of chicken wire large enough to protrude 1 to $1\frac{1}{2}$ inches above the rim, or a piece of foam at least 3 inches square and high enough to protrude 1 to $1\frac{1}{2}$ inches above the rim of the container. For the tall vase use shredded foam as a filler, topped with a piece of foam cut to fit the opening of the vase. The block of foam should be 2 to 4 inches high according to the weight of the flowers being used and, similarly, should protrude 1 to $1\frac{1}{2}$ inches above the rim of the vase.
3. A fastener for the holder—floral clay to secure the pin-point holder, or a staple, attached in the base of the shallow container, on which to impale the block of foam.
4. Flowers—hardened and with all foliage below the waterline removed. Twelve round flowers of one kind and of uniform size and development (anemones, asters, cosmos, carnations, daisies, zinnias, etc.). If there is some variation in the size of the flowers available, use the smaller and less developed flowers for the upper and outer flowers of the arrangement.
5. Foliage—several good-quality pieces of the natural foliage or other appropriate foliage.

Procedure

1. Secure the holder in the center of the shallow container. It can be placed at the left of center if the container

is large. If the tall vase is being used, stuff it with foam to a tightness appropriate for the flower being used— tight enough to hold the flowers where they are inserted, but not so tight that insertion is difficult. Fit the block of foam on top of the shredded foam. When the tall vase is used, the stems of the flowers should be cut long enough to pass completely through the block of foam and deeply into the shredded foam. Since this method anchors the block very securely, no other attachment is necessary.

2. Fill the container with water fortified with cut-flower preservative.

3. Select a very straight, good-quality flower as flower #1. Its length should be such that it will provide the desired overall height of the centerpiece when inserted. (Be sure that the width of the container is not more than $\frac{1}{2}$ the height above its rim of flower #1, or, if it is a taller vase or bowl, that its height is not more than $\frac{2}{3}$ the height above its rim of flower #1.) Insert it to the left of the center of the holder, tilted slightly to the left. (9, 4)

NOTE: A right-handed asymmetrical arrangement will be described. If a left-handed centerpiece is desired, simply turn the arrangement around when it is completed.

4. Flower #2 should be the same length as flower #1. Insert it from the right on the centerline of the holder just above the rim of the container, tilted very slightly below horizontal. (3, $-\frac{1}{2}$)

5. Flower #3 should be slightly shorter than flower #1. Insert it from the left just above the rim of the container in the center of the left-hand edge of the holder so that the flower is slightly below the halfway point between vertical and horizontal. (9, 2)

6. Flower #4 should be $\frac{3}{4}$ the length of flower #1. Insert it just to the right of center of the holder, tilted to the right and forward, so that the flower appears slightly closer to vertical than horizontal. (4, 3)

7. Flower #5 should be slightly shorter than flower #1. Insert it just behind the center of the holder, tilted backward and slightly to the right so that the flower appears slightly above midway between vertical and horizontal. (1, 3) (Fig. 150A)

8. Flower #6 should be slightly more than $\frac{2}{3}$ the length of flower #1. Insert it near the front edge of the holder forward and left of flower #1, tilted forward and to the left so that it appears to be midway between vertical and horizontal. (8, $2\frac{1}{2}$)

9. Flower #7 should be slightly less than $\frac{2}{3}$ the length of flower #1. Insert it near the back edge of the holder behind and slightly to the right of flower #1, tilted backward so that the flower is slightly below midway between horizontal and vertical. (12, 2)

10. Flower #8 should be $\frac{2}{3}$ the length of flower #1. Insert it in the side of the holder with the stem directed to the center of the holder, just above the rim of the container, so that it is $\frac{1}{3}$ of the way from the forward to the right direction, tilted slightly above horizontal. (5, 1)

11. Flower #9 should be $\frac{3}{4}$ the length of flower #1. Insert it near the back of the left-hand edge of the holder, tilted to the left and backward so that the flower appears midway between vertical and horizontal and midway between the left and the backward direction. (10:30, $2\frac{1}{2}$) (Fig. 150B)

12. Flower #10 should be slightly more than $\frac{1}{2}$ the length of flower #1. Insert it near the back edge of the holder toward the back right-hand corner, tilted to the right and backward so it balances flower #6. (2, 2)

13. Flower #11 should be slightly more than half the length of flower #1. Insert it near the front edge of the holder directly forward of flower #5, tilted for-

ward so that the flower is slightly closer to vertical than horizontal. (6, 3)

14. Flower #12 should be $\frac{2}{3}$ the length of flower #1. Insert it in the right-hand edge of the holder along the centerline and above flower #2, so that the flower appears slightly above horizontal. (3, 1) (Fig. 150C)

15. Insert filler flowers in the major voids. Insert foliage in any remaining voids so that the holder is disguised and the arrangement has balance. (Fig. 150D)

COMMENT: If a rounder centerpiece is desired, remove flower #2. Cut it the same length as flower #4. Insert it just above horizontal and just below flower #10, tilted to the right and backward. (2, $\frac{1}{2}$) (Fig. 150E, F)

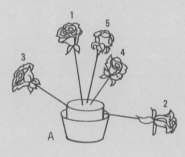

A

Fig. 150. Asymmetrical centerpiece of twelve round flowers. (A) Steps 1–7. (B) Steps 8–11. (C) Steps 12–14. (D) Step 15. (E,F) This centerpiece has been made rounder by moving the position of flower #2.

D

B

E

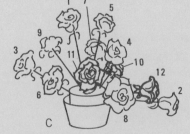

C

F

Asymmetrical Centerpiece of
Twelve Spike Flowers

Materials

1. Container—a circular, square, or rectangular shallow container or a tall vase with an opening at least 3 inches in diameter.

2. A holder for flowers—a medium-to-large pin-point holder for the shallow container fitted with a cap of chicken wire large enough to protrude 1 to $1\frac{1}{2}$ inches above the rim, or a piece of foam at least 3 inches square and high enough to protrude 1 to $1\frac{1}{2}$ inches above the rim of the container. For the tall vase use shredded foam as a filler topped with a piece of foam cut to fit the opening of the vase. The block of foam should be 2 to 4 inches high according to the weight of the flowers being used and, similarly, should protrude 1 to $1\frac{1}{2}$ inches above the rim of the vase.

3. A fastener for the holder—floral clay to secure the pin-point holder, or a staple, attached in the base of the shallow container, on which to impale the block of foam.

4. Flowers—hardened and with all foliage below the waterline removed. Twelve spike flowers of uniform size and development (delphiniums, gladioli, larkspurs, liatris, snapdragons, stock, etc.). If there is some variation in the size of the flowers available, use the smaller and less developed flowers for the upper and outer flowers of the arrangement.

5. Foliage—several good-quality pieces of the natural foliage, or other appropriate foliage.

Procedure

1. Secure the holder in the center of the shallow container. It can be placed at the left of center if the container is large. If the tall vase is being used, stuff it with foam to a tightness appropriate for the flower being used— tight enough to hold the flowers where they are inserted, but not so tight that insertion is difficult. Fit the block of foam on top of the shredded foam. When the tall vase is used, the stems of the flowers should be cut long enough to pass completely through the block of foam and deeply into the shredded foam. Since this method anchors the block very securely, no other attachment is necessary.

2. Fill the container with water fortified with cut-flower preservative.

3. Select a very straight good-quality flower as flower #1. Its length should be such that it will provide the desired overall height of the centerpiece when inserted. (The width of the container should not be more than $\frac{1}{2}$ the height above its rim of flower #1, or, if it is a tall vase or bowl, its height should not be more than $\frac{2}{3}$ of the height above its rim of flower #1.) Insert flower #1 straight up, 1 to $1\frac{1}{2}$ inches to the left of the center of the holder.

NOTE: A right-handed centerpiece will be described. If a left-handed centerpiece is desired, simply turn the arrangement around when it is completed.

4. Flower #2 should be slightly shorter than flower #1. Insert it from the right on the centerline of the holder, just above the rim of the container, tilted very slightly below horizontal. $(3, -\frac{1}{2})$

5. Flower #3 should be the same length as flower #2. Insert it from the left just above the rim of the container, in the center of the left-hand edge of the holder, directed toward the center of the holder, tilted about $\frac{1}{4}$ of the way from horizontal to vertical. (9, $1\frac{1}{2}$)

6. Flower #4 should be $\frac{3}{4}$ the length of flower #3. Insert it at the center of the right-hand edge of the holder, tilted to the right, so that the flower appears slightly above the midway point between flowers #1 and #2. (3, 3) (Fig. 151A)

7. Flower #5 should be the same length as flower #4. Insert it midway between flowers #1 and #4 and slightly back, tilted so that the flower appears midway between and slightly backward of flowers #1 and #4. (1, $3\frac{1}{2}$)

8. Flower #6 should be $\frac{3}{4}$ the length of flower #5. Insert it near the front edge of the holder, forward and slightly to the left of flower #1, tilted forward and to the left, so that the flower is midway between the left and forward directions and slightly above midway between horizontal and vertical. (7:30, 3)

9. Flower #7 should be the same length as flower #6. Insert it near the front edge of the holder, directly forward of flower #5, tilted forward and very slightly to the right, so that the flower is slightly closer to vertical than horizontal. (5, 3) (Fig. 151B)

10. Flower #8 should be the same length as flower #6. Insert it in the side of the holder in front of flower #2, just above the rim of the container and directed toward the center of the holder, tilted very slightly below horizontal. (4, $-\frac{1}{2}$) The flower should appear comfortably forward of flower #2.

(Opposite) Rhythmic, sophisticated arrangement of Fuji mums with dracena leaves and grape-ivy foliage. [Photograph courtesy of Florists' Transworld Delivery Association]

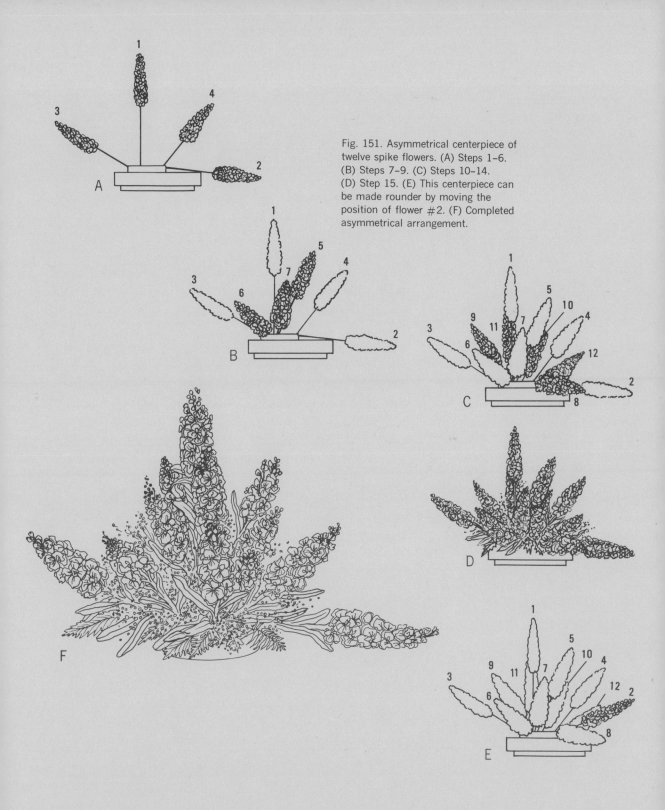

Fig. 151. Asymmetrical centerpiece of twelve spike flowers. (A) Steps 1–6. (B) Steps 7–9. (C) Steps 10–14. (D) Step 15. (E) This centerpiece can be made rounder by moving the position of flower #2. (F) Completed asymmetrical arrangement.

(Opposite) Nicely balanced and elegant arrangement of red roses.
[Photograph courtesy of Florists' Transworld Delivery Association]

11. Flower #9 should be a little longer than flower #8. Insert it near the back of the left-hand edge of the holder, tilted to the left and backward, so that the flower is midway between the left and the backward directions and midway between vertical and horizontal. (10:30, $2\frac{1}{2}$)

12. Flower #10 should be the same length as flower #8. Insert it near the back edge of the holder toward the back right corner, tilted to the right and backward, so that it balances flower #6. (1, 3)

13. Flower #11 should be $\frac{1}{2}$ the length of flower #1. Insert it near the back edge of the holder directly behind flower #1, tilted backward, so that it is midway between vertical and horizontal. (12, $2\frac{1}{2}$)

14. Flower #12 should be the same length as flower #10. Insert it in the side of the holder near the back right-hand corner, just above the rim of the container, tilted sharply to the right and slightly backward, so that the flower appears slightly behind midway between flowers #2 and #10. (2:30, 2) (Fig. 151C)

15. Insert filler flowers in the major voids. Insert foliage in any remaining voids so that the holder is disguised and the arrangement has balance. (Fig. 151D)

COMMENT: If you want a more circular and more symmetrical centerpiece, insert flower #2 in the same location, but tilted slightly upward, above the rim of the container. (3, $1\frac{1}{2}$) (Fig. 151E)

Symmetrical Three-Quarter Triangular Arrangement with Fifteen Flowers

Materials

1. Container—a shallow bowl, a deep bowl, or a tall vase with an opening at least 4 inches in diameter.

2. A holder for flowers—a large pin-point holder with an attached cap of chicken wire that will protrude about $1\frac{1}{2}$ inches above the rim of the shallow container, or a block of foam that is about 4 to 5 inches square and high enough to protrude $1\frac{1}{2}$ inches above the rim of the container. For the deep bowl or tall vase, use shredded foam or crushed chicken wire as the filler, topped by a block of foam cut to fit the opening of the bowl or vase, and at least 4 inches thick.

3. A fastener for the holder—floral clay to secure the pin-point holder in the base of the shallow container, or two or three staples, fastened in the base of the shallow container with tape, on which to impale the foam.

4. Flowers—hardened and with all foliage below the waterline removed. Two spike flowers of one kind (delphiniums, gladioli, larkspur, lilacs, snapdragons, etc.), five larger round flowers of one kind (anemones, asters, carnations, chrysanthemums, geraniums, irises, etc.), seven smaller round flowers (daisies, roses, tulips, etc.), one large feature flower to be used as the focal point (amaryllis, large chrysanthemum, gerbera, magnolia, etc.), and a quantity of filler flowers (candytuft, baby's breath, statice, etc.).

5. Foliage—a quantity of good-quality natural foliage of the flowers used.

6. A number of 18-inch florist wires of heavy and medium weights, to reinforce stems when necessary.

Procedure

1. Secure the pin-point holder or the block of foam in the center of the shallow container. If the deep bowl or tall vase is used, fill it with the shredded foam or crumpled chicken wire; stuff it to the tightness that will

hold stems where they have been inserted but will not make insertion difficult. Insert the block of foam on top of the filler. For the large number of flowers in this arrangement, it is advisable to anchor the foam with a cross of tape as described earlier.

2. Fill the container with water fortified with cut-flower preservative.

NOTE: In what follows, all dimensions will be for the length of the flower showing above the top or sides of the holder. In actually cutting the flowers, add to the lengths given the amount needed for insertion into the holder. For a large number of flowers the amount needed must be varied in order to avoid "collisions" between stems. While some judgment is necessary, the added length will generally be greatest for the early and vertical insertions of the flowers. The shorter flowers, particularly those inserted almost horizontally, require much less added length. See page 89 for a rapid way of cutting flowers to the right length.

3. Select a good-quality spike flower with a straight stem as flower S#1. Cut it so that it is equal to the desired height of the finished arrangement, making sure that it is not less than twice the diameter of the shallow container or not less than $1\frac{1}{2}$ times the height of the tall vase. Insert it straight up, 1 to $1\frac{1}{2}$ inches back of the center of the holder.

4. Spike flower S#2 should be $\frac{7}{8}$ the length of S#1. Insert it slightly to the left of S#1, tilted very slightly to the left. (9, $4\frac{1}{2}$) (Fig. 152A)

5. Large round flower LR#1 should be $\frac{2}{3}$ the length of S#2. Insert it slightly in front of S#1, tilted slightly forward and very slightly to the left. (6:30, 4)

6. Large round flower LR#2 should be a little shorter than LR#1. Insert it slightly in front of LR#1, tilted very slightly forward—just enough to prevent the flowers from crushing each other. (6, 3)

7. Large round flower LR#3 should be the same length as LR#2. Insert it horizontally from the right, on the centerline of the holder just above the rim of the container. (3, 0)

8. Large round flower LR#4 should be slightly shorter than LR#3. Insert it horizontally from the left, on the centerline of the holder just above the rim of the container. (9, 0)

9. Large round flower LR#5 should be $\frac{1}{2}$ the length of LR#1. Insert it in the side of the holder, just above the rim of the container, with the stem pointed toward the center of the holder at an angle, halfway between the left and forward directions, tilted very slightly below horizontal. (7:30, $-\frac{1}{2}$) (Fig. 152B)

10. Small round flower SR#1 should be the same length as LR#4. Insert it to the right of S#1, tilted to the right and slightly forward. (4:30, 3)

11. Small round flower SR#2 should be the same length as LR#2. Insert it to the left of S#2, tilted to the left and very slightly forward. (8:30, 3)

12. Small round flower SR#3 should be slightly shorter than LR#5. Insert it midway between LR#2 and LR#4, tilted so that the flower appears midway between LR#2 and LR#4. (7:30, 2)

13. Small round flower SR#4 should be the same length as LR#5. Insert it in front of the holder below LR#2 and slightly to the left, tilted so that it is slightly left of midway between LR#2 and horizontal. (6:30, $1\frac{1}{2}$)

14. Small round flower SR#5 should be the same length as SR#3. Insert it slightly to the right of the center of the front of the holder, with the stem pointed to the center of the holder just above the rim of the container, and tilted slightly below horizontal. (5:30, $-\frac{1}{2}$)

15. Small round flower SR#6 should be slightly shorter than SR#4. Insert it in the right-hand edge of the

A

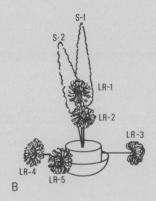

B

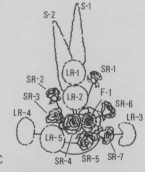

C

Fig. 152. Symmetrical three-quarter triangular arrangement with fifteen flowers (two gladioli, five large chrysanthemums, seven roses, and one poppy). (A) Steps 1–4. (B) Steps 5–9. (C) Steps 10–17.

holder, midway between LR#1 and LR#3, tilted so that the flower appears slightly below midway between LR#1 and LR#3. (3:30, 2)

16. Small round flower SR#7 should be the same length as SR#6. Insert it midway between LR#3 and SR#5, tilted very slightly above horizontal, so that the flower appears midway between LR#3 and SR#5. $(4:30, \frac{1}{2})$

17. Feature flower F#1 should be shorter than SR#3. Insert it near the front right-hand edge of the holder midway between LR#2 and SR#7 and tilted so that the flower appears midway between LR#2 and SR#7. (5, 2) (Fig. 152C)

18. Insert filler flowers in the voids in the arrangement. The filler flowers should be cut to lengths shorter than the average lengths of the flowers surrounding any void to be filled. The major voids are:

   A. Behind SR#6 $(3, 2\frac{1}{2})$
   B. Above and behind the feature flower (5, 3)
   C. Area surrounded by LR#1, SR#2, and SR#3 (7:30, 3)

19. Add foliage wherever necessary to hide bare stems, disguise the holder, or maintain balance. Use foliage very sparingly and be careful that it does not disturb the triangular shape of the arrangement or overpower the flowers. (Fig. 152D)

D   Fig. 152. (D) Steps 18–19.

Symmetrical Three-Quarter Triangular Arrangement of Twenty-One Flowers

Materials

1. Container—a shallow bowl, a deep bowl, or a tall vase with an opening that is at least 4 inches in diameter.

2. A holder for flowers—a large pin-point holder with an attached cap of chicken wire that will protrude about $1\frac{1}{2}$ inches above the rim of the shallow container, or a block of foam that is about 4 to 5 inches square and high enough to protrude $1\frac{1}{2}$ inches above the rim of the container. For the deep bowl or the tall vase, use shredded foam or crushed chicken wire as the filler, topped by a block of foam cut to fit the opening of the bowl or vase, and at least 4 inches thick.

3. A fastener for the holder—floral clay to secure the pin-point holder in the base of the shallow container, or two or three staples, attached in the base of the shallow container with tape, on which to impale the foam.

4. Flowers—hardened and with all foliage below the waterline removed. Three spike flowers of one kind (delphiniums, gladioli, larkspur, lilacs, snapdragons, etc.), nine larger round flowers of one kind (anemones, asters, carnations, geraniums, irises, etc.), seven smaller round flowers of one kind (anemones, asters, carnations, daisies, etc.), two feature flowers to be used as the focal point (amaryllis lilies, chrysanthemums, gerberas, magnolias, tuberous rooted begonias, etc.), and a quantity of filler flowers (candytuft, baby's breath, statice, etc.).

5. Foliage—some good-quality natural foliage of the flowers used.

6. A number of 18-inch florist wires of heavy and medium weights, to reinforce stems when necessary.

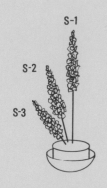

S-1

S-2

S-3

A

Procedure

1. Secure the pin-point holder or the block of foam in the center of the shallow container. If the deep bowl or the tall vase is used, fill it with the shredded foam or crumpled chicken wire; stuff it to the tightness that will hold stems where they have been inserted, but that will not make insertion difficult. Insert the block of foam on top of the filler. For the large number of flowers in this arrangement it is advisable to anchor the foam with a cross of tape as described earlier.

2. Fill the container with water fortified with cut-flower preservative.

NOTE: In what follows, all the dimensions will be for the length of the flower showing above the top or sides of the holder. In actually cutting the flowers, add to the lengths given the amount needed for insertion into the holder. For a large number of flowers the amount added must be varied in order to avoid "collisions" between stems. While some judgment is necessary, the added length will generally be greatest for the early and vertical insertions of the flowers. The shorter flowers, particularly those inserted nearly horizontally, require much less added length. See page 89 for a rapid method of cutting flowers to the right length.

3. Select a good-quality spike flower with a straight stem as S#1. Cut it so that it is equal to the desired height of the finished arrangement, making sure that it is not less than twice the diameter of the shallow container or not less than $1\frac{1}{2}$ times the height of the tall vase. Insert it straight up, 1 to $1\frac{1}{2}$ inches in back of the center of the holder.

4. Spike flower S#2 should be $\frac{2}{3}$ the length of S#1. Insert it to the left of S#1, tilted slightly backward and to the left so that it is $\frac{1}{3}$ of the way from vertical to horizontal. (10:30, $3\frac{1}{2}$)

5. Spike flower S#3 should be $\frac{1}{2}$ the length of S#1. Insert it to the left of S#1 and S#2 near the left-hand edge of the holder, tilted to the left so that it is just below midway between vertical and horizontal. (9, 2) (Fig. 153A)

6. Large round flower LR#1 should be slightly less than $\frac{2}{3}$ the length of S#1. Insert it forward of S#1, tilted very slightly forward, just enough so that the flower is not crushed by S#1. (6, $4\frac{1}{2}$)

7. Large round flower LR#2 should be $\frac{1}{3}$ the length of S#1. Insert it in front of LR#1, tilted slightly forward, just enough so that its flower is not crushed by LR#1. (6, 4)

8. Large round flower LR#3 should be $\frac{1}{2}$ the length of LR#2. Insert it forward and very slightly to the left of LR#2, tilted forward so that its flower appears just below and very slightly to the left of LR#2, approximately midway between the rim of the container and LR#2. (6:30, 2)

9. Large round flower LR#4 should be slightly less than $\frac{1}{2}$ the length of S#1. Insert it to the right of S#1, tilted very slightly backward and slightly to the right so that it is about $\frac{1}{3}$ the way from vertical to horizontal. (2, $3\frac{1}{2}$)

10. Large round flower LR#5 should be slightly shorter than LR#1. Insert it from the left along the centerline of the holder just above the rim of the container, tilted very slightly below horizontal. (9, $-\frac{1}{2}$)

11. Large round flower LR#6 should be $\frac{2}{3}$ the length of LR#5. Insert it from the right along the centerline of the holder, slightly above the rim of the container, tilted very slightly below horizontal. (3, $-\frac{1}{2}$)

12. Large round flower LR#7 should be slightly shorter than LR#6. Insert it slightly forward of midway between LR#4 and LR#6, tilted so it appears slightly

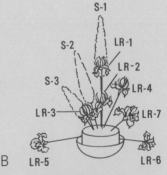

Fig. 153. Symmetrical three-quarter triangular arrangement of twenty-one flowers (lupins, asters, roses, and geraniums). (A) Steps 1–5. (B) Steps 6–12.

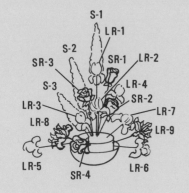

C

forward of midway between LR #4 and LR #6. (3, 2) (Fig. 153B)

13. Small round flower SR #1 should be the same length as LR #1. Insert it midway between LR #1 and LR #4, tilted so that the flower appears to be between LR #1 and LR #4, but very slightly closer to LR #1. $(3, 4\frac{1}{2})$

14. Small round flower SR #2 should be slightly longer than LR #2. Insert it slightly in back of midway between LR #2 and LR #7, tilted so that the flower appears slightly in back of midway between LR #2 and LR #7. (4, 4)

15. Small round flower SR #3 should be slightly longer than SR #2. Insert it slightly to the left and very slightly backward of LR #2, tilted slightly to the left and very slightly forward so that it balances SR #2. (8, 4)

16. Large round flower LR #8 should be $\frac{2}{3}$ the length of SR #3. Insert it near the left-hand edge of the holder, very slightly forward of midway between LR #5 and SR #3, tilted so that the flower appears to be slightly forward of midway between LR #5 and SR #3. $(8:30, 1\frac{1}{2})$

17. Large round flower LR #9 should be the same length as LR #4. Insert it in the right-hand side of the holder toward the back, with the stem directed to the center of the holder slightly above the rim of the container, tilted slightly above horizontal and approximately $\frac{1}{3}$ the way from the right-hand to the backward directions. (2, 1)

18. Small round flower SR #4 should be $\frac{3}{4}$ of the length of SR #2. Insert it in the front of the holder with the stem directed to the center of the holder, slightly above the rim of the container $\frac{1}{3}$ the way from the forward to the right-hand directions, tilted very slightly below horizontal. $(7, -\frac{1}{2})$ (Fig. 153C)

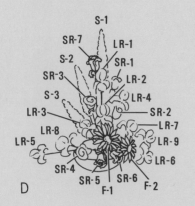

D

19. Small round flower SR#5 should be the same length as SR#4. Insert it along the front centerline of the holder, slightly above the rim of the container and tilted slightly below horizontal. (6, −1) This flower cascades more than SR#4 and SR#6.

20. Small round flower SR#6 should be the same length as SR#4. Insert it in the front of the holder with the stem directed to the center of the holder, slightly above the rim of the container so that it is slightly more than $\frac{1}{3}$ the way from the forward to the right-hand directions, tilted very slightly below horizontal. (4:45, $-\frac{1}{2}$)

21. Small round flower SR#7 should be $\frac{3}{4}$ the length of S#1. Insert it to the left of S#1, tilted very slightly to the left and very slightly forward. (8, $4\frac{1}{2}$)

22. Feature flower F#1 should be slightly longer than LR#3. Insert it to the right of LR#3 above the midpoint between SR#5 and SR#6, tilted so that the flower appears in the middle of the triangle formed by LR#2, SR#5, and SR#6. (5:30, $1\frac{1}{2}$)

23. Feature flower F#2 should be the same length as F#1. Insert it in the front of the holder, with its stem pointed toward the center of the holder midway between SR#6 and LR#6, and tilted very slightly below horizontal. (4, $-\frac{1}{2}$) (Fig. 153D)

24. Insert filler flowers in the voids in the arrangement. The filler flowers should be cut to lengths shorter than the average length of the flowers surrounding the void to be filled. The major voids are:

    A. Between LR#7 and LR#9 (2:30, $1\frac{1}{2}$)
    B. Between SR#3 and S#2 (9, $3\frac{1}{2}$)

25. Add foliage wherever necessary to hide bare stems, disguise the holder, or maintain balance. Use foliage very sparingly and be careful that it does not disturb the triangular shape of the arrangement or overpower the flowers.

E

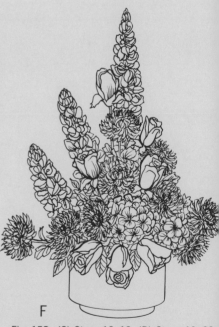

F

Fig. 153. (C) Steps 13–18. (D) Steps 19–23. (E, F) Completed arrangements.

Three-Quarter Arrangement
Symmetrical Triangle
#1

Materials

1. Container—a shallow bowl, a deep bowl, or a tall vase with an opening that is at least 4 inches in diameter.

2. A holder for flowers—a large pin-point holder with an attached cap of chicken wire that will protrude about $1\frac{1}{2}$ inches above the rim of the shallow container, or a block of foam that is about 5 inches square and high enough to protrude $1\frac{1}{2}$ inches above the rim of the container. For the deep bowl or tall vase, use shredded foam or crushed chicken wire as the filler, topped by a block of foam cut to fit the opening of the bowl or vase and at least 4 inches thick.

3. A fastener for the holder—floral clay to secure the pin-point holder in the base of the shallow container, or two or three staples, fastened in the base of the shallow container with tape, on which to impale the foam.

4. Flowers—hardened and with all foliage below the waterline removed. Four spike flowers of one kind (delphiniums, gladioli, larkspurs, lilacs, snapdragons, etc.), twelve larger round flowers of one kind (anemones, asters, carnations, geraniums, irises, etc.), nine smaller round flowers (daisies, roses, tulips, zinnias, etc.), one large feature flower to be used as the focal point (amaryllis lily, chrysanthemum, gerbera, magnolia, etc.), and a quantity of filler flowers (candytuft, baby's breath, statice, etc.).

5. Foliage—some good-quality natural foliage of the flowers used.

6. A number of 24-inch florist wires of heavy and medium weights, to reinforce stems when necessary.

Procedure

1. Secure the pin-point holder or the block of foam in the center of the shallow bowl. If the deep bowl or tall vase is used, fill it with shredded foam or crumpled chicken wire; stuff it to the tightness that will hold the stems where they have been inserted but will not make insertion difficult. Insert the block of foam on top of the filler. For the large number of flowers in this arrangement it is advisable to anchor the foam with a cross of tape as described earlier.

2. Fill the container with water fortified with cut-flower preservative.

NOTE: In what follows, all dimensions given will be for the length of the flower showing above the rim of the container. In actually cutting the flowers, add to the lengths given the amount needed for insertion into the holder. For a large number of flowers the amount added must be varied in order to avoid "collisions" between stems. While some judgment is necessary, the added length will generally be greatest for the early and vertical insertions of the flowers. The shorter flowers, particularly those inserted almost horizontally, require much less added length. See page 89 for a rapid method of cutting flowers to the right length.

3. Select a good-quality spike flower with a straight stem as S#1. Cut it so that it is equal to the desired height

A

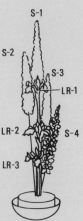

B

of the finished arrangement, making sure that it is not less than twice the diameter of the shallow container or not less than $1\frac{1}{2}$ times the height of the tall vase. Insert it straight up, 1 to $1\frac{1}{2}$ inches in back of the center of the holder.

4. Spike flower S#2 should be $\frac{7}{8}$ the length of S#1. Insert it slightly to the left of S#1, tilted very slightly to the left and very slightly backward. (11, $4\frac{1}{2}$)

5. Spike flower S#3 should be a little less than $\frac{3}{4}$ the length of S#1. Insert it slightly to the right of S#1, tilted very slightly to the right and slightly backward. (1:30, $4\frac{1}{2}$) (Fig. 154A)

6. Large round flower LR#1 should be the same length as S#3. Insert it slightly in front of S#1, tilted very slightly forward—just enough to prevent the flowers from crushing each other. (6, $4\frac{1}{2}$)

7. Large round flower LR#2 should be $\frac{1}{2}$ the length of S#1. Insert it slightly in front of LR#1, tilted slightly forward—just enough so that the flower is not crushed by any part of the flower or stem of LR#1. (6, 4)

8. Spike flower S#4 should be $\frac{2}{3}$ the length of S#2. Insert it slightly to the right of LR#2, tilted slightly to the right and very slightly forward. (4, 4)

9. Large round flower LR#3 should be $\frac{2}{3}$ the length of S#4. Insert it slightly in front of LR#2, tilted slightly forward—just enough so that the flower is not crushed by any part of the flower or stem of LR#2. (6, $3\frac{1}{2}$) (Fig. 154B)

10. Large round flower LR#4 should be slightly longer than LR#2. Insert it horizontally from the right just above the rim of the container, and on the centerline of the holder. (3, 0)

11. Large round flower LR#5 should be the same length as LR#4. Insert it horizontally from the left just above the rim of the container, and on the centerline of the holder. (9, 0)

12. Large round flower LR#6 should be slightly less than $\frac{1}{2}$ the length of LR#1. Insert it in the side of the holder, just above the rim of the container, so that the stem is pointed toward the center of the holder at an angle halfway between left and forward, tilted very slightly below horizontal. (7:30, $-\frac{1}{2}$)

13. Large round flower LR#7 should be $\frac{2}{3}$ the length of LR#1. Insert it slightly to the left of LR#2, tilted slightly to the left. (9, 4)

14. Large round flower LR#8 should be the same length as LR#1. Insert it midway between, but behind, S#1 and S#3, tilted very slightly to the right and very slightly backward—just enough so that its flower is not crushed by either S#1 or S#3. (1, $4\frac{1}{2}$) This flower does not show in the illustration but adds depth to the arrangement. (Fig. 154C)

15. Large round flower LR#9 should be $\frac{2}{3}$ the length of S#2. Insert it slightly to the left of S#2, tilted slightly to the left and slightly backward so that it leans backward slightly more than LR#8. (11, 4)

16. Large round flower LR#10 should be $\frac{1}{2}$ the length of LR#9. Insert it slightly behind LR#4, tilted very slightly above horizontal and slightly backward from LR#4. (2:30, $\frac{1}{2}$)

17. Smaller round flower SR#1 should be the same length as LR#10. Insert it slightly to the left of LR#3, tilted to the left and forward. (7:30, $3\frac{1}{2}$)

18. Smaller round flower SR#2 should be slightly shorter than $\frac{1}{2}$ the length of LR#1. Insert it to the right of S#4, tilted to the right and slightly backward. (2, 3)

19. Smaller round flower SR#3 should be $\frac{1}{3}$ the length of LR#1. Insert it in front of LR#3, tilted slightly forward from it. (6, 3) (Fig. 154D)

20. Feature flower F#1 should be $\frac{1}{2}$ the length of LR#3. Insert it to the right of SR#3, tilted forward and slightly to the right. (5, $2\frac{1}{2}$)

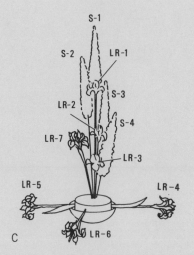

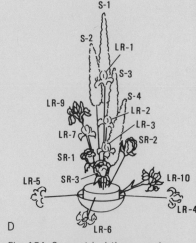

Fig. 154. Symmetrical three-quarter triangular arrangement #1 (four larkspurs, twelve irises, nine roses, and one gerbera). (A) Steps 1–5. (B) Steps 6–9. (C) Steps 10–14. (D) Steps 15–19.

21. Smaller round flower SR#4 should be $\frac{3}{4}$ the length of SR#1. Insert it to the right and below F#1, with its stem directed to the center of the holder, and tilted slightly above horizontal. (4, 1) Its flower should be located midway between SR#3 and LR#4 and should balance SR#3 on the other side of F#1.

22. Smaller round flower SR#5 should be $\frac{2}{3}$ the length of SR#1. Insert it midway between but slightly above LR#5 and LR#6 with its stem pointed to the center of the holder and tilted very slightly above horizontal. (8, $\frac{1}{2}$)

23. Smaller round flower SR#6 should be the same length as LR#6. Insert it midway between LR#5 and LR#7, tilted to the left and very slightly backward so that the flower appears slightly behind the plane of LR#5 and LR#7 but midway between them. (9:30, 2) (Fig. 154E)

24. Smaller round flower SR#7 should be the same length as SR#1. Insert it just below SR#4 with its stem pointed to the center of the holder and tilted very slightly below horizontal. (4, $-\frac{1}{2}$)

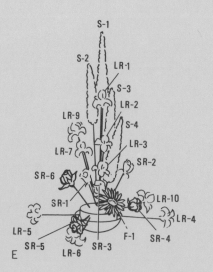

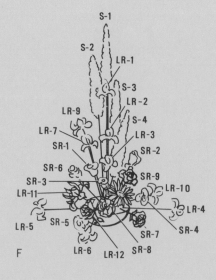

25. Large round flower LR #11 should be the same length as SR #5. Insert it midway between LR #6 and LR #7, tilted so that its flower is in the same plane as LR #6 and LR #7 and midway between them. (8, 2)

26. Smaller round flower SR #8 should be $\frac{1}{2}$ the length of SR #1. Insert it just below SR #3, tilted slightly above horizontal and slightly to the left. (6:30, 1)

27. Small round flower SR #9 should be slightly longer than F #1. Insert it midway between SR #2 and F #1, tilted so that the flower appears midway between SR #2 and F #1. (3, 3)

28. Large round flower LR #12 should be slightly shorter than SR #8. Insert it between SR #3 and LR #6, tilted so that its flower is in the same plane. (7, 1) (Fig. 154F)

29. Insert filler flowers in the voids in the arrangement. The filler flowers should be cut to lengths shorter than the average length of the flowers surrounding any void to be filled. The major voids are:

    A. Between SR #4 and LR #10   (3, 1)
    B. Between SR #5 and SR #6   (9, 1)
    C. Between SR #6 and LR #7   (9, 3)
    D. Between SR #3 and SR #2   (4, 4)
    E. Between SR #4 and SR #8   (5, 1)

30. Add foliage wherever necessary to hide bare stems, fill voids, or maintain balance. Use foliage very sparingly and be careful that it does not disturb the triangular shape of the arrangement.

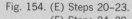

Fig. 154. (E) Steps 20–23.
(F) Steps 24–28.
(G) Completed arrangement.

G

Three-Quarter Arrangement
Symmetrical Triangle
#2

Materials

1. Container—a shallow bowl, a deep bowl, or a tall vase with an opening at least 4 inches in diameter.

2. A holder for flowers—a large pin-point holder with an attached cap of chicken wire that will protrude about $1\frac{1}{2}$ inches above the rim of the shallow container, or a block of foam about 5 inches square and high enough to protrude $1\frac{1}{2}$ inches above the rim of the container. For the deep bowl or the tall vase, use shredded foam or crushed chicken wire as the filler, topped by a block of foam cut to fit the opening of the bowl or vase and at least 4 inches thick.

3. A fastener for the holder—floral clay to secure the pin-point holder in the base of the shallow container, or two or three staples, attached in the base of the shallow container with tape, on which to impale the foam.

4. Flowers—hardened and with all foliage below the waterline removed. Eleven spike flowers of one kind (delphiniums, gladioli, larkspur, lilacs, snapdragons, etc.), seven larger round flowers of one kind (anemones, asters, carnations, geraniums, irises, etc.), six smaller round flowers (daisies, roses, tulips, zinnias, etc.), one large feature flower to be used as the focal point (amaryllis lily, chrysanthemum, gerbera, magnolia), and a quantity of filler flowers (candytuft, baby's breath, statice, etc.).

5. Foliage—some good-quality natural foliage of the flowers used.

6. A number of 24-inch florist wires of heavy and medium weights, to reinforce stems when necessary.

Procedure

1. Secure the pin-point holder or the block of foam in the center of the shallow holder. If the deep bowl or the tall vase is used, fill it with the shredded foam or crumpled chicken wire; stuff it to the tightness that will hold stems where they have been inserted, but that will not make insertion difficult. Insert the block of foam on top of the filler. For the large number of flowers in this arrangement it is advisable to anchor the foam with a cross of tape as described earlier.

2. Fill the container with water fortified with cut-flower preservative.

NOTE: In what follows, all the dimensions will be for the length of the flower showing above the rim of the container. In actually cutting the flowers, add to the lengths given the amount needed for insertion into the holder. For a larger number of flowers the amount added must be varied in order to avoid "collisions" between stems. While some judgment is necessary, the added length will generally be greatest for the early and vertical insertions of the longest flowers. The shorter flowers, particularly those inserted nearly horizontally, require much less added length. See page 89 for a rapid way of cutting flowers to the right length.

3. Select a good-quality spike flower with a straight stem as S#1. Cut it so that it is equal to the desired height of the finished arrangement, making sure that it is not less than twice the diameter of the shallow container or not less than $1\frac{1}{2}$ times the height of the tall vase. Insert it straight up, 1 to $1\frac{1}{2}$ inches in back of the center of the holder.

4. Spike flower S#2 should be a little over $\frac{2}{3}$ the length of S#1. Insert it to the left of the center of the holder, tilted slightly to the left. (9, 4)

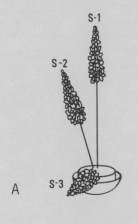

A

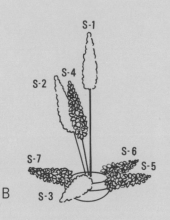

B

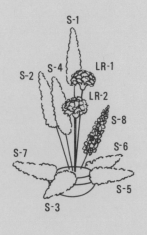

C

5. Spike flower S#3 should be $\frac{2}{3}$ the length of S#2. Insert it horizontally in the side of the holder, just above the rim of the container, so that the stem is pointed toward the center of the holder at an angle $\frac{2}{3}$ the way from the left to the forward directions. (7, 0) (Fig. 155A)

6. Spike flower S#4 should be the same length as S#2. Insert it midway between and forward of S#1 and S#2, tilted so that its flower appears between S#2 and the stem of S#1, but slightly forward. (8:30, $4\frac{1}{2}$)

7. Spike flower S#5 should be a little shorter than S#3. Insert it horizontally from the right on the centerline of the container and just above the rim of the container. (3, 0)

8. Spike flower S#6 should be the same length as S#3. Insert it horizontally in the side of the holder, just above the rim of the container, so that the stem is pointed toward the center of the holder at an angle halfway between the right and the backward directions. (1:30, 0)

9. Spike flower S#7 should be $1\frac{1}{2}$ times the length of S#6. Insert it horizontally in the side of the holder, just above the rim of the container, so that the stem is pointed toward the center of the holder at an angle $\frac{1}{6}$ the way between the left and the backward directions. (9:30, 0) (Fig. 155B)

10. Large round flower LR#1 should be the same length as S#2. Insert it to the right and slightly forward of S#1, tilted very slightly to the right. (3, $4\frac{1}{2}$)

11. Spike flower S#8 should be $\frac{3}{4}$ the length of LR#1. Insert it to the right of S#1, tilted slightly to the right and backward. (1:30, 4)

12. Large round flower LR#2 should be the same length as S#8. Insert it in front of S#1, tilted slightly forward. (6, 4) (Fig. 155C)

13. Spike flower S#9 should be slightly longer than S#8.

Insert it in front of LR #1, tilted very slightly to the right. (3, 4½)

14. Large round flower LR #3 should be slightly less than ½ the length of S #4. Insert it in front of S #9, tilted to the right and forward. (5, 3)

15. Large round flower LR #4 should be ½ the length of S #7. Insert it horizontally, just above the rim of the container, with the stem pointed toward the center of the holder, so that its flower is just forward of S #7. (8, 0)

16. Large flower LR #5 should be a little longer than LR #4. Insert it horizontally, just above the rim of the container, with the stem pointed toward the center of the holder, so that its flower is just forward of S #5. (4, 0)

17. Large round flower LR #6 should be the same length as LR #3. Insert it midway between LR #2 and LR #4, tilted so that the flower appears midway between and slightly behind LR #2 and LR #4. (8, 2½) (Fig. 155D)

18. Small round flower SR #1 should be the same length as LR #4. Insert it in front of S #4, tilted forward and slightly to the left. (7:30, 3)

19. Spike flower S #10 should be the same length as S #6. Insert it midway between S #3 and S #7, tilted so that the flower appears midway between and slightly above S #3 and S #7. (8, 1)

20. Small round flower SR #2 should be a little shorter than SR #1. Insert it in front of LR #2, tilted sharply forward. (6, 2)

21. Feature flower F #1 should be a little shorter than SR #2. Insert it to the right of SR #2, tilted so that its flower appears just to the right of SR #2. (5:30, 2)

22. Small round flower SR #3 should be the same length as SR #1. Insert it horizontally just above the rim of

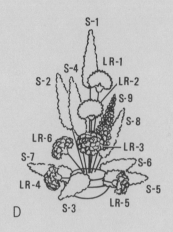

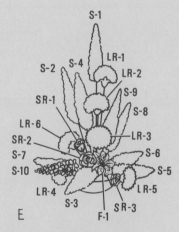

Fig. 155. Symmetrical three-quarter triangular arrangement #2.
(A) Steps 1–5. (B) Steps 6–9.
(C) Steps 10–12. (D) Steps 13–17.
(E) Steps 18–22.

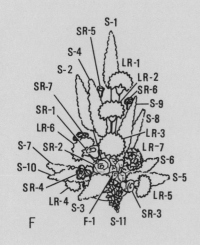

F

G

Fig. 155. (F) Steps 23–28.
(G) Completed
arrangement.

the container so that its flower is below and slightly to the right of F#1, with its stem directed toward the center of the holder. (4:30, 0) (Fig. 155E)

23. Small round flower SR#4 should be a little longer than F#1. Insert it horizontally midway between S#3 and S#10. (7:30, 0)

24. Small round flower SR#5 should be the same length as S#8. Insert it midway between, but behind, S#1 and S#2, tilted very slightly to the left and very slightly backward, just enough so that its flower is not crushed by either S#1 or S#2. (11, $4\frac{1}{2}$) This flower hardly shows in the illustration, but it adds depth to the arrangement.

25. Large round flower LR#7 should be the same length as F#1. Insert it midway between S#5 and S#9, tilted so that its flower appears midway between and in the same plane as S#5 and S#9. (3, 2)

26. Spike flower S#11 should be the same length as S#5. Insert it in the front of the holder slightly to the right of center, with the stem pointed toward the center of the holder and tilted slightly below horizontal. (5:30, $-\frac{1}{2}$)

27. Small round flower SR#6 should be slightly shorter than LR#2. Insert it to the right of S#1, tilted very slightly to the right and backward. (2, $4\frac{1}{2}$) This flower hardly shows in the illustration, but it adds depth to the arrangement.

28. Small round flower SR#7 should be $\frac{2}{3}$ the length of SR#5. Insert it to the left of S#2, tilted sharply to the left of S#2, and backward. (10, 2) (Fig. 155F)

29. Insert filler flowers in any voids in the arrangement. The filler flowers should be cut to lengths shorter than the average length of the flowers surrounding any void to be filled. If the flowers used are of appropriate sizes and the arrangement is executed properly, there should be no voids, and filler flowers will not be needed.

Arrangement of Spike and Round Flowers
(*Three-Quarter, Symmetrical, Fan-Shaped*)

Materials

1. Container—a shallow circular container or a tall vase with an opening at least 3 inches in diameter.
2. A holder for flowers—a medium-to-large pin-point holder for the shallow container, fitted with a cap of chicken wire large enough to protrude 1 to $1\frac{1}{2}$ inches above the rim of the container. For the tall vase use shredded foam as a filler topped with a block of foam cut to fit the opening of the vase. The block of foam should be 2 to 4 inches high according to the weight of the flowers being used and should protrude 1 to $1\frac{1}{2}$ inches above the rim of the vase.
3. A fastener for the holder—floral clay to secure the pin-point holder, or a staple, attached in the base of the shallow container with tape, on which to impale the block of foam.
4. Flowers—hardened and with all foliage below the waterline removed. Ten spike flowers of one kind and of uniform size and development (delphiniums, gladioli, larkspur, liatris, snapdragons, stock, etc.), and fourteen round flowers (asters, carnations, chrysanthemums, daffodils, irises, roses, tulips, zinnias, etc.). The largest and most beautiful flower should be identified and held for the focal point of the arrangement. In this recipe it will be round flower R#11.
5. Foliage—several good-quality pieces of the natural foliage of the flowers used or other appropriate foliage.

Procedure

1. Secure the holder in the center of the shallow container. If a tall vase is being used, stuff it with shredded foam to a tightness appropriate for the flowers being used—

tight enough to hold the flowers where they are inserted, but not so tight that insertion is difficult. Fit
the block on top of the shredded foam. When the tall
vase is used, the stems of the flower should be cut long
enough to pass completely through the block of foam
and deeply into the shredded foam. Since this method
anchors the block very securely, no other attachment
is necessary.

2. Fill the container with water fortified with cut-flower
   preservative.

3. Select a spike flower with a very straight stem as
   flower S#1. If there is a variation in size, this flower
   should be one of the smallest and least developed. If
   the shallow container is being used, cut flower S#1
   so that it is equal to the length required for insertion
   in the holder plus at least twice the diameter of the
   container. If the tall vase is being used, flower S#1
   should be the length required for insertion plus at least
   twice the height of the vase. Insert it straight up about
   1 to $1\frac{1}{2}$ inches in back of the center of the holder. Spike
   flowers should always be inserted face-forward. If they
   are conical, the best florets should always show toward
   the front of the arrangement. Round flowers high in
   the arrangement are inserted so they appear in profile.
   The lowest are full-faced, with a gradual transition in
   between.

NOTE: In what follows, the extra length required for insertion will not be mentioned; the length of only that part
of the flower showing above the rim of the container will
be given. It is understood, however, that the length needed
for insertion is to be added in each case.

4. Select spike flower S#2. It should be $\frac{3}{4}$ the length
   of S#1. Insert it to the right of S#1, tilted slightly
   to the right and very slightly forward. (3:30, 4)

5. Select spike flower S#3. It should be the same length as S#2. Insert it to the left of S#1, tilted slightly to the left and very slightly forward. (8, 4)

6. Select spike flower S#4. It should be $\frac{7}{8}$ of the length of S#3. Insert it from the left along the centerline of the holder, just above the rim of the container, tilted slightly above horizontal. (9, 1)

7. Select spike flower S#5. It should be the same length as S#4. Insert it from the right along the centerline of the holder, just above the rim of the container, tilted slightly above horizontal. (3, 1)

8. Select spike flower S#6. It should be $\frac{1}{2}$ the length of S#2. Insert it along the centerline of the holder, just above the rim of the container and midway between the left and the forward directions, tilted slightly above horizontal. (7:30, 1)

9. Select spike flower S#7. It should be the same length as S#6. Insert it along the centerline of the holder, just above the rim of the container and midway between the right and forward directions, tilted slightly above horizontal. (4:30, 1) (Fig. 156A)

10. Select spike flower S#8. It should be $\frac{2}{3}$ the length of S#1. Insert it midway between S#2 and S#5, tilted slightly to the right and very slightly backward, so that its flower appears midway between, but slightly in back of, S#2 and S#5. (2:30, 3)

11. Select spike flower S#9. It should be the same length as S#4. Insert it midway between S#3 and S#4, tilted to the left and very slightly backward, so that its flower appears midway between, but slightly in back of, S#3 and S#4. (10, $2\frac{1}{2}$)

12. Select spike flower S#10. It should be $\frac{1}{3}$ the length of S#1. Insert it horizontally in the center front of the holder, so that the flower points directly forward, and the stem is just above the rim. (6, $\frac{1}{2}$)

13. Select spike foliage of good quality, preferably the natural foliage of the spike flowers used. Cut it to various lengths, all shorter than spike flower S#1. Insert the foliage tilted slightly backward in the voids between the flowers, and add finishing touches to the back of the arrangement. (Fig. 156B)

14. Select round flower R#1. It should be $\frac{3}{4}$ the length of S#1. Insert it just in front of S#1, tilted very slightly forward. (6, $4\frac{1}{2}$)

15. Select round flower R#2. It should be $\frac{3}{4}$ the length of R#1. Insert it in front of S#9, tilted to the left, so that its flower appears in front of S#9. (9, $2\frac{1}{2}$)

16. Select round flower R#3. It should be the same length as R#2. Insert it in front of S#8, tilted to the right, so that its flower appears in front of S#8. (3, 3)

17. Select round flower R#4. It should be the same length as R#2. Insert it in front of R#1 almost straight up. (6, $4\frac{1}{2}$) (Fig. 156C)

18. Select round flower R#5. It should be $\frac{2}{3}$ the length of R#1. Insert it between S#5 and S#7, tilted sharply to the right and forward so that its flower appears between S#5 and S#7, closer to S#7 and tilted upward from it. (4, $1\frac{1}{2}$)

19. Select round flower R#6. It should be the same length as R#5. Insert it between S#4 and S#6, tilted sharply to the left and forward, so that its flower appears between S#4 and S#6, closer to S#6 and tilted upward from it. (8, $1\frac{1}{2}$)

20. Select round flower R#7. It should be the same length as R#6. Insert it between R#4 and R#6, tilted slightly to the left and forward, so that the flower appears midway between, but slightly forward of, R#4 and R#6. (7:30, $2\frac{1}{2}$)

21. Select round flower R#8. It should be slightly shorter than R#7. Insert it midway between R#5 and R#7, tilted so that its flower appears midway between, but

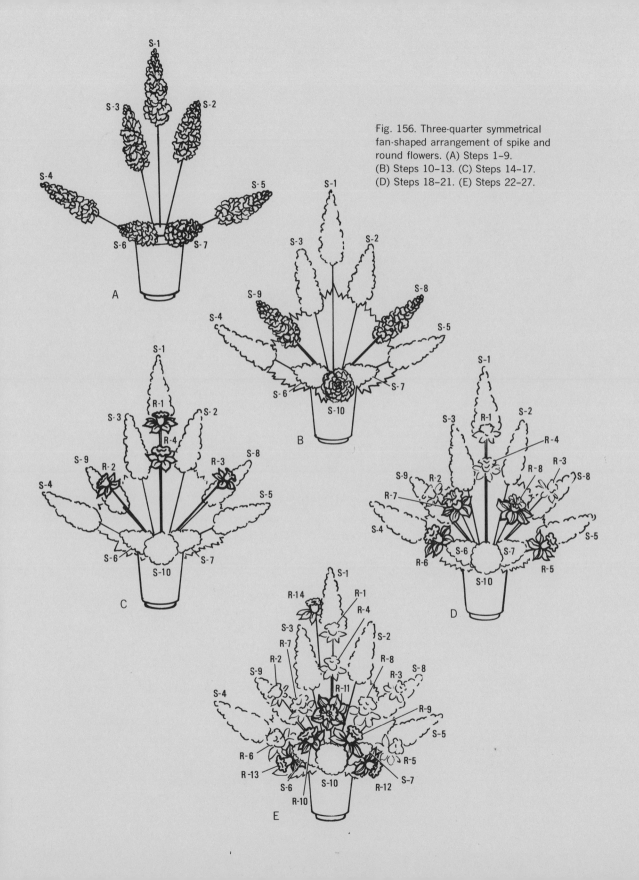

Fig. 156. Three-quarter symmetrical fan-shaped arrangement of spike and round flowers. (A) Steps 1–9. (B) Steps 10–13. (C) Steps 14–17. (D) Steps 18–21. (E) Steps 22–27.

F

Fig. 156. (F) Completed arrangement of daffodils and snapdragons.

very slightly above, R#5 and R#7. (5, 2) Round flowers R#6, R#7, R#8, and R#5 should form a smooth curve. (Fig. 156D)

22. Select round flower R#9. It should be $\frac{1}{2}$ the length of R#1. Insert it between S#7 and S#10, tilted so that its flower appears midway between, but slightly above, S#7 and S#10. (5:15, 1)

23. Select round flower R#10. It should be the same length as R#9. Insert it between S#6 and S#10, tilted so that its flower appears midway between, but slightly above, S#6 and S#10. (6:45, 1)

24. Select round flower R#11. It should be the same length as R#9. Insert it just behind S#10, tilted so that its flower appears just above S#10. (6, $1\frac{1}{2}$)

25. Select round flower R#12. It should be the same length as R#5. Insert it to the right of S#7, tilted so that its flower cascades slightly below the rim of the container between, but below, S#7 and R#5. (4:15, $-\frac{1}{2}$)

26. Select round flower R#13. It should be the same length as R#12. Insert it to the left of S#6, tilted so that its flower cascades slightly below the rim of the container between, but below, S#6 and R#6. (7:45, $-\frac{1}{2}$)

27. Select round flower R#14. It should be a little shorter than S#1. Insert it between S#1 and S#3, tilted very slightly backward and very slightly to the left. (10, $4\frac{1}{2}$) This flower adds depth to the arrangement. (Fig. 156E)

28. Add filler flowers wherever necessary to fill voids. Tuck in pieces of foliage sparingly to fill in remaining voids, and to hide bare stems. Some foliage should cascade over the rim of the holder to enhance the curves made by flowers S#6, S#7, and S#10. (Fig. 156F–H)

COMMENT: If you are short of flowers, steps 25, 26, and 27 can be omitted, and the arrangement will still be attractive.

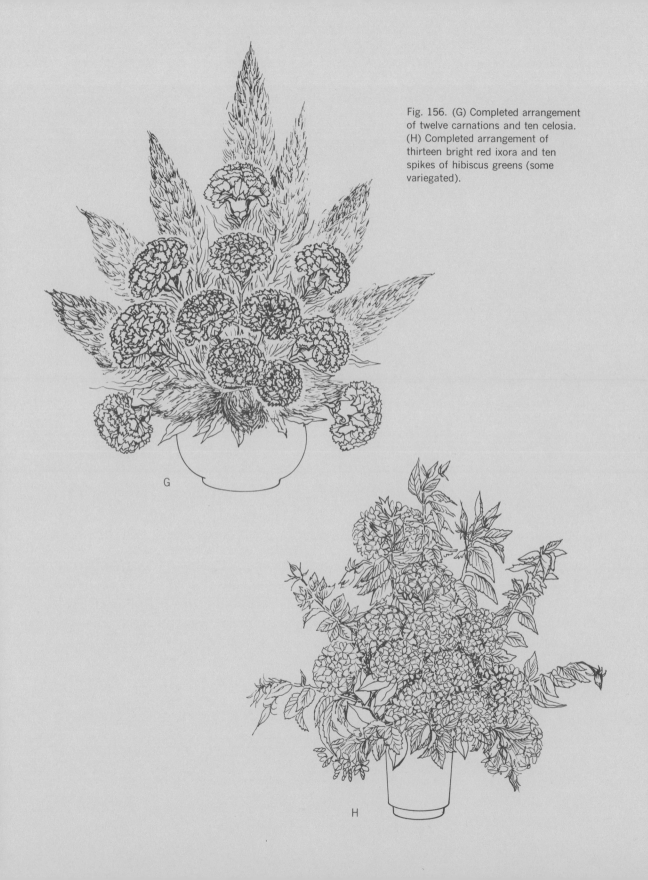

Fig. 156. (G) Completed arrangement of twelve carnations and ten celosia. (H) Completed arrangement of thirteen bright red ixora and ten spikes of hibiscus greens (some variegated).

G

H

Modified T-Shape Arrangement # 1

Materials

1. Container—a shallow bowl with an opening that is at least 4 inches in diameter.
2. A holder for flowers—a large pin-point holder with an attached cap of chicken wire that will protrude $1\frac{1}{2}$ inches above the rim of the container, or a block of foam about 4 to 5 inches square and high enough to protrude $1\frac{1}{2}$ inches above the rim of the container.
3. A fastener for the holder—floral clay to secure the pin-point holder on the base of the container, or two to three staples, fastened with tape in the base of the container, on which to impale the foam.
4. Flowers—hardened and with all foliage below the waterline removed. Six spike flowers (delphiniums, gladioli, larkspur, etc.), eleven different spike flowers (delphiniums, gladioli, larkspur, lupins), four round flowers (anemones, asters, carnations, geraniums, irises, etc.), and six different round flowers (anemones, asters, carnations, daffodils, irises, etc.). Spike flowers should be of uniform size and development. Round flowers should be of the same size or slightly different in size and shape. One feature flower.
5. Some good-quality natural foliage of the flowers used.
6. A number of 18-inch florist wires of heavy and medium weights, to reinforce stems when necessary.

Procedure

1. Secure the pin-point holder or the block of foam in the center of the container.
2. Fill the container with water fortified with cut-flower preservative.

NOTE: In what follows, all dimensions given will be for the length of the flower showing above the top or sides of the holder. In actually cutting the flowers, add the amount needed for insertion into the holder. For a larger number of flowers, the amount added must be varied in order to avoid "collisions" between stems. While some judgment is necessary, the added length will generally be greatest for the early and vertical insertions of the flowers. The shorter flowers, particularly those inserted almost horizontally, require much less added length. See page 89 for a rapid method of cutting flowers to the right length.

3. Select a good-quality spike flower with a straight stem as S#1. Cut it so that it is equal to the desired height of the finished arrangement, making sure that the length is not less than twice the diameter of the container. Insert the flower straight up, 1 to $1\frac{1}{2}$ inches back of the center of the holder.

4. Spike flower S#2 should be $\frac{3}{4}$ the length of S#1. Insert it very slightly to the left of S#1, tilted very slightly to the left. $(9, 4\frac{1}{2})$

5. Spike flower S#3 should be $\frac{3}{4}$ of the length of S#2. Insert it very slightly to the left of S#2, tilted slightly to the left. $(9, 4)$

6. Spike flower S#4 should be approximately the same length as S#2. Insert it very slightly to the right of S#1, tilted very slightly to the right. $(3, 4\frac{1}{2})$ (Fig. 157A)

7. A different spike flower DS#1 should be $\frac{3}{4}$ the length of S#2. Insert it slightly forward of midway between S#1 and S#4, tilted very slightly to the right and very slightly forward. $(4:30, 4\frac{1}{2})$ It may be necessary to remove some of the lower florets from S#1 to insert it this close. S#1, S#2, and DS#1 should be so close together that they look almost like a single flower.

8. Another different spike flower DS#2 should be the same length as S#3. Insert it from the left along the left centerline of the holder, just above the rim of the container, tilted slightly below horizontal. $(9, -\frac{1}{2})$

9. Round flower R#1 should be the same length as

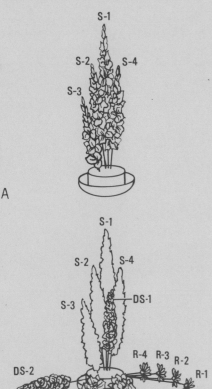

A

B

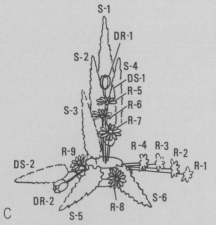

C

DS#2. Insert it from the right along the right center-line of the holder just above the rim of the container, tilted slightly below horizontal. $(3, -\frac{1}{2})$

10. Round flower R#2 should be $\frac{5}{6}$ the length of R#1. Insert it from the right along the centerline of the holder, tilted slightly above R#1, so that the flower appears slightly above it. $(3, 0)$

11. Round flower R#3 should be $\frac{2}{3}$ the length of R#1. Insert it from the right along the centerline of the holder, tilted slightly above R#2, so that the flower appears slightly above it. $(3, \frac{1}{2})$

12. Round flower R#4 should be $\frac{1}{2}$ the length of R#3. Insert it from the right along the centerline of the holder, tilted slightly above R#3 so the flower appears slightly above R#3. $(3, 1)$ Round flowers R#1, R#2, R#3, and R#4 form a garland that functions as a spike flower and balances DS#2.

13. Spike flower S#5 should be slightly shorter than DS#2. Insert it in the side of the holder just above the rim of the container so that the stem is pointed toward the center of the holder at an angle halfway between left and forward, tilted slightly below horizontal. $(7:30, -\frac{1}{2})$

14. Spike flower S#6 should be the same length as S#5. Insert it in the side of the holder just above the rim of the container, so that the stem is pointed toward the center of the holder at an angle halfway between right and forward, tilted slightly below horizontal. $(4:30, -\frac{1}{2})$ (Fig. 157B)

15. A different round flower DR#1 should be $\frac{2}{3}$ the length of S#1. Insert it slightly in front of S#1, tilted very slightly forward. $(6, 4\frac{1}{2})$

16. Round flower R#5 should be slightly more than $\frac{3}{4}$ the length of DR#1. Insert it slightly to the right and

(Opposite, left) Charming basket arrangement of yarrow, strawflowers, and other dried materials, lifted out of the ordinary by the effective placement of pheasant feathers. (Right) Sweet and colorful miniature centerpiece of strawflowers, baby's breath, and field flowers, perkily set in a copper bowl. [Photographs courtesy of Florists' Transworld Delivery Association]

forward of DR#1, tilted slightly forward and very slightly to the right. (5:45, 4)

17. Round flower R#6 should be $\frac{3}{4}$ the length of R#5. Insert it slightly to the left and forward of R#5, tilted very slightly forward and very slightly to the left of R#5. (6, $3\frac{1}{2}$)

18. Round flower R#7 should be $\frac{1}{2}$ the length of R#5. Insert it slightly to the right and forward of R#6, tilted forward and very slightly to the right. (5, 3)

19. Round flower R#8 is slightly more than $\frac{1}{2}$ the length of R#6. Insert it in the front of the holder slightly to the right of center, just above the rim of the container, with the stem pointed toward the center of the holder, and tilted slightly below horizontal so that the flower appears close to S#6. (5, $-\frac{1}{2}$)

20. Round flower R#9 should be a little shorter than R#8. Insert it slightly above midway between S#5 and DS#2, tilted so that the flower appears slightly above midway between S#5 and DS#2. (8:15, 2)

21. Different round flower DR#2 should be almost twice the length of R#9. Insert it midway between S#5 and DS#2, slightly above the rim of the container, with the stem directed to the center of the holder, and tilted slightly below horizontal so that the flower appears slightly below midway between S#5 and DS#2. (8:15, -1) (Fig. 157C)

22. Different round flower DR#3 should be a little longer than R#9. Insert it midway between DR#2 and R#9, just above the rim of the container, with the stem directed to the center of the holder, and tilted above horizontal so the flower appears slightly forward of midway between DR#2 and R#9. (8, $\frac{1}{2}$)

23. Different spike flower DS#3 should be approximately the same length as S#6. Insert it in the side of the holder, slightly above the rim of the container, with

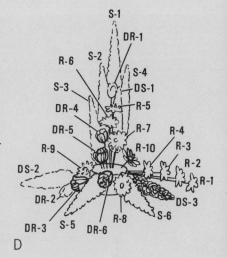

D

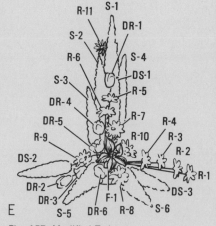

E

Fig. 157. Modified T-shape arrangement #1. (A) Steps 1–6. (B) Steps 7–14. (C) Steps 15–21. (D) Steps 22–27. (E) Steps 28 and 29.

(Opposite, top) Fireside basket with flowers carefully placed to preserve the lines of the basket. The red Ti leaves, heather, pink carnations, and red and purple anemones harmonize to present a pleasant rhythmic arrangement. (Bottom) Two hand-painted ceramic watering cans, the one at left with a dainty arrangement of roses, daisies, and carnations, and the other with green plants enhanced by tube-inserted fresh flowers. [Photographs courtesy of Florists' Transworld Delivery Association]

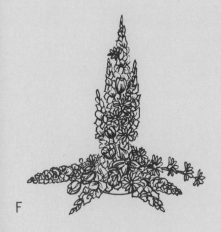

F

the stem directed toward the center of the holder, and tilted slightly below horizontal so that the flower appears midway between S#6 and R#1. (3:45, $-\frac{1}{2}$)

24. Different round flower DR#4 should be slightly shorter than R#6. Insert it slightly to the left of R#6, tilted slightly forward and very slightly to the left. (7, 4)
25. Different round flower DR#5 should be slightly shorter than R#7. Insert it slightly to the left of R#7, tilted forward and very slightly to the left. (6:30, 3)
26. Different round flower DR#6 should be slightly shorter than DR#5. Insert it in the front of the holder, midway between R#8 and S#5, slightly above the rim of the container, with the stem pointed toward the center of the holder, and tilted horizontally so that the flower appears slightly above midway between R#8 and S#5. (6:15, 0)
27. Round flower R#10 should be slightly more than $\frac{1}{2}$ the length of R#7. Insert it midway between R#7 and R#4, tilted so the flower appears midway between R#7 and R#4. (4, 2) (Fig. 157D)

Fig. 157. (F, G) Steps 30 and 31.
(H) Modified T-shape arrangement using snapdragons, stocks, daffodils, anemones, and one large double daffodil as feature flower.
(I) Asymmetrical modified T-shape arrangement using delphiniums, stocks, roses, and daisies.
(J) Modified T-shape arrangement using six asters, five stocks, three miniature gladioli, seven small carnations, one geranium, and daisies for fill.

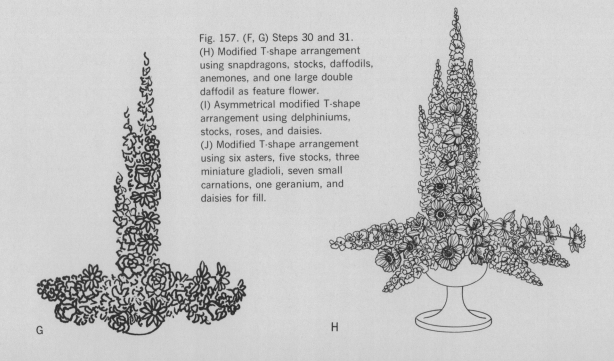

G

H

28. Round flower R#11 should be slightly shorter than S#1. Insert it to the left of S#1, tilted very slightly to the left and backward. $(11, 4\frac{1}{2})$

29. Feature flower F#1 should be slightly shorter than DR#5. It should be a beautiful round flower or a fine specimen of one of the other round flowers in this arrangement. Insert it midway between R#7 and R#8, tilted so that the flower appears slightly to the right of R#7 and R#8. $(4:30, 1\frac{1}{2})$ (Fig. 157E)

30. The major voids are behind R#9 and R#10. They must be filled with very short filler flowers. Fill the voids so the arrangement is attractive from the front and sides, being careful to maintain the T shape.

31. Add foliage wherever necessary to hide bare stems, fill voids, disguise the holder, or maintain balance. Use foliage very sparingly and be careful that it does not disturb the T shape of the arrangement or cover the flowers. (Fig. 157F–J)

I   J

Modified T-Shape Arrangement # 2

Materials

1. Container—a shallow bowl with an opening that is at least 4 inches in diameter.
2. A holder for flowers—a large pin-point holder with an attached cap of chicken wire that will protrude $1\frac{1}{2}$ inches above the rim of the container, or a block of foam about 4 to 5 inches square and high enough to protrude $1\frac{1}{2}$ inches above the rim of the container.
3. A fastener for the holder—floral clay to secure the pin-point holder in the base of the container, or two or three staples, fastened with tape in the base of the container, on which to impale the foam.
4. Flowers—hardened and with all foliage below the waterline removed. Eleven spike flowers of one kind (delphiniums, gladioli, larkspur, lilacs, etc.), four larger round flowers of one kind (anemones, asters, carnations, geraniums, irises, etc.), and eleven smaller round flowers of one kind (daisies, marigolds, roses, tulips, zinnias, etc.). Select the most beautiful, fully developed small round flower and retain it for the focal point, flower SR # 10 in this arrangement. A quantity of filler flowers (candytuft, baby's breath, statice, etc.).
5. Some good-quality natural foliage of the flowers used.
6. A number of 18-inch florist wires of heavy and medium weights, to reinforce stems when necessary.

Procedure

1. Secure the pin-point holder or the block of foam in the center of the container.
2. Fill the container with water fortified with cut-flower preservative.

NOTE: In what follows, all dimensions given will be for the length of the flower showing above the top or sides of the holder. In actually cutting the flowers, add the amount needed for insertion into the holder. For a large number of flowers, the amounts added must be varied in order to avoid "collisions" between stems. While some judgment is necessary, the added length will generally be greatest for the early and vertical insertions of the flowers. The shorter flowers, particularly those inserted almost horizontally, require much less added length. See page 89 for a rapid method of cutting flowers to the right length.

3. Select a good-quality spike flower with a straight stem as $S\#1$. Cut it so that it equals the desired height of the finished arrangement, making sure that the length is not less than twice the diameter of the container. Insert the flower straight up, 1 to $1\frac{1}{2}$ inches in back of the center of the holder.

4. Spike flower $S\#2$ should be $\frac{7}{8}$ the length of $S\#1$. Insert it very slightly to left of $S\#1$, tilted very slightly to the left and very slightly backward. $(10{:}30, 4\frac{1}{2})$

5. Spike flower $S\#3$ should be slightly longer than $S\#2$. Insert it very slightly to the right of $S\#1$, tilted very slightly to the right and very slightly backward. $(1, 4\frac{1}{2})$ Flowers $S\#1$, $S\#2$, and $S\#3$ should be so close together that they look almost like a single flower.

6. Spike flower $S\#4$ should be $\frac{2}{3}$ the length of $S\#3$. Insert it slightly to the left of $S\#2$, tilted slightly to the left. $(9, 4)$

7. Spike flower $S\#5$ should be $\frac{2}{3}$ the length of $S\#1$. Insert it slightly forward of $S\#3$, tilted slightly to the right and very slightly forward. $(4, 4)$

8. Spike flower $S\#6$ should be the same length as $S\#4$. Insert it from the right along the right centerline of the holder, just above the rim of the container, tilted very slightly below horizontal. $(3, -\frac{1}{2})$

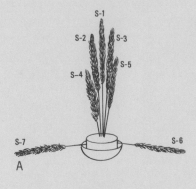

A

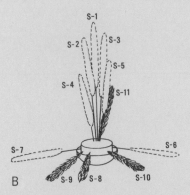

B

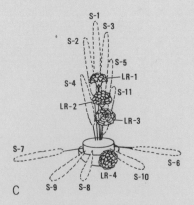

C

9. Spike flower S#7 should be the same length as S#5. Insert it from the left along the left centerline of the holder just above the rim of the container, tilted very slightly below horizontal. $(9, -\frac{1}{2})$ (Fig. 158A)

10. Spike flower S#8 should be $\frac{1}{2}$ the length of S#1. Insert it slightly to the left of the centerline of the holder, just above the rim of the container, tilted very slightly to the left and below horizontal. $(6:30, -\frac{1}{2})$

11. Spike flower S#9 should be the same length as S#7. Insert it in the side of the holder between S#7 and S#8, just above the rim of the container with the stem directed toward the center of the holder, tilted so that the flower appears between S#7 and S#8, but slightly closer to S#8 and very slightly below horizontal. $(7:30, -\frac{1}{2})$

12. Spike flower S#10 should be slightly shorter than S#8. Insert it in the front of the holder between S#8 and S#6, slightly above the rim of the container, with the stem pointed toward the center of the holder, tilted so that the flower appears between S#8 and S#6 but slightly closer to S#6, and very slightly below horizontal. $(4:30, -\frac{1}{2})$

13. Spike flower S#11 should be $\frac{1}{2}$ the length of S#3. Insert it slightly to the right of S#3, tilted slightly to the right and slightly backward. $(2:30, 4)$ S#11 should be very close to the stem of S#3. (Fig. 158B)

14. Large round flower LR#1 should be slightly shorter than S#4. Insert it slightly in front of S#1, tilted very slightly forward. $(6, 4\frac{1}{2})$

15. Large round flower LR#2 should be $\frac{3}{4}$ the length of S#11. Insert it in front of LR#1, tilted slightly forward. $(6, 4)$

16. Large round flower LR#3 should be $\frac{1}{2}$ the length of LR#1. Insert it slightly to the right and forward of LR#2, tilted slightly forward and very slightly to the right. (5, 4)

17. Large round flower LR#4 should be the same length as LR#3. Insert it in the front of the holder, slightly to the right of midway between S#8 and S#10 and just above the rim of the container, with the stem pointed toward the center of the holder, and tilted slightly below horizontal so that the flower appears between S#8 and S#10 but slightly closer to S#10. (5:30, $-\frac{1}{2}$) (Fig. 158C)

18. Small round flower SR#1 should be slightly shorter than LR#1. Insert it slightly to the left of LR#2, tilted slightly to the left and very slightly forward. (7, 4)

19. Small round flower SR#2 should be slightly longer than LR#3. Insert it in front of SR#1, tilted forward and very slightly to the left. (6:30, 3)

20. Small round flower SR#3 should be $\frac{1}{3}$ the length of S#8. Insert it in the front of the holder midway between LR#4 and S#8, slightly above the rim of the container, with the stem pointed toward the center of the holder, and tilted very slightly below horizontal so that the flower appears midway between LR#4 and S#8. (6, $-\frac{1}{2}$)

21. Small round flower SR#4 should be slightly shorter than SR#2. Insert it midway between S#7 and S#9, slightly above the rim of the container, with the stem directed to the center of the holder, and tilted slightly above horizontal so that the flower appears slightly above midway between S#7 and S#9. (8:15, $\frac{1}{2}$)

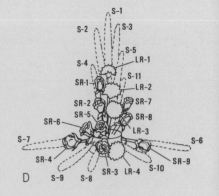

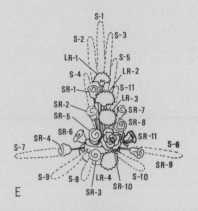

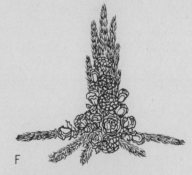

Fig. 158. Modified T-shape arrangement #2. (A) Steps 1–9. (B) Steps 10–13. (C) Steps 14–17. (D) Steps 18–26. (E) Steps 27 and 28. (F) Steps 29 and 30.

22. Small round flower SR#5 should be $\frac{4}{5}$ the length of SR#4. Insert it in the front of the holder very slightly to the right of midway between SR#2 and S#8, tilted so that the flower appears slightly to the right of midway between SR#2 and S#8. (6, $1\frac{1}{2}$)

23. Small round flower SR#6 should be slightly shorter than SR#5. Insert it slightly above midway between SR#5 and SR#4, tilted so that the flower appears slightly above midway between SR#4 and SR#5. (7, $1\frac{1}{2}$)

24. Small round flower SR#7 should be slightly longer than SR#5. Insert it forward of S#11, tilted slightly to the right. (3, 4)

25. Small round flower SR#8 should be slightly shorter than LR#3. Insert it forward and very slightly to the right of SR#7, tilted to the right. (3, 3)

26. Small round flower SR#9 should be slightly longer than SR#4. Insert it between S#6 and S#10, slightly above the rim of the container, with the stem directed toward the center of the holder, and tilted very slightly above horizontal, so that the flower appears slightly above midway between S#6 and S#10. (3:45, $\frac{1}{2}$) (Fig. 158D)

G

H

27. Small round flower SR#10 should be $\frac{2}{3}$ the length of SR#6. It should be a beautiful, fully developed flower. Insert it midway between LR#3 and LR#4, tilted so that the flower appears midway between LR#3 and LR#4. (5:15, 2)

28. Small round flower SR#11 should be slightly longer than SR#8. Insert it midway between SR#8 and SR#9, tilted so that the flower appears midway between SR#8 and SR#9. (4, 1) (Fig. 158E)

29. The major voids are behind SR#8 and SR#11 and behind SR#6. They must be filled in with very short filler flowers. Fill the voids so that the arrangement is attractive from the front and sides but be careful to maintain the T shape.

30. Add foliage wherever necessary to hide bare stems, fill voids, disguise the holder, or maintain balance. Use foliage very sparingly and be careful that it does not disturb the T shape of the arrangement or cover the flowers. (Fig. 158F–J)

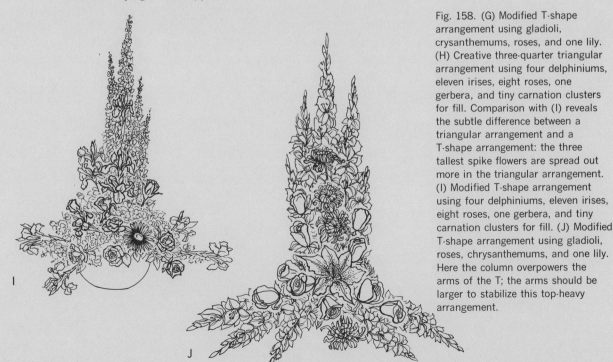

Fig. 158. (G) Modified T-shape arrangement using gladioli, crysanthemums, roses, and one lily. (H) Creative three-quarter triangular arrangement using four delphiniums, eleven irises, eight roses, one gerbera, and tiny carnation clusters for fill. Comparison with (I) reveals the subtle difference between a triangular arrangement and a T-shape arrangement: the three tallest spike flowers are spread out more in the triangular arrangement. (I) Modified T-shape arrangement using four delphiniums, eleven irises, eight roses, one gerbera, and tiny carnation clusters for fill. (J) Modified T-shape arrangement using gladioli, roses, chrysanthemums, and one lily. Here the column overpowers the arms of the T; the arms should be larger to stabilize this top-heavy arrangement.

Airy Round Centerpiece

Materials

1. Container—a circular, square, or rectangular shallow container or a tall vase with an opening at least 3 inches in diameter.

2. A holder for flowers—a medium-to-large pin-point holder for the shallow container fitted with a cap of chicken wire large enough to protrude 1 to $1\frac{1}{2}$ inches above the rim, or a piece of foam at least 3 inches square and high enough to protrude 1 to $1\frac{1}{2}$ inches above the rim of the container. For the tall vase use shredded foam as a filler topped with a piece of foam cut to fit the opening of the vase. The block of foam should be 2 to 4 inches high according to the weight of the flowers being used and, similarly, should protrude 1 to $1\frac{1}{2}$ inches above the rim of the vase.

3. A fastener for the holder—floral clay to secure the pin-point holder, or a staple, attached in the base of the shallow container, on which to impale the block of foam.

4. Flowers—hardened, with the below-water foliage removed. Twenty-three spike flowers of uniform size and development (delphiniums, larkspur, liatrus, snapdragons, stock, etc.). Gladioli are acceptable but not ideal since they are a front-facing rather than a conical flower. Seven round flowers of uniform size and development that have the appropriate relationship in size to the spike flowers (asters, carnations, chrysanthemums, daffodils, irises, roses, tulips, zinnias, etc.). If there are some variations in the size of the flowers available, use the smaller and less developed flowers for the upper and outer flowers of the arrangement.

5. Foliage—several pieces of good-quality natural foliage of the flowers used or of other appropriate foliage.

Procedure

1. Secure the holder in the center of the shallow container. If the tall vase is being used, stuff it with foam to a tightness appropriate for the flowers being used—tight enough to hold the flowers where they are inserted, but not so tight that insertion is difficult. Fit the block of foam on top of the shredded foam. When the tall vase is used, the stems of the flowers should be cut long enough to pass completely through the block of foam and deeply into the shredded foam. Since this method anchors the block very securely, no other attachment is necessary.

2. Fill the container with water fortified with cut-flower preservative.

3. Select a very straight good-quality flower as flower S#1. Its length should be such that, when inserted, it will provide the desired overall height of the center-piece. The width of the container should be not more than $\frac{1}{2}$ the height of flower S#1, or, if a tall vase or bowl is used, its height should be not more than $\frac{2}{3}$ the height of the flower above its rim. Insert spike flower S#1 straight up in the center of the holder.

NOTE: In what follows, the extra length required for insertion will not be included in the measurements given. These will refer only to the parts of the stem and the flower that are exposed outside the holder. It should be understood, however, that the additional length needed for insertion is to be added in each case.

4. Spike flower S#2 should be the same length as S#1. Insert it horizontally from the left along the centerline of the holder, just above the rim of the container. (9, 0)

5. Spike flower S#3 should be the same length as S#2. Insert it horizontally from the right along the center-line of the holder, just above the rim of the container. (3, 0)

6. Spike flower S#4 should be $\frac{3}{4}$ the length of S#1. Insert it to the left of S#1, tilted to the left $\frac{1}{3}$ of the way from vertical to horizontal. (9, $3\frac{1}{2}$)

7. Spike flower S#5 should be the same length as S#4. Insert it to the right of S#1, tilted to the right $\frac{1}{3}$ of the way from vertical to horizontal. (3, $3\frac{1}{2}$) (Fig. 159A)

8. Spike flower S#6 should be $\frac{2}{3}$ the length of S#1. Insert it horizontally in the left side of the holder in front of S#2, just above the rim of the container, and with the stem pointed toward the center of the holder so it is $\frac{1}{3}$ of the way from the left to the forward directions. (8, 0)

9. Spike flower S#7 should be the same length as S#6. Insert it horizontally in the left side of the holder in back of S#2, just above the rim of the container, and with the stem pointed toward the center of the holder so it is $\frac{1}{3}$ of the way from the left to the backward directions. (10, 0)

10. Spike flower S#8 should be the same length as S#7. Insert it horizontally in the right side of the holder in front of S#3, just above the rim of the container, and with the stem pointed toward the center of the holder so it is $\frac{1}{3}$ of the way from the right to the forward directions. (4, 0)

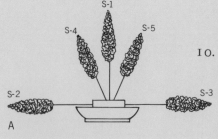

11. Spike flower S#9 should be the same length as S#8. Insert it horizontally in the right side of the holder in back of S#3, just above the rim of the container, and with the stem pointed toward the center of the holder so it is $\frac{1}{3}$ of the way from the right to the backward directions. (2, 0) (Fig. 159B)

12. Spike flower S#10 should be $\frac{3}{4}$ the length of S#9. Insert it in front of the holder slightly above the rim of the container, and with the stem pointed toward the center of the holder, tilted very slightly above horizontal and $\frac{2}{3}$ of the way from the left to the forward directions. $(7, \frac{1}{2})$

13. Spike flower S#11 should be the same length as S#10. Insert it in the front of the holder, slightly above the rim of the container, and with the stem pointed toward the center of the holder, tilted very slightly above horizontal and $\frac{2}{3}$ of the way from the right to the forward directions. $(5, \frac{1}{2})$

14. Spike flower S#12 should be the same length as S#9. Insert it in front of S#1, tilted forward $\frac{1}{3}$ of the way from vertical to horizontal. $(6, 3\frac{1}{2})$

15. Round flower R#1 should be slightly more than $\frac{1}{2}$ the length of S#1. Insert it between S#1 and S#4, tilted slightly to the left and very slightly forward so the flower appears slightly forward of midway between S#1 and S#4. (8, 4)

16. Round flower R#2 should be $\frac{7}{8}$ the length of R#1. Insert it midway between S#1 and S#5, tilted slightly to the right and slightly forward so the flower appears slightly forward of midway between S#1 and S#5. (4, 4)

Fig. 159. Airy round centerpiece.
(A) Steps 1–7. (B) Steps 8–11.
(C) Steps 12–18.

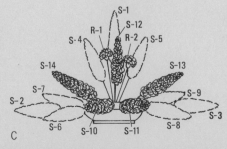

17. Spike flower S#13 should be the same length as S#12. Insert it between S#3 and S#5, tilted so the flower appears midway between S#3 and S#5. $(3, 1\frac{1}{2})$

18. Spike flower S#14 should be the same length as S#12. Insert it between S#2 and S#4, tilted so the flower appears midway between S#2 and S#4. $(9, 1\frac{1}{2})$ (Fig. 159C)

19. Spike flower S#15 should be the same length as S#12. Insert it between R#1 and S#6, tilted so the flower is slightly above midway between R#1 and S#6. $(8, 2\frac{1}{2})$

20. Spike flower S#16 should be slightly shorter than S#12. Insert it between S#10 and S#12, tilted so the flower is between S#10 and S#12 and somewhat closer to S#12 and forward of R#1. $(6:30, 2\frac{1}{2})$

21. Spike flower S#17 should be the same length as S#16. Insert it between R#2 and S#11, tilted so the flower is slightly above midway between R#2 and S#11, and balancing S#16. $(5, 2\frac{1}{2})$

22. Round flower R#3 should be $\frac{1}{2}$ the length of R#2. Insert it between R#1 and S#10, tilted so the flower appears slightly below midway between R#1 and S#10. $(7, 2)$

23. Round flower R#4 should be slightly shorter than R#2. Insert it between R#2 and S#8, tilted so the flower is midway between R#2 and S#8. $(4, 2)$ (Fig. 159D)

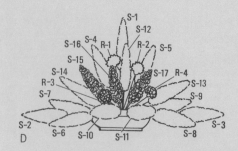

24. Turn the arrangement completely around and turn the clock face with it so that 12 is now the forward direction.

25. Spike flower S#18 should be the same length as S#12. Insert it in front of S#1, tilted forward $\frac{1}{3}$ of the way between vertical and horizontal. (12, $3\frac{1}{2}$)

26. Spike flower S#19 should be the same length as S#10. Insert it in the front of the holder, slightly above the rim of the container, and with the stem pointed toward the center of the holder, tilted very slightly above horizontal and $\frac{2}{3}$ of the way from the right to the forward directions. (11, $\frac{1}{2}$)

27. Spike flower S#20 should be the same length as S#19. Insert it in the front of the holder, slightly above the rim of the container, and with the stem pointed toward the center of the holder, tilted very slightly above horizontal and $\frac{2}{3}$ of the way from the left to the forward directions. (1, $\frac{1}{2}$)

28. Round flower R#5 should be very slightly shorter than R#1. Insert it between S#1 and S#18, tilted so the flower is very slightly to the right of midway between S#1 and S#18. (11:30, 4) (R#5 is not visible in the illustration.)

29. Round flower R#6 should be $\frac{2}{3}$ the length of R#5. Insert it between R#5 and S#9, tilted so the flower appears midway between R#5 and S#9 but closer to R#5, and also midway between S#5 and S#20. (1:30, $2\frac{1}{2}$)

Fig. 159. (D) Steps 19–23.
(E) Steps 24–32.

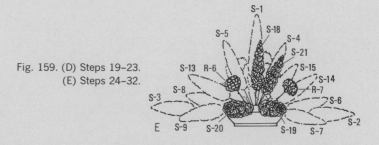

30. Spike flower S#21 should be slightly shorter than S#4. Insert it between S#1 and S#19, tilted so the flower is midway between S#1 and S#19. (11, 3)

31. Round flower R#7 should be approximately the same length as R#6. Insert it between S#7 and S#21, tilted so the flower is slightly above midway between S#7 and S#21 and also midway between S#4 and S#19. (10:30, $1\frac{1}{2}$)

32. Spike flower S#22 should be the same length as S#12. Insert it horizontally from the back along the centerline of the holder, slightly above the rim of the container. (6, 0) (S#22 is not visible in the illustration.) (Fig. 159E)

33. Spike flower S#23 should be the same length as S#22. Insert it horizontally from the front along the center-line of the holder, slightly above the rim of the container. (12, 0) (Fig. 159F)

34. Insert filler flowers in any voids in the arrangement. The filler flowers should be shorter than flowers surrounding any void. If the flowers used in the arrangement are of appropriate sizes and the arrangement is executed properly, there should be no voids and the filler flowers will not be needed.

35. Add foliage wherever necessary to hide bare stems, fill voids, or maintain balance. Use foliage very sparingly and be careful that it does not overpower any flowers or disturb the shape of the arrangement. (Fig. 159G)

Fig. 159. (F) Steps 33 and 34. (G) Step 35.

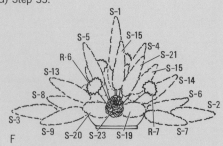

Compact Round Centerpiece

Materials

1. Container—a circular, square, or rectangular shallow container or a tall vase with an opening at least 3 inches in diameter.

2. A holder for flowers—a medium-to-large pin-point holder for the shallow container fitted with a cap of chicken wire large enough to protrude 1 to $1\frac{1}{2}$ inches above the rim, or a piece of foam at least 3 inches square and high enough to protrude 1 to $1\frac{1}{2}$ inches above the rim of the container. For the tall vase use shredded foam as a filler topped with a piece of foam cut to fit the opening of the vase. The block of foam should be 2 to 4 inches high according to the weight of the flowers being used and, similarly, should protrude 1 to $1\frac{1}{2}$ inches above the rim of the vase.

3. A fastener for the holder—floral clay to secure the pin-point holder, or a staple, attached in the base of the shallow container, on which to impale the block of foam.

4. Flowers—hardened, with all the foliage below the waterline removed. Seventeen spike flowers of uniform size and development (delphiniums, larkspur, liatris, snapdragons, stock, etc.). Gladioli are acceptable but not ideal since they are a front-facing rather than a conical flower. Fourteen round flowers of uniform size and development that have an appropriate relationship in size to the spike flowers (asters, carnations, chrysanthemums, daffodils, irises, roses, tulips, zinnias, etc.). If there are some variations in the size of the flowers available, use the smaller and less developed flowers for the upper and outer flowers of the arrangement.

5. Foliage—several pieces of good-quality natural foliage of the flowers used or of other appropriate foliage.

Procedure

1. Secure the holder in the center of the shallow container. If the tall vase is being used, stuff it with foam to a tightness appropriate for the flowers being used—tight enough to hold the flowers where they are inserted, but not so tight that insertion is difficult. Fit the block of foam on top of the shredded foam. When the tall vase is used, the stems of the flowers should be cut long enough to pass completely through the block of foam and deeply into the shredded foam. Since this method anchors the block very securely, no other attachment is necessary.

2. Fill the container with water fortified with cut-flower preservative.

3. Select a very straight good-quality spike flower as flower S#1. Its length should be such that, when inserted, it will provide the desired overall height of the centerpiece. The width of the container should not be more than $\frac{1}{2}$ the height of flower S#1, or, if it is a tall vase or bowl, its height should be not more than $\frac{2}{3}$ of the height of the flower above its rim. Insert spike flower S#1 straight up in the center of the holder.

NOTE: In what follows, the extra length required for insertion will not be included in the measurements given. These will refer only to those parts of the stem and the flower that are exposed outside the holder. It should be understood, however, that the additional length needed for insertion is to be added in each case.

4. Spike flower S#2 should be the same length as S#1. Insert it horizontally from the left along the centerline of the holder, just above the rim of the container. (9, 0)

5. Spike flower S#3 should be the same length as S#2. Insert it horizontally from right along the centerline of the holder, just above the rim of the container. (3, 0)

6. Spike flower S#4 should be $\frac{3}{4}$ the length of S#1. Insert it between S#1 and S#2, tilted slightly above midway so the flower appears between S#1 and S#2, but slightly closer to S#1. (9, 3)

7. Spike flower S#5 should be the same length as S#4. Insert it between S#1 and S#3, tilted slightly above midway, so the flower appears between S#1 and S#3, but slightly closer to S#1. (3, 3) (Fig. 160A)

8. Spike flower S#6 should be $\frac{2}{3}$ the length of S#1. Insert it horizontally in the left side of the holder in front of S#2, just above the rim of the container, and with the stem pointed toward the center of the holder, so it is $\frac{1}{3}$ of the way from the left to the forward directions. (8, 0)

9. Spike flower S#7 should be the same length as S#6. Insert it horizontally in the left side of the holder back of S#2, just above the rim of the container, and with the stem pointed toward the center of the holder so it is $\frac{1}{3}$ of the way from the left to the backward directions. (10, 0)

10. Spike flower S#8 should be the same length as S#7. Insert it horizontally in the right side of the holder in front of S#3, just above the rim of the container, and with the stem pointed toward the center of the holder so it is $\frac{1}{3}$ of the way from the right to the forward directions. (4, 0)

11. Spike flower S#9 should be the same length as S#8. Insert it horizontally in the right side of the holder in back of S#3, just above the rim of the container, and with the stem pointed toward the center of the holder so it is $\frac{1}{3}$ of the way from the right to the backward directions. (2, 0) (Fig. 160B)

12. Spike flower S#10 should be $\frac{3}{4}$ the length of S#9.

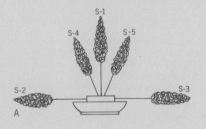

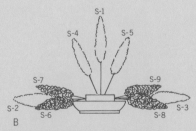

Fig. 160. Compact round centerpiece. (A) Steps 1–7. (B) Steps 8–11.

Insert it in the front of the holder slightly above the rim of the container, with the stem pointed toward the center of the holder, tilted very slightly above horizontal, and $\frac{2}{3}$ of the way from the left to the forward directions. $(7, \frac{1}{2})$

13. Spike flower S#11 should be the same length as S#10. Insert it in the front of the holder, slightly above the rim of the container, with the stem pointed toward the center of the holder, tilted very slightly above horizontal, and $\frac{2}{3}$ of the way from the right to the forward directions. $(5, \frac{1}{2})$

14. Spike flower S#12 should be the same length as S#9. Insert it in front of S#1, tilted slightly above midway between horizontal and vertical. $(6, 3)$

15. Round flower R#1 should be slightly more than $\frac{1}{2}$ the length of S#1. Insert it midway between S#1 and S#4, tilted slightly to the left and very slightly forward, so the flower appears slightly forward of midway between S#1 and S#4. $(8, 4)$

16. Round flower R#2 should be $\frac{7}{8}$ the length of R#1. Insert it between S#1 and S#5, tilted slightly to the right and very slightly forward, so the flower appears slightly forward of midway between S#1 and S#5. $(4, 4)$

17. Round flower R#3 should be $\frac{4}{5}$ the length of R#2. Insert it between S#3 and S#5, tilted so the flower appears midway between S#3 and S#5. $(3, 1\frac{1}{2})$

18. Round flower R#4 should be the same length as R#3. Insert it midway between S#2 and S#4, tilted so that the flower appears midway between S#2 and S#4. $(9, 1\frac{1}{2})$ (Fig. 160C)

19. Round flower R#5 should be slightly shorter than R#4. Insert it between R#1 and S#6, tilted so the flower appears very slightly forward of midway between R#1 and S#6. $(7:30, 2\frac{1}{2})$

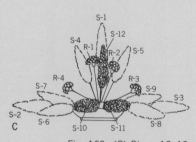
Fig. 160. (C) Steps 12–18.

20. Round flower R#6 should be the same length as R#5. Insert it between R#2 and S#8, tilted so the flower appears slightly forward of midway between R#2 and S#8. (4:30, $2\frac{1}{2}$)

21. Round flower R#7 should be $\frac{3}{4}$ the length of R#5. Insert it between S#12 and S#10, tilted so the flower appears slightly to the right of midway between S#12 and S#10. (7, $1\frac{1}{2}$)

22. Round flower R#8 should be the same length as R#7. Insert it between R#2 and S#11, tilted so the flower appears midway between R#2 and S#11. (5, 2) (Fig. 160D)

23. Turn the arrangement completely around and turn the clock face with it so that 12 is now the forward direction.

24. Spike flower S#13 should be the same length as S#12. Insert it in front of S#1, tilted forward so it is slightly above midway between horizontal and vertical. (12,3)

25. Spike flower S#14 should be the same length as S#10. Insert it in the front of the holder, slightly above the rim of the container, with the stem pointed toward the center of the holder, tilted very slightly above horizontal and $\frac{2}{3}$ of the way from the right to the forward directions. (11, $\frac{1}{2}$)

26. Spike flower S#15 should be the same length as S#14. Insert it in the front of the holder, slightly above the rim of the container, with the stem pointed toward the center of the holder, tilted slightly above horizontal and $\frac{2}{3}$ of the way from the left to the forward directions. (1, $\frac{1}{2}$)

27. Round flower R#9 should be slightly longer than R#1. Insert it between S#1 and S#13, tilted so the flower is midway between S#1 and S#13. (12, 4) This flower does not show in the illustration.

28. Round flower R#10 should be the same length as

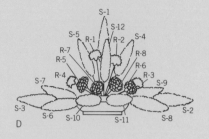

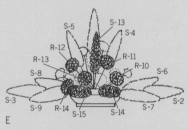

Fig. 160. (D) Steps 19–23. (E) Steps 24–32.

R#6. Insert it between S#4 and S#14, tilted so the flower appears slightly forward of midway between S#4 and S#14 and slightly closer to S#7. (10:30, 1½)

29. Round flower R#11 should be ⅔ the length of R#9. Insert it between S#4 and S#13, tilted so the flower appears slightly forward of midway between S#4 and S#13. (11, 3)

30. Round flower R#12 should be ¾ the length of R#9. Insert it between S#9 and S#13, tilted so the flower appears midway between S#9 and S#13 and slightly closer to S#13. (1:30, 2½)

31. Round flower R#13 should be ½ the length of R#12. Insert it between S#13 and S#15, tilted so the flower appears midway between S#13 and S#15. (12:30, 2)

32. Round flower R#14 should be the same length as R#10. Insert it between S#9 and S#15, tilted so the flower appears midway between S#9 and S#15. (1:30, ½) (Fig. 160E)

33. Spike flower S#16 should be the same length as S#12. Insert it from the back along the centerline of the holder, slightly above the rim of the container, and tilted slightly above horizontal. (6, 1) (S#16 is not visible in the illustration.)

34. Spike flower S#17 should be the same length as S#16. Insert it from the front along the centerline of the holder, slightly above the rim of the container, and tilted slightly above horizontal. (12, 1) (Fig. 160F)

35. Insert filler flowers in any voids in the arrangement. The filler flowers should be shorter than flowers surrounding any void. If the flowers used in the arrangement are of appropriate sizes and the arrangement is executed properly, there should be no voids, and the filler flowers will not be needed.

36. Add foliage wherever necessary to hide bare stems, fill voids, or maintain balance. Use foliage very sparingly and be careful that it does not overpower any flowers or disturb the shape of the arrangement. (Fig. 160G)

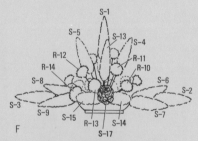

Fig. 160. (F) Steps 33 and 34.
(G) Steps 35 and 36.

Airy Centerpiece
(Long and Narrow)

Materials

1. Container—a circular, square, or rectangular shallow container or a tall vase with an opening at least 3 inches in diameter.

2. A holder for flowers—a medium-to-large pin-point holder for the shallow container fitted with a cap of chicken wire large enough to protrude 1 to $1\frac{1}{2}$ inches above the rim, or a piece of foam at least 3 inches square and high enough to protrude 1 to $1\frac{1}{2}$ inches above the rim of the container. For the tall vase, use shredded foam as a filler, topped with a piece of foam cut to fit the opening of the vase. The block of foam should be 2 to 4 inches high according to the weight of the flowers being used and, similarly, should protrude 1 to $1\frac{1}{2}$ inches above the rim of the vase.

3. A fastener for the holder—floral clay to secure the pin-point holder, or a staple, attached in the base of the shallow container, on which to impale the block of foam.

4. Flowers—hardened, with the below-water foliage removed. Seventeen spike flowers of uniform size and development (delphiniums, larkspur, liatris, snapdragons, stock, etc.). Gladioli are acceptable but not ideal since they are a front-facing rather than a conical flower. Fifteen round flowers of uniform size and development that have an appropriate relationship in size to the spike flowers (asters, carnations, chrysanthemums, daffodils, irises, roses, tulips, zinnias, etc.). If there are some variations in the size of the flowers available, use the smaller and less developed flowers for the upper and outer flowers of the arrangement.

5. Foliage—several pieces of good-quality natural foliage of the flowers used or of other appropriate foliage.

Procedure

1. Secure the holder in the center of the shallow container. If the tall vase is being used, stuff it with foam to a tightness appropriate for the flower being used—tight enough to hold the flowers where they are inserted, but not so tight that insertion is difficult. Fit the block of foam on top of the shredded foam. When the tall vase is used, the stems of the flowers should be cut long enough to pass completely through the block of foam and deeply into the shredded foam. Since this method anchors the block very securely, no other attachment is necessary.

2. Fill the container with water fortified with cut-flower preservative.

3. Select a very straight good-quality spike flower as flower $S\#1$. Its length should be such that, when inserted, it will provide the desired overall height of the centerpiece. The width of the container should be not more than $\frac{1}{2}$ the height of flower $S\#1$, or, if a tall vase or bowl is used, its height should not be more than $\frac{2}{3}$ of the height of the flower above its rim. Insert spike flower $S\#1$ straight up in the center of the holder.

NOTE: In what follows the extra length required for insertion will not be included in the measurements given. These will refer only to that part of the stem and the flower that is exposed outside the holder. It should be understood, however, that the additional length needed for insertion is to be added in each case.

4. Spike flower $S\#2$ should be the same length as $S\#1$. Insert it horizontally from the left along the centerline of the holder, just above the rim of the container. (9, 0)

5. Spike flower $S\#3$ should be the same length as $S\#2$. Insert it horizontally from the right along the center-

line of the holder, just above the rim of the container. (3, 0)

6. Spike flower S#4 should be $\frac{3}{4}$ the length of S#1. Insert it to the left of S#1, tilted to the left, $\frac{1}{3}$ of the way from vertical to horizontal. (9, $3\frac{1}{2}$)

7. Spike flower S#5 should be the same length as S#4. Insert it to the right of S#1, tilted to the right $\frac{1}{3}$ of the way from vertical to horizontal. (3, $3\frac{1}{2}$) (Fig. 161 A)

8. Spike flower S#6 should be $\frac{2}{3}$ the length of S#1. Insert it horizontally in the left side of the holder in front of S#2, just above the rim of the container with the stem pointed toward the center of the holder, so it is $\frac{1}{3}$ of the way from the left to the forward directions. (8, 0)

9. Spike flower S#7 should be the same length as S#6. Insert it horizontally in the left side of the holder in back of S#2, just above the rim of the container, and with the stem pointed toward the center of the holder so it is $\frac{1}{3}$ of the way from the left to the backward directions. (10, 0)

10. Spike flower S#8 should be the same length as S#7. Insert it horizontally in the right side of the holder in front of S#3, just above the rim of the container, and with the stem pointed toward the center of the holder, so it is $\frac{1}{3}$ of the way from the right to the forward directions. (4, 0)

11. Spike flower S#9 should be the same length as S#8. Insert it horizontally in the right side of the holder in back of S#3, just above the rim of the container, and with the stem pointed toward the center of the holder so it is $\frac{1}{3}$ of the way from the right to the backward directions. (2, 0) (Fig. 161 B)

12. Spike flower S#10 should be $\frac{3}{4}$ the length of S#9. Insert it in the front of the holder slightly above the rim of the container, with the stem pointed toward the

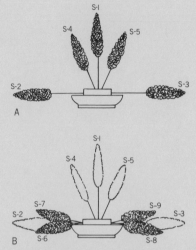

Fig. 161. Airy centerpiece (long and narrow). (A) Steps 1–7. (B) Steps 8–11.

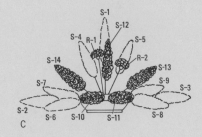

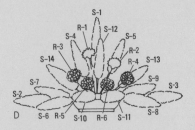

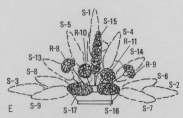

Fig. 161. (C) Steps 12–18. (D) Steps
19–23. (E) Steps 24–31.

center of the holder, tilted very slightly above horizontal and $\frac{2}{3}$ of the way from the left to the forward directions. $(7, \frac{1}{2})$

13. Spike flower S#11 should be the same length as S#10. Insert it in the front of the holder, slightly above the rim of the container, with the stem pointed toward the center of the holder, tilted very slightly above horizontal and $\frac{2}{3}$ of the way from the right to the forward directions. $(5, \frac{1}{2})$

14. Spike flower S#12 should be the same length as S#8. Insert it in front of S#1, tilted slightly above midway between horizontal and vertical. $(6, 3\frac{1}{2})$

15. Round flower R#1 should be slightly longer than $\frac{1}{2}$ the length of S#1. Insert it midway between S#1 and S#4, tilted slightly to the left and very slightly forward so the flower appears slightly forward of midway between S#1 and S#4. $(8, 4)$

16. Round flower R#2 should be slightly shorter than R#1. Insert it midway between S#5 and S#12, tilted so the flower appears slightly to the right of midway between S#5 and S#12. $(4{:}30, 3\frac{1}{2})$

17. Spike flower S#13 should be the same length as S#5. Insert it midway between S#3 and S#5, tilted so the flower appears midway between S#3 and S#5. $(3, 2)$

18. Spike flower S#14 should be the same length as S#4. Insert it midway between S#2 and S#4, tilted so the flower appears midway between S#2 and S#4. $(9, 2)$ (Fig. 161C)

19. Round flower R#3 should be very slightly shorter than R#2. Insert it midway between R#1 and S#6, tilted so the flower appears midway between R#1 and S#6 and slightly closer to R#1. $(8, 2\frac{1}{2})$

20. Round flower R#4 should be the same length as R#3. Insert it between R#2 and S#8, tilted so the flower appears slightly forward of midway between R#2 and S#8. $(4{:}30, 1\frac{1}{2})$

21. Round flower R#5 should be slightly shorter than R#3. Insert it midway between S#10 and S#12, tilted so the flower appears midway between S#10 and S#12. (6:30, $1\frac{1}{2}$)

22. Round flower R#6 should be $\frac{1}{2}$ the length of R#4. Insert it midway between R#4 and R#5, tilted so the flower appears midway between R#4 and R#5. (5:30, $1\frac{1}{2}$) (Fig. 161D)

23. Turn the arrangement completely around and turn the clock face with it so that 12 is now the forward direction.

24. Spike flower S#15 should be the same length as S#12. Insert it in front of S#1, tilted slightly above midway between horizontal and vertical. (12, $3\frac{1}{2}$)

25. Spike flower S#16 should be the same length as S#10. Insert it in the front of the holder, slightly above the rim of the container, with the stem pointed toward the center of the holder, tilted very slightly above horizontal and $\frac{2}{3}$ of the way from the right to the forward directions. (11, $\frac{1}{2}$)

26. Spike flower S#17 should be the same length as S#16. Insert it in the front of the holder, slightly above the rim of the container, with the stem pointed toward the center of the holder, tilted very slightly above horizontal and $\frac{2}{3}$ of the way from the left to the forward directions. (1, $\frac{1}{2}$)

27. Round flower R#7 should be $\frac{2}{3}$ the length of S#1. Insert it midway between S#1 and S#15, tilted so the flower is midway between S#1 and S#15. (12, 4) This flower does not show in the illustration.

28. Round flower R#8 should be $\frac{2}{3}$ the length of R#7. Insert it between S#5 and S#9, tilted so the flower appears midway between S#5 and S#9. (2, 2)

29. Round flower R#9 should be $\frac{4}{5}$ the length of R#7. Insert it between S#14 and S#16, tilted so the flower

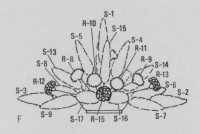

Fig. 161. (F) Steps 32–35. (G) Steps 36 and 37.

appears slightly above midway between S#14 and S#16. (10:30, 2)

30. Round flower R#10 should be $\frac{3}{4}$ the length of R#8. Insert it between S#5 and S#17, tilted so the flower is very slightly to the right of midway between S#5 and S#17. (1, 2)

31. Round flower R#11 should be slightly more than $\frac{1}{2}$ the length of R#10. Insert it between R#7 and R#9, tilted so the flower appears slightly forward of midway between R#7 and R#9. (11, 3) (Fig. 161E)

32. Round flower R#12 should be slightly longer than $\frac{1}{2}$ the length of S#3. Insert it midway between S#3 and S#13, tilted so the flower appears midway between S#3 and S#13. (3, 1)

33. Round flower R#13 should be slightly longer than $\frac{1}{2}$ the length of S#2. Insert it between S#2 and S#14, tilted so the flower appears midway between S#2 and S#14. (9, 1)

34. Round flower R#14 should be $\frac{1}{2}$ the length of S#10. Insert it horizontally from the back along the center-line of the holder, slightly above the rim of the container. (6, 0) This flower does not show in the illustration.

35. Round flower R#15 should be $\frac{1}{2}$ the length of S#16. Insert it horizontally from the front along the center-line of the holder, slightly above the rim of the container. (12, 0) (Fig. 161F)

36. Insert filler flowers in any voids in the arrangement. The filler flowers should be shorter than the flowers surrounding any void. If the flowers used in the arrangement are of appropriate sizes and the arrangement is executed properly, there should be no voids and the filler flowers will not be needed.

37. Add foliage wherever necessary to hide bare stems, fill voids, or maintain balance. Use foliage very sparingly and be careful that it does not overpower any flowers or disturb the shape of the arrangement. (Fig. 161G)

Compact Centerpiece
(*Long and Narrow*)

Materials

1. Container—a circular, square, or rectangular shallow container or a tall vase with an opening at least 3 inches in diameter.

2. A holder for flowers—a medium-to-large pin-point holder for the shallow container fitted with a cap of chicken wire large enough to protrude 1 to $1\frac{1}{2}$ inches above the rim, or a piece of foam at least 3 inches square and high enough to protrude 1 to $1\frac{1}{2}$ inches above the rim of the container. For the tall vase, use shredded foam as a filler topped with a piece of foam cut to fit the opening of the vase. The block of foam should be 2 to 4 inches high according to the weight of the flowers being used and, similarly, should protrude 1 to $1\frac{1}{2}$ inches above the rim of the vase.

3. A fastener for the holder—floral clay to secure the pin-point holder, or a staple, attached in the base of the shallow container, on which to impale the block of foam.

4. Flowers—hardened, with the below-water foliage removed. Fifteen spike flowers of uniform size and development (delphiniums, larkspur, liatris, snapdragons, stock, etc.). Gladioli are acceptable but not ideal since they are a front-facing rather than a conical flower. Sixteen round flowers of uniform size and development that have an appropriate relationship in size to the spike flowers (asters, carnations, chrysanthemums, daffodils, irises, roses, tulips, zinnias, etc.). If there are some variations in the size of the flowers available, use the smaller and less developed flowers for the upper and outer flowers of the arrangement.

5. Foliage—several pieces of good-quality natural foliage of the flowers used or of other appropriate foliage.

Procedure

1. Secure the holder in the center of the shallow container. If the tall vase is used, stuff it with foam to a tightness appropriate for the flowers being used—tight enough to hold the flowers where they are inserted, but not so tight that insertion is difficult. Fit the block of foam on top of the shredded foam. When the tall vase is used, the stems of the flowers should be cut long enough to pass completely through the block of foam and deeply into the shredded foam. Since this method anchors the block very securely, no other attachment is necessary.

2. Fill the container with water fortified with cut-flower preservative.

3. Select a very straight good-quality spike flower as flower S#1. Its length should be such that when inserted it will provide the desired overall height of the centerpiece. The width of the container should not be more than $\frac{1}{2}$ the height of flower S#1, or, if a tall vase or bowl is used, its height should not be more than $\frac{2}{3}$ of the height of the flower above its rim. Insert spike flower S#1 straight up in the center of the holder.

NOTE: In what follows, the extra length required for insertion will not be included in the measurements given. These will refer only to those parts of the stem and the flower that are exposed outside the holder. It should be understood, however, that the additional length needed for insertion is to be added in each case.

4. Spike flower S#2 should be the same length as S#1. Insert it horizontally from the left along the centerline of the holder, just above the rim of the container. (9, 0)

5. Spike flower S#3 should be the same length as S#2. Insert it horizontally from the right along the centerline of the holder, just above the rim of the container. (3, 0)

6. Spike flower S#4 should be $\frac{3}{4}$ the length of S#1. Insert it between S#1 and S#2, tilted slightly above midway, so the flower appears between S#1 and S#2, but slightly closer to S#1. (9, 3)

7. Spike flower S#5 should be the same length as S#4. Insert it between S#1 and S#3, tilted slightly above midway, so the flower appears between S#1 and S#3, but slightly closer to S#1. (3, 3) (Fig. 162A)

8. Spike flower S#6 should be $\frac{2}{3}$ the length of S#1. Insert it horizontally in the left side of the holder in front of S#2, with the stem pointed toward the center of the holder, just above the rim of the container, so it is $\frac{1}{3}$ of the way from the left to the forward directions. (8, 0)

9. Spike flower S#7 should be the same length as S#6. Insert it horizontally in the left side of the holder in back of S#2, just above the rim of the container, and with the stem pointed toward the center of the holder, so it is $\frac{1}{3}$ of the way from the left to the backward directions. (10, 0)

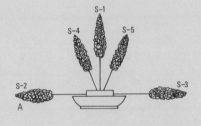

10. Spike flower S#8 should be the same length as S#7. Insert it horizontally in the right side of the holder in front of S#3, just above the rim of the container, and with the stem pointed toward the center of the holder, so it is $\frac{1}{3}$ of the way from the right to the forward directions. (4, 0)

11. Spike flower S#9 should be the same length as S#8. Insert it horizontally in the right side of the holder in back of S#3, just above the rim of the container, and with the stem pointed toward the center of the holder, so it is $\frac{1}{3}$ of the way from the right to the backward directions. (2, 0) (Fig. 162B)

12. Spike flower S#10 should be $\frac{3}{4}$ the length of S#9. Insert it in the front of the holder slightly above the rim of the container, with the stem pointed toward the center of the holder, tilted very slightly above hori-

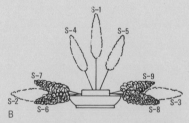

Fig. 162. Compact centerpiece, long and narrow. (A) Steps 1–7. (B) Steps 8–11.

zontal and $\frac{2}{3}$ of the way from the left to the forward directions. $(7, \frac{1}{2})$

13. Spike flower S#11 should be the same length as S#10. Insert it in the front of the holder, slightly above the rim of the container, with the stem pointed toward the center of the holder, tilted very slightly above horizontal and $\frac{2}{3}$ of the way from the right to the forward directions. $(5, \frac{1}{2})$

14. Spike flower S#12 should be the same length as S#9. Insert it in front of S#1, tilted slightly above midway between horizontal and vertical. $(6, 3)$

15. Round flower R#1 should be slightly more than $\frac{1}{2}$ the length of S#1. Insert it midway between S#1 and S#4, tilted slightly to the left and very slightly forward, so the flower appears slightly forward of midway between S#1 and S#4. $(8, 4)$

16. Round flower R#2 should be $\frac{3}{4}$ the length of R#1. Insert it midway between S#1 and S#5, tilted slightly to the right and very slightly forward, so the flower appears slightly forward of midway between S#1 and S#5. $(4, 4)$

17. Round flower R#3 should be $\frac{4}{5}$ the length of R#2. Insert it midway between S#3 and S#5, tilted so the flower appears midway between S#3 and S#5. $(3, 1\frac{1}{2})$

18. Round flower R#4 should be the same length as R#3. Insert it midway between S#2 and S#4, tilted so the flower appears midway between S#2 and S#4. $(9, 1\frac{1}{2})$ (Fig. 162C)

19. Round flower R#5 should be slightly shorter than R#4. Insert it midway between R#1 and S#6, tilted so the flower appears very slightly forward of midway between R#1 and S#6. $(7:30, 2)$

20. Round flower R#6 should be the same length as R#5. Insert it between R#2 and S#8, tilted so the flower appears slightly forward of midway between R#2 and S#8. $(4:30, 2)$

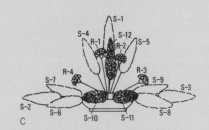

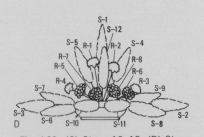

Fig. 162. (C) Steps 12–18. (D) Steps 19–22.

21. Round flower R#7 should be $\frac{3}{4}$ the length of R#5. Insert it midway between S#12 and S#10, tilted so the flower appears slightly to the right of midway between S#12 and S#10. (6:30, $1\frac{1}{2}$)

22. Round flower R#8 should be the same length as R#7. Insert it midway between R#2 and S#11, tilted so the flower appears midway between R#2 and S#11. (5, 2) (Fig. 162D)

23. Turn the arrangement completely around and turn the clock face with it so 12 is now the forward direction.

24. Spike flower S#13 should be the same length as S#12. Insert it in front of S#1, tilted so it is slightly above midway between horizontal and vertical. (12, 3)

25. Spike flower S#14 should be the same length as S#10. Insert it in the front of the holder, slightly above the rim of the container, with the stem pointed toward the center of the holder, tilted very slightly above horizontal and $\frac{2}{3}$ of the way from the right to the forward directions. (11, $\frac{1}{2}$)

26. Spike flower S#15 should be the same length as S#14. Insert it in the front of the holder, slightly above the rim of the container, and with the stem pointed toward the center of the holder, tilted very slightly above horizontal and $\frac{2}{3}$ of the way from the left to the forward directions. (1, $\frac{1}{2}$)

27. Round flower R#9 should be slightly longer than R#1. Insert it midway between S#1 and S#13, tilted so the flower is midway between S#1 and S#13. (12, 4) This flower does not show in the illustration.

28. Round flower R#10 should be the same length as R#6. Insert it between S#4 and S#14, tilted so the flower appears slightly to the right of midway between S#4 and S#14 and slightly closer to S#14. (10:30, $1\frac{1}{2}$)

29. Round flower R#11 should be $\frac{2}{3}$ the length of R#9. Insert it between S#4 and S#13, tilted so the flower

appears slightly forward of midway between S#4 and S#13. (11, 3)

30. Round flower R#12 should be $\frac{3}{4}$ the length of R#9. Insert it between S#9 and S#13, tilted so the flower appears between S#9 and S#13 and slightly closer to S#13. (1:30, $2\frac{1}{2}$)

31. Round flower R#13 should be $\frac{1}{2}$ the length of R#12. Insert it midway between S#13 and S#15, tilted so the flower appears midway between S#13 and S#15. (12:30, 2)

32. Round flower R#14 should be the same length as R#10. Insert it midway between S#9 and S#15, tilted so the flower appears midway between S#9 and S#15. (1:30, $\frac{1}{2}$)

33. Round flower R#15 should be the same length as R#6. Insert it from the back along the centerline of the holder, slightly above the rim of the container, tilted slightly above horizontal. (6, 1) This flower does not show in the illustration.

34. Round flower R#16 should be the same length as R#15. Insert it from the front along the centerline of the holder, slightly above the rim of the container, tilted slightly above horizontal. (12, 1) (Fig. 162E)

35. Insert filler flowers in any voids in the arrangement. The filler flowers should be shorter than flowers surrounding any void. If the flowers used in the arrangement are of appropriate sizes and the arrangement is executed properly, there should be no voids, and the filler flowers will not be needed.

36. Add foliage wherever necessary to hide bare stems, fill voids, or maintain balance. Use foliage very sparingly and be careful that it does not overpower any flowers or disturb the shape of the arrangement. (Fig. 162F)

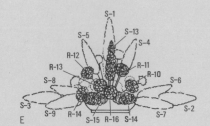

Fig. 162. (E) Steps 24–34. (F) Steps 35 and 36.

Appendix A

Dish Gardens and Water Gardens

☐ One way of always having a lovely centerpiece or a touch of green in your home is to design a dish garden or a water garden. A dish garden is a grouping of foliage plants arranged in soil in a metal or ceramic container and designed so that it can be used as a centerpiece or a three-quarter arrangement. A water garden, in contrast, is composed of plants growing in water in a container. With proper care, these gardens will last indefinitely and give you a great deal of pleasure.

Making a Dish Garden

In a dish garden, varieties in shape, texture, and color all contribute to the beauty of the composition. In selecting and placing the plants, you should apply all the principles described in connection with flower arrangements. In addition, you must pay some attention to the fact that a dish garden continues to live and grow.

The intended location of the dish garden will determine the type, color, shape, and size of the container, but your selection of plants will depend on several other factors. The number and size of plants you can use will be dictated by

Fig. 163. Plants that require the same amount of exposure and watering should be used together in a dish garden.

Fig. 164. Members of the cactus family can be grouped together.

the size and depth of the container. In addition, you must select plants that grow at the same rate in order to retain the balanced shape and lines of the arrangement over a long period. If one plant grew so large that it becam out of scale with the rest of the composition, it would eve tually have to be either pruned or replaced. Finally, to insure the uniform good health of your garden you must assemble plants that require the same exposure and watering. For example, philodendron, nephthytis, dracena, pittosporum, and ivy are congenial companions requiring subdued lighting, moderate watering, and rich soil. Members of the cactus family, on the other hand, require sandy soil, little water, and much sunlight. (Figs. 163, 164)

The plants used in dish gardens are generally sold in small pots, and it is best to leave them in their pots until you have decided exactly where you want to place each one in the final arrangement. A good way to work out your design is to lay a large sheet of paper on a flat surface and trace the outline of your container on the paper. Then around this tracing draw another line that follows the outline of the container but is fifty percent larger—that is, a four-inch dimension becomes six inches, a six-inch dimension becomes nine inches, and so on. Now position your plants, still in their pots, within this outline until you achieve the arrangement you want, remembering that in your final design the horizontal spacing will be compressed while the heights will remain unchanged. Obviously, the plants you select should all be in pots of approximately the same height. This method will help you avoid overcrowding and enable you to create a design that is properly balanced.

Prepare your container by covering the bottom with a one-inch layer of pebbles or pieces of broken flower pots. This will provide a limited amount of drainage and aeration for your plants. When you are ready to transfer the plants to the container, remove them carefully from their pots in order to keep their balls of earth intact. To do this, take a plant from one corner of your test arrangement and lay one hand on top of the soil, with your fingers straddling the stem of the plant. Invert the pot and tap its rim on the edge of a table so that the ball of earth drops easily and gently into your hand. (If the plant is very short and compact, you can support it by cupping your hand over the entire crown as you tap it out.) Carefully place the plant in the corresponding corner of the container. (Figs. 165, 166)

Fig. 165. Tap the rim of the pot against the edge of a table. The ball of earth will fall easily and gently into your hand.

Repeat this for each of the plants in order until all are transferred to their proper positions in the container. You may have to press the balls of earth carefully together in order to fit them in. As you position the plants, make sure that the tops of the balls of soil are all at the same level. If it is necessary to raise some of them, add a layer of soil under the balls of earth wherever it is needed. Use sterilized potting soil, which can be purchased from your florist or garden center. (Fig. 167)

When all the plants have been transferred to the container, check your design and make any necessary adjustments. Then fill in the voids between the plants with more potting soil, tamp down the earth around the plants, and water them thoroughly. Finally, add a top dressing of moss or of white or colored pebbles. This serves not only as a decorative finish but aids in retaining moisture. You can find moss on the ground in wooded areas or you may be able to purchase it at your flower shop. Colored stones, if you prefer them, also can be purchased from your florist.

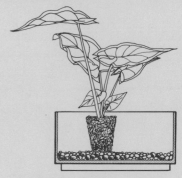

Fig. 166. Line the bottom of your planter with a one-inch layer of pebbles or pieces of broken pots. This will provide drainage and aeration for your plants.

Caring for a Dish Garden

Proper watering is crucial to the good health of a dish garden. Since it does not have any real drainage, it must not be overwatered. The best approach is to check it regu-

Fig. 167. After you have removed the plants from their pots, place the balls of earth in the container in their selected spots, pressing the balls closely togeth or separating them as your desi   ctates.

Fig. 168. Water sprayer.

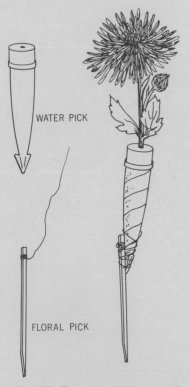

WATER PICK

FLORAL PICK

Fig. 169. The water pick is covered with floral tape, and the wire of the floral pick is tightly wrapped around one end.

larly and water it only when the soil becomes dry to the touch. The most satisfactory watering method is to fill your sink to a depth slightly greater than the height of the container. Use water at room temperature. Immerse the container until air stops bubbling from the soil, then lift it straight up in order not to disturb the surface finish. Place the container on the drain board and let the excess water run off. It is also a good idea to spray the foliage lightly with a fine spray of water. If the foliage is dusty, you can clean it with a soft cloth or facial tissue and then spray it with a commercial leaf shine. Follow the directions carefully when using these products. (Fig. 168)

Rotate your garden every few days so that it does not become lopsided as the plants seek sunlight. Try to keep the plants growing at the same rate in order to maintain the balanced appearance and good lines of the garden. Since the amount of soil is small, it is also important to add fertilizer once a month.

For a bit of extra color or variety, you can add flowers to your dish garden from time to time. To do this, you need water picks and floral picks. Cover the water picks with green floral tape, and attach each one to a floral pick. Insert these assemblies in the garden wherever you want to place a flower. Simply push the floral picks into the soil; they are so thin that there is no danger of damaging the roots of your plants. Then fill the picks with water and insert your flowers. You must add water to the tubes every day since their capacity is small and the water is quickly absorbed by the flowers. (Fig. 169)

The flowers you select must be in scale with the rest of the garden and be of appropriate colors and textures. They should also be in keeping with the existing mood. Most important, they should enhance the feeling of natural beauty. As you place them, keep in mind the elements of design. But remember that your objective is to create the impression of a flowering garden rather than a full-blown floral arrangement. (Fig. 170)

Making a Water Garden

A water garden is similar to a dish garden, except that the plants are growing without soil in a ceramic, glass, or metal container filled with water enriched with a liquid fertilizer. You can select from a wide variety of materials since many plants thrive in water. Philodendron, pothos, nephthytis, coleus, ivy, and Chinese evergreens are just a few examples. As with dish gardens, you can make an effective centerpiece or three-quarter arrangement if you adhere to the fundamentals of design in selecting and placing your plants. The addition of a few flowers to this ever-living, ever-changing foundation of greenery will provide you with an economical, effective, and almost instantaneous flower arrangement.

The success of a water garden depends on your handling the plants conscientiously at each step in its design and development. As with dish gardens you will probably purchase the plants in small pots of soil. Tap them out of the pots as described above. Then hold them under running water and gently crush the balls of earth to wash all the soil away from the roots. Use water at or slightly above room temperature so as not to shock the roots. And catch the soil in a bucket or dishpan to avoid clogging your plumbing. As soon as you have cleaned each plant, place it in a bowl of water at room temperature while you prepare the others. (Fig. 171)

As you visualize the placement of your plants in the arrangement, keep in mind all the fundamentals of design. While the container is still dry, use floral clay to attach pin-point holders as accurately as you can in the positions

Fig. 170. Dish garden with three wild calla lilies. The flowers you select to insert in the camouflaged tubes should be in scale and in keeping with the mood already set.

Fig. 171. Preparing plants for water gardens. After the soil has been carefully removed from the roots of the plants, you are ready to create your water garden.

where you want to place the plants. Use only nonrusting holders so that the water will remain clean and attractive.

Fill the container with water and impale the plants on the pin points exactly where you want them in your final design. Press them down just to the point where the soil lines of the plants are even with the surface of the water. It is particularly important not to submerge any parts of the stems that are normally above ground, since this would prevent them from breathing and induce rot.

When all your plants are in place and the design meets with your approval, you can conceal the pin-point holders by spreading pebbles among the roots in the bottom of the bowl. This will also help to hold the plants in place, add some visual weight, and provide a small amount of mineral nutrition.

As the roots adjust to their new environment, they will shed small bits of material that cloud the water and promote the growth of bacteria. Because of this it is advisable to change the water as soon as it appears cloudy. Let room-temperature water flow into the container until the stale water has been completely replaced or, if you find it more convenient, draw the water off with a syringe and then add fresh water. After a few changes, the system will become stable and the water should remain clear for long periods of time. Once the garden is established, you will need to add water from time to time only to replenish the losses from evaporation and transpiration. You should also add liquid fertilizer regularly to insure healthy growth.

Besides being a beautiful living arrangement in itself, your water garden can function as a background for cut flowers. Impale the flowers in appropriate spots in the pin-point holders or, if necessary, add some additional holders. After the cut flowers have died and been removed, you should change the water completely to remove any bacterial growth introduced by the stems. (Figs. 172, 173)

Arrangements of Cut Greens

Arrangements made exclusively of cut greens are somewhat akin to water gardens. Because of the wonderful texture and great variety of the colors of their foliage, cut greens make very effective decorations. It is wise to use greens that have a long-lasting quality, such as podocarpus, Scotch broom, eucalyptus, magnolia, and pachysandra. The greens also provide a ready background for cut flowers. The more conscientious you are about water changes, the longer your greens will last. They also benefit from frequent spraying with lukewarm water.

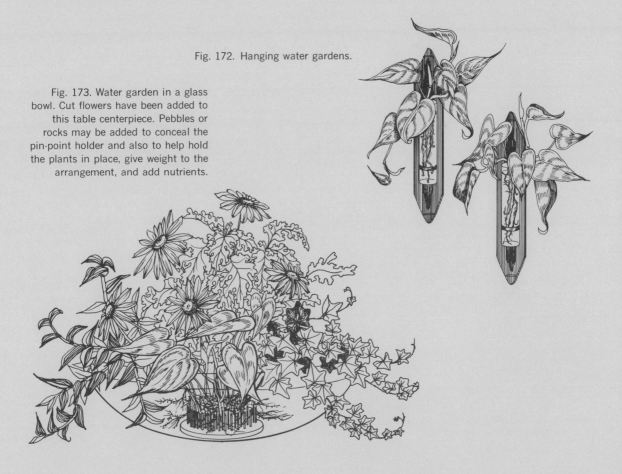

Fig. 172. Hanging water gardens.

Fig. 173. Water garden in a glass bowl. Cut flowers have been added to this table centerpiece. Pebbles or rocks may be added to conceal the pin-point holder and also to help hold the plants in place, give weight to the arrangement, and add nutrients.

Appendix

The Art of Preserving Flowers

B

Fig. 174. Flowers can be dried in an upright position.

☐ The art of drying flowers and designing waterless arrangements is a truly creative hobby that has flourished for centuries. Its continuing popularity today is easy to understand. For one thing, improved techniques now result in many truly fine specimens. The muted tones of preserved flowers harmonize well with most environments, and they can be arranged in containers that do not hold enough water to maintain fresh flowers. (They are ideal for use on a cherished piece of furniture where a water spot would be disastrous.) Dried arrangements also are a boon to the busy housewife who enjoys the color and beauty of flowers but lacks the time to give them daily attention. And the absence of pollen makes them popular with people who suffer from hay fever.

Although techniques have improved greatly in recent years, the basic objective in all methods of preserving flowers is to remove all moisture while minimizing changes in shape, texture, and color. The most popular methods today are (1) air-drying flowers in either an upright or a hanging position and (2) embedding them for a period of time in any of several drying powders.

Air-Drying Flowers

It is very simple to air-dry flowers in an upright position. Just arrange the grasses and flowers very loosely in containers and place them in a very dry, warm, dark area. (Attics are ideal.) Since the key to success is rapid dehydration, the drier the area the better will be the results. A free flow of air is also very helpful. The flowers will be dry and ready to arrange in just a few days. Because the flowers develop slightly during the initial stages of the drying process, they should be cut just before they reach full maturity. Flowers that respond most satisfactorily to this treatment are celosia, hydrangea, sumac, and most grasses and weeds. (Figs. 174, 175)

The stems of flowers dried upright in containers will normally remain straight. If you want curved stems, you must mold them by hand before drying. For more controlled curves, place a heavy wire along the stem, wrap it with a fine wire, and then bend it to the shape you want. Remove the wires when the stem has dried. If the stem is hollow, you can insert a heavy wire into the opening and bend it as desired. In this case, leave the wire in place after drying; removing it might crack the dried stem and, in any case, it is invisible.

Drying flowers in a hanging position is another simple procedure. As when drying them upright in containers, you should cut the flowers just before they reach maturity. Some of the many materials that can be dried in this way are

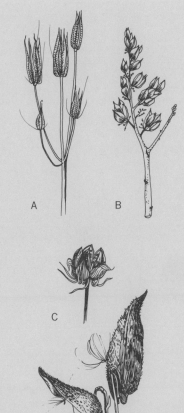

Fig. 175. Common seedpods that can be gathered in the fall and used in dried arrangements. (A) Columbine. (B) Lilac. (C) Hibiscus. (D) Milkweed.

Fig. 176. Flowers can be dried in a hanging position.

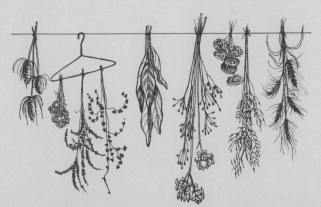

acacia, yarrow, goldenrod, dock, grasses, milkweed, and sumac. (Fig. 176)

To hang the flowers, tie the cut ends of the stems with short pieces of string and attach them to a rod or stretched rope in a very dry, warm, dark area, preferably where there is a free passage of air. You can increase your drying area by hooking clothes hangers over the stretched line and attaching your flowers to the crossbars. You must hang large flowers singly, but you can save time and space by putting small flowers in bunches held together with elastic bands or "Twistems." Use string, pipe cleaners, or "Twistems" to attach the bunches to the rod or line. Although different materials dry at different rates, most will be ready within a few days. Check the drying room periodically and remove any thoroughly dried plants. The stems naturally dry straight, but you can introduce any curves you want by the methods described above.

Drying Powders

Simplicity is the great advantage of air-drying flowers. Unfortunately, however, the selection of flowers that respond to this treatment is somewhat limited, and the colors obtained are restricted to muted tones of beige, orange, brown, and yellow. Embedding the flowers in a drying medium, though more complex, is a much more reliable means for preserving the original shape, color, and texture of the flowers.

The objective of this method is to immobilize every part of the flower in all its three-dimensional beauty throughout the drying process. This is accomplished by completely embedding the flower in a fine rigid powder and leaving it undisturbed during the entire dehydration. The powder may be inert and serve no function other than mechanical support during the drying. Or it may actively absorb moisture from the flower or react chemically with it while it is providing mechanical support.

Some of the many kinds of powder that are used include:

A. Silica gel, a commercial preparation that can be purchased from florists

B. Equal portions of pumice and yellow cornmeal, plus three tablespoons of ordinary uniodized table salt for each quart of the mixture

C. Plain borax

D. Equal portions of borax and yellow cornmeal, plus three tablespoons of uniodized salt for each quart of the mixture

E. One part of borax and two parts of fine building sand

F. Specially prepared sand with some additional ingredients as described below

For any of these preparations, the ingredients must be very dry and thoroughly mixed. All of them can be stored indefinitely in sealed, air-tight glass or metal containers. They can be reused many times provided they are dried by heating after each use. It is good practice to put them in their storage containers and seal them tightly while the mixtures are still warm. When not in use, they never should be allowed to stand in the open at room temperature for any length of time.

How to Prepare Sand for Use

Although sand requires some special treatment, it has the advantage of being cheap. The best choice is fine builder's sand. Do not use seashore sand since it contains too many impurities. Begin by passing the sand through the finest sieve you can find in order to remove all the coarse grains.

After this is done, wash the sand very carefully. Fill a one-gallon container about two-thirds full of sand and then fill it to the top with warm water. Stir thoroughly from the bottom up until the sand is completely wet, adding more water if necessary. When all the sand is soaked, agitate it for a few minutes and then let the sand settle. Now tip the container and drain off the water from the top of the sand. Repeat this process until the water that runs off is quite clean and clear.

Now add more water, along with one tablespoon of detergent or soap powder, and thoroughly agitate the sand until you feel that each grain has been treated. Let the sand settle and drain off as much of the soapy water as you can. Rinse the sand repeatedly with fresh water until the rinse water comes away clear and free of suds. Do not cut corners at this stage since your ultimate success depends very heavily on the cleanliness of the sand.

The next step is to dry the sand. Spread it in a large pan and heat it in a slow oven at 250°F. Stir it from time to time. This step will require four to five hours.

After the sand has thoroughly dried, heat about twenty pounds of it to a temperature of 300°F in your oven. When it is uniformly hot, stir in four tablespoons of melted paraffin. Continue stirring until each grain is coated with paraffin. You will be able to tell when you have stirred enough by the evenness of the slightly darker color imparted to the sand by the paraffin. Then let the sand cool completely and mix in one tablespoon of bicarbonate of soda and one tablespoon of silica gel. The sand is now ready for use.

Processing Flowers in the Drying Medium

When you finally are ready to select flowers for drying, cut them at whatever stages you need for your planned arrangement. If you have no particular design in mind, make a selection at all stages of development—some buds, some partially opened flowers, and some mature blooms.

Each flower must be crisp, fresh, and in perfect condition since any imperfection becomes more apparent after drying. Do not try to process too many flowers at one session, for your success will depend on the meticulous execution of each step in the process.

Cut the flowers on a sunny afternoon and make sure they are completely dry. Use the corner of a paper towel or a toothpick tipped with absorbent cotton to remove any drops of water on the surface or hidden in the hearts of the flowers. If you are a beginner, you may want to remove the stems before drying since the flower heads alone require much less drying medium and are considerably easier to handle. You can dry the stems separately in air or you can add artificial stems after the flowers are dry. If you decide to leave the stems attached, strip off all the leaves except for two or three near the blossom.

For the actual drying you will need a selection of appropriate containers. These can be of almost any material, but they must satisfy three important requirements. They must be rigid enough to maintain their shape when filled with the drying medium; they should have the maximum possible surface area; and they must be large enough so that there is at least one inch of drying medium between any part of the flower or stem and the nearest wall of the container. Rigid wooden boxes and deep glass, pottery, or metal baking dishes all work well. Cardboard boxes and aluminum foil dishes generally are less satisfactory.

Select a container of the appropriate size for the flower or flowers you are preparing and cover the bottom with one inch of drying powder. Place the flower on the powder and add powder around it until the flower is supported and

Fig. 177. Cover the bottom of the container with one inch of drying powder. Place the flower on the powder and add powder around it until the flower is supported and will stand by itself. Continue to add powder very carefully without disturbing the flower. Avoid any trapped-air spaces that cannot be filled with powder.

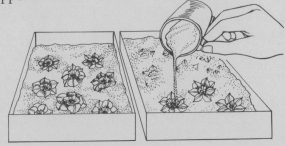

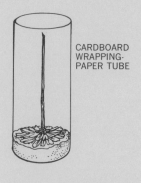

CARDBOARD
WRAPPING-
PAPER TUBE

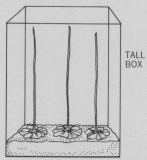

TALL
BOX

Fig. 178. Drying single-petaled flat flowers with their stems. After the flowers are placed in the medium, the container is filled with the drying powder.

will stand by itself. Normally the flower is placed with its face up. In any case, it should be positioned so that no cup-shaped areas face down. Single-petaled flat flowers can be placed face down in the medium with their stems attached. The medium is then carefully added until the flower and stem are completely submerged. The important thing is to avoid any trapped-air spaces that cannot be filled with powder. (Figs. 177, 178)

Once the flower is fixed in position, continue to add powder very carefully without disturbing it. Make sure that each minute structure in the flower is completely surrounded and supported by the powder. When the flower is entirely embedded, cover it with about one inch of the lighter powders. If you are using sand, add only about a quarter of an inch on top since the sand is quite heavy and can distort some of the more delicate structures.

If you are drying a flower with the stem attached, you will need a container long enough to hold the stem in a horizontal position. Put about one inch of powder in the bottom where the flower head will be but add much more where the stem will be so that, when you position the stem, the flower head will be just above the powder in its end of the container. Then slowly add powder until all parts of the flower are surrounded and supported without being disturbed. (Fig. 179)

For beginners it is best to process just one flower to a container. After you become more experienced, you can easily process several identical flowers in one large flat box as long as you make sure that all the flowers are at least one inch apart.

Once the flowers are completely embedded in the drying medium, you should tap the container lightly on all sides

ADD MORE POWDER
TO SUPPORT STEM

1-INCH POWDER

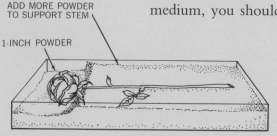

Fig. 179. The container should be long enough to hold the stem in a horizontal position.

and place it in a warm dry location. Mark it with an identifying label including the date, type of flower, and expected drying time so that you will know what it contains and when to test it.

How Long Will It Take?

The length of time required for complete drying depends on so many factors that it is impossible to give any precise figures. Temperature, humidity, the size and type of flowers being dried, and the kind of medium being used all play a role. Even so, the following summary should be helpful as a rough guide to the necessary processing times. All flowers are not included, but others of the same sizes, thicknesses, and textures as those listed require about the same drying times.

In general, four to six days are enough for columbines, cornflowers, cosmos, daffodils, daisies and painted daisies, delphiniums, larkspurs, lilies of the valley, narcissi, pansies, Queen Anne's lace, and sweet peas. (Fig. 180)

Six to eight days are needed for baby gladioli, spray chrysanthemums and pompoms, dahlias, day lilies, single peonies, snapdragons, tulips, and zinnias. (Fig. 181)

Eight to ten days are necessary for black-eyed susans, liatris, lilacs, all lilies other than day lilies, marigolds, all types of roses, and stock. (Fig. 182)

The precise drying time is more critical for some media

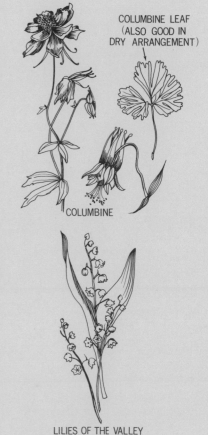

COLUMBINE LEAF
(ALSO GOOD IN
DRY ARRANGEMENT)

COLUMBINE

LILIES OF THE VALLEY

Fig. 180. The drying time for flowers such as columbines and lilies of the valley is usually four to six days.

Fig. 181. Six to eight days are needed to dry flowers such as day lilies, single peonies, and zinnias.

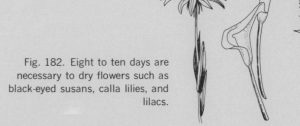

Fig. 182. Eight to ten days are necessary to dry flowers such as black-eyed susans, calla lilies, and lilacs.

Fig. 183. In the case of ball-type flowers, first cover the calyx with glue, then brush glue on the underside of the outer petals, and finally, drip glue on the tops of the bases of all the petals.

than for others. In borax or silica gel the flower starts to turn brown if you leave it in the medium after it is completely dry. You can leave a dried flower in prepared sand for a much longer time without ill effects.

In any case you must have some way of testing the dryness of the flowers. This is a delicate operation and must be done very carefully. First remove most of the powder above the flower and then dig a small hole next to the dried blossom. Gently shake the powder from around the highest part of the flower into the hole. You can also blow through a soda straw to remove the powder. When a small part of the flower is exposed, examine it carefully and test it very gently with a toothpick. If it appears stiff and springy it is probably ready to be taken out. If it appears at all soft or limp, it should be carefully recovered and tested a day or two later.

When the flower is completely dry, remove the top layer of powder until the flower is just about exposed. Then gradually remove the powder from around the edges of the container until it begins to fall away from the flower. Continue until the flower is completely exposed, then remove it, preferably handling it only by the calyx or stem. (Some flowers are rugged enough so that you can simply pour the powder out of the container through your fingers until you retrieve the blossom.) After you have removed the flower, let it stand for about twenty-four hours to stabilize so that it will be easier to handle.

Preparing Dried Flowers for Arrangement

Several additional steps are necessary to strengthen dried flowers and prevent further change. First of all, you should reinforce the heart of each flower with a glue composed of equal parts of nail polish remover and acetate cement. Use a fine brush or a toothpick to drip glue into the heart

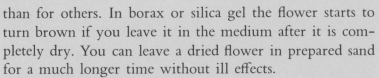

Fig. 184. Use a fine camel's-hair brush to remove remaining grains of the medium.

of the flower. Tilt the flower so the glue runs around the base of each petal and continue adding glue until the bases of all the petals are coated. In the case of ball-type flowers, such as zinnias or chrysanthemums, first cover the calyx with glue, then brush glue on the underside of the bases of the outer petals, and finally drip glue on the tops of the bases of all the petals. Tilt the flower and work the glue in until all the glue-covered areas are connected. This makes a very strong bond. In all cases be very careful not to get any glue on the parts of the petals that show. If a petal should fall off, you can reattach it with Elmer's Glue. (Fig. 183)

After the glue dries, the flower is ready for its final cleanup. Use a small camel's-hair brush or a toothpick covered with absorbent cotton to gently remove any grains of the medium that remain on the flower. At this point you can also restore the texture of velvety petals by lightly stroking them with a brush dipped in vegetable oil. (Fig. 184)

If your dried flower has no stem, now is the time to provide one. Stems that were dried separately can be reunited with the flower by using a needle as a dowel. To do this, coat the eye end of the needle with glue and push it into the end of the stem. Then coat the point with glue and, using the stem as a handle, push the needle into the short stem of the flower. Just before pressing the two ends of the stem together, add some glue to the gap. Then press the stem until the ends are in tight contact and wipe off any excess glue that is squeezed out. (Fig. 185)

Since flower stems become quite faded when dried, you may want to dye them to restore their fresh color. Oil paints mixed in nail polish remover produce excellent results. You can make a good basic green from six parts dark green and one part cadmium yellow, plus an optional dash of white and burnt sienna. Adjust this to the exact shade of green

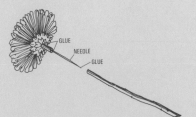

Fig. 185. Stems that were dried separately can be reunited with the flower.

Fig. 186. To make a wire stem, dip the end of the wire in glue, insert it into the short natural stem, and wrap it with floral tape.

you want by adding small amounts of yellow or blue. Keep the mixture quite liquid, since you want a dyeing rather than a painting action. The mixture will keep indefinitely in a tightly capped bottle.

Some flower dryers are willing to accept wire stems. To make one, you should first select a piece of wire of the correct gauge for the size of the flower—usually 18 gauge for large flowers and 22 gauge for smaller ones. Dip the end of the wire in glue, insert it into the short natural stem of the flower, and wrap it with light green, dark green, or brown floral tape. For a more lifelike appearance, you can later dye the tape with the mixture described above. You can bend the wire stem into any desired curve, and, if it turns out to be too weak, you can easily add a stronger wire. (Fig. 186)

Wire serves another function in the art of preserving flowers. Although spike flowers can be dried in one stalk, the effect is lost if even a single floret falls off. However, if you are willing to do the painstaking work, you can reconstruct a spike flower with wired florets. Wire each floret with very fine wire and cover the wire with tape. Then tape the wired florets to a heavy wire representing the spine of the spike. It is important to attach the florets in the correct size relationship to each other and at the proper angles. Although the operation is tedious, the lasting quality of the wired spike makes it well worth the effort. (Fig. 187)

How to Compensate for Color Changes

In selecting flowers for preservation in a drying medium, you must keep in mind the fact that different colors are affected differently by the drying process. Moreover, the results vary in different media and under different conditions so you will have to rely on your own experience to predict exactly what will happen. In general, you can expect the following results with most flowers:

1. Pinks, oranges, and blues dry reasonably true to color.
2. Reds and purples darken somewhat.
3. Greens dry true to color but should be dyed since they rather quickly turn to gray or an insipid yellow.
4. Yellows fade both during drying and after exposure to light.
5. White tends to become transparent during the drying and later turns to beige.

While you may not care to compensate for these changes in your first efforts, later you probably will want to try. You can adjust the colors with aerosol spray dyes, liquid dyes, or chalk dyes. Whatever method you select, you must make your color adjustments on fresh specimens, since the dried flowers are too fragile for treatment.

Aerosol sprays are available from your florist and are the simplest to use. However, the colors are quite crude and there is no way to blend them. To color a flower with aerosol dye, cover the areas you do not want to color with foil and apply the dye as directed on the can.

Liquid dyes, also available at flower shops, provide you with the opportunity to mix exactly the color you want. Simply dip the flower into the dye and hold it there for a second; then remove it and rinse it in cold water. The longer you hold the flower in the dye, the deeper the color will be. If the first try does not give a deep enough tint, shake off the water and dip the flower again. When the color meets with your satisfaction, let the flower dry with its stem in water to keep it fresh. If necessary, you can later touch up the color with a small brush dipped in liquid dye. The dye will remain usable for about six months if it is stored in tightly closed jars.

The powdered-chalk method is also excellent. You can

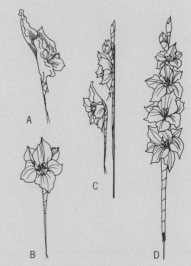

Fig. 187. A spike flower can be reconstructed by wiring. (A) Wire each floret with a very fine wire. (B) Cover the wire with tape. (C) Tape the wired florets to the heavy wire that serves as the spine of the flower. (D) The florets should be in the correct size relationship to one another and at the proper angles.

A   ¼-INCH THICK
     NEWSPAPER

B

Fig. 188. Preserving foliage by
pressing. (A) Place newspaper
(¼-inch thick) on a smooth, hard, dry
surface. Spread a single layer of
leaves on top. Add another ¼ inch of
newspaper. (B) Place a heavy,
smooth board on the top of the
completed stack. Weight it uniformly
with bricks or cinder blocks and leave
it for four weeks.

blend the chalks to obtain subtle colors, and there is no need
to wait for the color to dry before processing the flowers.
Buy high-quality colored chalks from an artists' supply
store and pulverize each color separately. After blending to
obtain the color you want, pour the mixture into a plastic
bag. Place your flower in the bag and, holding it closed,
gently shake the bag. Remove the flower, shake off the
excess chalk, and transfer it to the drying medium. You
can later make some color adjustments or cover blemishes
by using a small brush dipped in chalk of the correct color.

How to Preserve Foliage

Since most of the leaves should be removed from the
flowers before processing, you will need additional foliage
when you are ready to make a dried arrangement. Although
the best method is to embed the foliage in a drying medium,
much of it responds quite well to air-drying. Some of the
best for air-drying are artemesia, eucalyptus, andromeda,
lemon, huckleberry, iris, daffodil, and gladiolus foliage.

Dogwood, beech, maple, sumac, oak, and many other
thin flat leaves can be preserved by pressing. This is a particularly good method for capturing autumn colors. Select
healthy specimens and clean them with salt-free vegetable
oil or olive oil. Place a pad of newspaper about ¼ inch thick
on a smooth, hard, dry surface, spread a single layer of
leaves on top, and then add another ¼-inch layer of newspapers. You can press more than one layer of leaves at a time
if you separate each layer with about a ¼ inch of newspapers.
Place a heavy, smooth board on top of the completed stack,
weight it uniformly with several bricks or cinder blocks,
and leave it undisturbed for about four weeks. When the
leaves are dry, you can give them a sheen by rubbing them
again with vegetable oil. You can also change their color
by dyeing them as you would dye stems (see pages 267–

268) or by tinting them with liquid shoe polish or even with oil stains made for use on wood. (Fig. 188)

Coleus, funkia, maple, and caladium leaves are best preserved if they are pressed with an iron. Cut prime leaves, clean them with vegetable oil, and arrange them in a single layer between two sheets of waxed paper. Place this sandwich on several sheets of newspaper over a flat hard surface, cover it with several more sheets of newspaper, and press with a warm iron until the leaves are completely dry. (Fig. 189)

Fig. 189. Preserving foliage by pressing with an iron.

Skeletonized leaves can be quite attractive in some dried flower arrangements. To prepare them, simmer the leaves for forty-five minutes in a quart of water in which you have dissolved two tablespoons of household lye. Make sure the leaves are completely covered by the solution. Then rinse the leaves with cool water and spread them in a single layer on absorbent material that will soak up excess water. Gently scrape away the substance of the leaf until only the veins and the outline remain. If you now soak the skeletonized leaves for one hour in a solution of two tablespoons of household bleach to one quart of water, they will fade to a beige color. After two hours of soaking, they will turn white. When you have achieved the color you want, spread the leaves in a single layer between paper towels, place a board and a weight on top, and let them dry for twenty-four hours. (Fig. 190)

Many types of foliage can be preserved by the glycerin method. Laurel, fire thorn, viburnum, andromeda, mountain ash, wild huckleberry, ilex, cotoneaster, beech, rhododendron, galax, and magnolia all respond well to this treatment. Note that glycerin changes the color of foliage depending on its type and the time of year when it is picked. Generally, foliage processed in the spring tends toward redness, whereas leaves picked in the fall turn brownish.

To treat the foliage, fill a jar with a solution of one part

Fig. 190. Skeletonized leaves.

glycerin to two parts water. Slit the stems and lightly scrape two inches of bark from the stem ends. Insert the stems vertically in the jar and place it where there is plenty of air circulation. Every day polish both sides of each leaf with a cloth saturated with glycerin. When the level of liquid in the jar stops dropping, you will know that the foliage is saturated and can be removed. Another clue is that tiny beads of moisture begin to ooze from the leaves when the treatment is complete. The whole process should take less than two weeks. It will be even less for greens picked in the warm season since they absorb the solution more readily. Sometimes the thinner types of leaves begin to droop during treatment. When this happens, hang them upside down for a few days after removing them from the glycerin.

Ivy stems and individual leaves of ivy, philodendron, or similar greens can also be preserved by the glycerin method. They assume a beautiful shade of green that is very attractive in many arrangements. Simply submerge the sprays or single leaves in the glycerin solution for four days and then rinse off the glycerin with cold water.

Once the glycerin treatment is over, it is not necessary to keep the foliage in water. All that is required is an occasional wiping to keep the leaves free of dust. You will find that they are very useful for adding at least an illusion of reality to arrangements of artificial flowers, if you have a spot where fresh flowers simply cannot be kept.

Fig. 191. Arrangement of preserved flowers using pink tea roses, daisies, and heather.

Arranging Preserved Flowers

When you compose an arrangement with dried flowers, you should apply the same basic principles of design that you would if you were working with fresh flowers. In this case, however, you will have an even greater choice of containers since the flowers do not require any water. If you want, you can even arrange them with no container. (Fig. 191)

If you are arranging the flowers on a flat tray—or even on a place mat—you can attach a piece of styrofoam to the tray or mat with a bit of floral clay and then insert the stems in the foam. You can also use a plain ball of clay for the holder. (Fig. 192)

For shallow dishes, a good holder is a piece of styrofoam attached with melted paraffin. You can camouflage the foam with materials such as dried moss, stones, or bits of colored glass.

Tall containers will need additional weight for stability. Fill them partway full with sand or pebbles and place crumpled chicken wire or a piece of styrofoam on top for a holder.

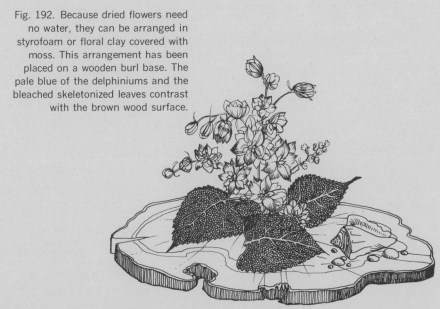

Fig. 192. Because dried flowers need no water, they can be arranged in styrofoam or floral clay covered with moss. This arrangement has been placed on a wooden burl base. The pale blue of the delphiniums and the bleached skeletonized leaves contrast with the brown wood surface.

Index

Accessories:
  in arrangements, 54
  placement of, 55
Air-drying of flowers, 259
Anemones, sample arrangement, 147
Anthuriums, sample arrangement, 153
Asters, sample arrangement, 194, 218
Asymmetry in arrangements, 22

Bacterial growth, preventing, 86
Balance, 19–22
  achieving, 20–21
  asymmetrical, 22
  clustering flowers to increase weight, 21
  color in, 22
  visual weight in, 19
Base (stand), flower, 55
Basket arrangement, 50
Begonia, tuberous, sample arrangement, 127
Bird of paradise, sample arrangement, 121
Borax as drying powder, 261
Branches in arrangements, 41, 46, 48, 52, 55, 124, 126, 127, 129, 131, 138, 140
Bulb flowers, treatment of, 95

Carnations, sample arrangement, 213, 218
Casual flowers, examples, 43
Cattails, sample arrangement, 145
Celosia, sample arrangement, 213
Centerpiece arrangement:
  focal point in, 37
  height of, 5
  recipes for (see Recipes for arrangements, by type and shape)
Chemical treatment, 89
Chenille stems, 61
Chicken-wire holder, 72–76
  construction of, 72
  with pin-point holder, 67, 73
  using, 75
Chrysanthemums, sample arrangement, 190, 224, 225
Circle-shaped arrangements, 10
Clay, floral, 59–60
Clematis, sample arrangement, 138
Coffee table, size of arrangement for, 5
Color:
  in arrangements, 23–32
    combining, 26
      tints, hues, tones, and shades, 31
    common-ingredient theory, 28
    complementary colors, 30

Color:
  in arrangements (*cont.*)
    monochromatic colors, 29
    number used, 26
    selection of, 28
    triadic color scheme, 30
  balance achieved by, 22
  of container, 26, 47
    changing, 52
  cool, 24
  of dried flowers, 268
  emotional response to, 23–24
  of focal point in arrangements, 35
  of interior of container, 48
  mood, matching by, 24–25
  warm, 24
Color wheel, 28–32
  complementary colors, 30
  intermediary colors, 29
  primary colors, 29
  secondary colors, 29
  shades, 31
  tints, 31
  tones, 31
  use of, 29–32
Common-ingredient theory of color
    harmony, 28
Complementary colors, 30
Containers, 45–53
  basic shapes of, 51
  changing color of, 52
  changing texture of, 52
  collection of, 51
  color of, 26, 47
  improvised, 52
    epergnes, 53
  pottery, handmade, 51
  for preserved flowers, 273
  selection guidelines, 45
    color, 47
    shape, 49
      effect of, 14

Containers:
  selection guidelines (*cont.*)
    style, 46
    texture, 51
    visual weight, 47
  size, 6
Cornmeal, yellow, for drying flowers, 261
Corsage thread, 60, 79
Cosmos, sample arrangement, 32, 140
Crescent-shaped arrangements, 10
Curves in arrangements, 34
Cutting flowers, 83
  development after, 84
  proper time for, 83
    roses, 93
  treatment after, 85
Cutting stems, 88

Daffodils:
  sample arrangement, 212, 218
  single-flower arrangement, 122
Daisies, sample arrangement, 168, 218
Decor:
  effect on arrangement, 25
  modern, traditional, and Victorian,
    arrangements for, 44
Delphiniums, sample arrangement, 172,
    185, 218, 225
Dining room, formal, arrangement for, 43
Dining-room table, size of
    arrangement for, 5
Dish gardens, 251–255
  caring for, 253
  flowers added to, 254
  making, 251
  planning, 252
  selection of plants for, 251
Dominant curve, 34
Dragon-fly holder, 77
Dried flowers:
  arrangement of, 273

Dried flowers (*cont.*)
  dyeing, 268
  preparation for arranging, 266
  sample arrangements, 50, 51, 272, 273
Driftwood, sample arrangement with dried
    flowers, 60
Drying flowers, 258–266
  air-drying, 259
  compensating for color changes, 268–270
  finishing, 266
  media for, 262–266
  powders for, 260
    borax, 261
    sand, 261–262
    silica gel, 261
    yellow cornmeal, 261
  preparation of flowers, 263
  procedures in drying media, 262
  time required, 265
Dyeing dried flowers, 268

Ellipse-shaped arrangements, 10
Epergnes, improvised, 53
Exotic arrangement, sample, 43

Fan-shaped arrangement, recipes for (*see*
    Recipes for arrangements, by type and
    shape)
Figurines in arrangements, 53
Floral clay, 59–60
Floral tape, 60
  waterproof, 60
Floral wires, 61
Florist's picks, 108
Flower arranging, checklist for, 111–115
Flower stands, 55
Focal point in arrangement, 35–38
  centerpiece, 37
  color of, 35
  creating, 35

Focal point in arrangement (*cont.*)
  position of, 35
  shape of, 37
Foliage:
  preserving, 270–272
  treatment of, 97
  types of, 98
  wiring, 106
  (*See also* Greens; Leaves)
"Forcing" flowering shrubs, 92
Formal dining room, arrangement for, 43
Formal flowers, examples of, 43
"Frog" (*see* Holders, pin-point)
Fuji mums, sample arrangement, 134

Geraniums, sample arrangement, 140, 157,
    194
Gerberas, sample arrangement, 200, 224,
    225
Gladioli, sample arrangement, 133, 143,
    151, 176, 190, 218, 224, 225
Glycerin method of preserving foliage, 271
Greens:
  arrangements of, 257
  size, relative to flowers, 8
  treatment of, 97
  types of, 97
  (*See also* Foliage; Leaves)

Hardening flowers, 87
Hardware-cloth holders, 76
Harmony in arrangement, 38–44
  achieving, 38
  definition of, 38
Hibiscus, sample arrangement, 35, 127,
    164
Hogarth curve, 9
Holders:
  Blue Ribbon, 68
  chicken-wire, 72

Holders:
  chicken-wire (*cont.*)
    construction of, 72
    securing, 74
    using, 75
  dragon-fly, 77
  hardware-cloth, 76
  miscellaneous, 68, 82
  pin-point, 61
    camouflaging, 67
    care of, 67
    chicken-wire caps for, 67, 73
    fastening in container, 62
    problems with, 65
    in tall vases, 63
    in transparent tall vases, 63
  plastic-foam, 69
    determining size of, 69
    securing, 70
  for preserved flowers, 273
  shredded styrofoam, 80
  twig, 78
  Vermiculite, 81
  waterproof-tape, 79
Hues of colors, 31

Irises:
  sample arrangement, 16, 200, 224, 225
    garden, 39, 161
Ixora, sample arrangement, 213

Jack-in-the-pulpit, sample arrangement, 44

Kenya, 63
Kenzan naoshi, 67

Larkspur, sample arrangement, 200, 224
Laurel, sample arrangement, 48

Leaves:
  preserving, 270–272
    by pressing, 270
    skeletonizing, 271
  (*See also* Foliage; Greens)
Lilacs:
  sample arrangement, 39
  treatment of, 93
Lilies, sample arrangement, 129, 225
L-shape arrangements, 9
  reversed, 9
Lupins, sample arrangement, 194

Magnolias, sample arrangement, 121, 125, 140
Mantel, arrangement for, 5
Materials for flower arranging, 58
Mechanical aids, 57–82
  chenille stems, 61
  chicken wire, 67
  corsage thread, 60, 79
  floral clay, 59
  floral tape, 60
    waterproof, 60
  floral wires, 61
  florist's picks, 108
  holders (*see* Holders)
  "Twistems," 61
Milky-sap flowers, treatment of, 94
Mimosa, sample arrangement, 50
Modern arrangement, example of, 42
Modern decor, arrangement for, 44
Monochromatic color scheme, 29
Moss for camouflaging holders, 67

"Oasis" plastic foam, 69
Orchid, cymbidium, sample arrangement, 126
Oriental arrangement, example of, 41, 48
  hanging, example of, 46

Outdoor terrace party, arrangement for, 44
Oval-shaped arrangements, 10

Pansies, sample arrangement, 154
Pebbles for camouflaging holders, 67
Pedestal vase, 50
    improvised, 53
Peonies:
    sample arrangement, 135
        with single flower, 140
Picks, florist's, 108
Pin-point holders (*see* Holders, pin-point)
Pitcher, arrangement in, 50
Plastic-foam holders (*see* Holders,
        plastic-foam)
Poinsettia blooms, treatment of, 95
Poppies, sample arrangement, 149
Powders for drying flowers (*see* Drying
        flowers, powders)
Preserved flowers, arrangement of, 273
Preserving arrangements, 100
Preserving flowers (*see* Drying flowers)
Preserving foliage, 270–272
Pressing leaves, 270
Primary colors, 29
Proportion or scale, 4, 6–8

Queen Anne's lace, sample arrangement,
    34
"Quickie" plastic foam, 69

Recipes for arrangements:
    locating flowers, 117–119
    by number of flowers:
        one, 120, 122, 124, 126, 128,
            130, 132
        two, 133, 137, 142
        three,144, 146, 148, 150, 152, 154
        four, 156

Recipes for arrangements:
    by number of flowers (*cont.*)
        five, 158, 160
        seven, 162
        twelve:
            asymmetrical centerpiece of round
                flowers, 178
            asymmetrical centerpiece of spike
                flowers, 182
            symmetrical fan-shaped, of conical
                spike flowers, 169
            symmetrical fan-shaped, of front-
                facing spike flowers, 173
            symmetrical fan-shaped, of round
                flowers, 165
        fifteen:
            symmetrical, three-quarter
                triangular, 186
        twenty-one:
            symmetrical, three-quarter
                triangular, 191
        twenty-four:
            symmetrical, fan-shaped,
                three-quarter, 207
        twenty-five:
            symmetrical, three-quarter
                triangular, 202
        twenty-six:
            modified T-shaped, 220
            symmetrical three-quarter
                triangular, 196
        twenty-eight:
            modified T-shaped, 214
        thirty:
            airy round centerpiece, 226
        thirty-one:
            compact, long and narrow
                centerpiece, 245
            compact, round centerpiece, 233
        thirty-two:
            airy, long and narrow centerpiece,
                239

Recipes for arrangements (*cont.*)
  positioning flowers, 118
  by type and shape:
    centerpieces:
      airy, long and narrow, with 32
        flowers, 239
      airy round, with 30 flowers, 226
      asymmetrical, with 12 round
        flowers, 178
      asymmetrical, with 12 spike
        flowers, 182
      compact long and narrow, with 31
        flowers, 245
      compact round, with 31 flowers,
        233
    fan-shaped, three-quarter symmetrical:
      12 round flowers, 165
      12 spike flowers, conical, 169
      12 spike flowers, front facing, 173
      24 spike and round flowers, 207
    T-shaped, modified:
      26 spike and round flowers, 220
      28 spike and round flowers, 214
    triangular, three-quarter symmetrical:
      15 spike and round flowers, 186
      21 spike and round flowers, 191
      25 spike and round flowers, 202
      26 spike and round flowers, 196
Rhythm in arrangements, 32–35
  achieving, 32
  definition of, 32
  ideal, example of, 39
  repetition in, 33
    departure from, 34
Room decor:
  effect on arrangement, 25
  modern, traditional, and Victorian,
    arrangements for, 44
Roses:
  sample arrangement, 36, 134, 136, 181,
    190, 194, 200, 218, 224, 225
  treatment of, 93

Sand for drying flowers, 261
Scale:
  within arrangement:
    height of flowers in shallow
      container, 6
    size of container, 6
  or proportion, 4, 6–8
Secondary colors, 29
Shades of color, 31
Shape of arrangement, 9–19
  circle, 10
  container, effect of, 14
  crescent, 10
  effect of flower shapes on, 14
  ellipse, 10
  fan (*see* Recipes for arrangements, by
    type and shape)
  Hogarth curve, 9
  L-shape, 9
    reversed, 9
  oval, 10
  selection of, 12
  torch, 9
  triangle, 10
    (*See also* Recipes for arrangements, by
      type and shape)
  T-shape, inverted, 13
    (*See also* Recipes for arrangements, by
      type and shape)
Shape of flowers, 16–19
  combining flowers to change shape, 19
Shaping flowers, 107
Shrubs, "forcing," 92
Silica gel drying powder, 261
Size of arrangement, 4
Skeletonizing leaves, 271
Snapdragons, sample arrangement, 212,
  218
Stands, flower, 55
Stems:
  on dried flowers, 267
  lengthening, 109

Stems (*cont.*)
  reinforcing delicate stems, 65
    hollow stems, 66
Stock, sample arrangement, 218
Styrofoam holder, shredded, 80

Table mat, enhancement of arrangement
  by, 56
Tape, floral, 60
  waterproof, 60
Teacup, arrangement in, 50
Teapot arrangement, 49
Temperature of water, 86
Texturizing containers, 52
Thread, corsage, 60, 79
Tints of color, 31
Tones of color, 31
Tools for flower arranging, 58
  use of, 104
Torch-shaped arrangements, 9
Traditional arrangement with wild flowers,
  40
Traditional house, arrangement for, 44
Treatment of flowers:
  bulb flowers, 95
  chemical, 89
  after cutting, 85
  lilacs, 93
  milky-sap flowers, 94
  miscellaneous, 96
  poinsettia, 95
  roses, 93
  woody-stemmed plants, 92
Treatment of foliage and greens, 97
Triadic color scheme, 30
Triangular arrangements, 10
  (*See also* Recipes for arrangements, by
    type and shape)
Tropical arrangement, example of, 49

T-shaped arrangement, inverted, 13
  (*See also* Recipes for arrangements, by
    type and shape)
Tulips, sample arrangement, 39, 50, 135,
  160
Twig holder, 78
"Twistems," 61

Vase, pedestal, 50
  improvised, 53
  (*See also* Containers)
Vermiculite holder, 81
Victorian house, arrangement for, 44
Viewing point for arrangement, 3
Visual weight of containers, 47

Water, temperature of, 86
Water gardens, 255–256
  caring for, 256
  preparing plants for, 255
Water picks, 109, 254
  in dish gardens, 254
Waterproof-tape holder, 79
Weight:
  in arrangements, 11
  visual:
    in arrangements, 19
    of container, 47
Wild flowers, traditional arrangement
  with, 40
Wires, floral, 61
Wiring flowers, 105
Wiring foliage, 106
Wooden shoe, arrangement in, 49
Woody-stemmed plants, treatment of, 92

Zinnias, sample arrangement, 23